Representing

RELIGION/CULTURE/CRITIQUE
Series editor: Elizabeth A. Castelli

How Hysterical: Identification and Resistance in the Bible and Film
By Eric Runions
(2003)

*Connected Places: Region, Pilgrimage, and Geographical
Imagination in India*
By Anne Feldhaus
(2003)

*Representing Religion in World Cinema: Filmmaking, Mythmaking,
Culture Making*
Edited by S. Brent Plate
(2003)

REPRESENTING RELIGION IN WORLD CINEMA

FILMMAKING, MYTHMAKING, CULTURE MAKING

EDITED BY S. BRENT PLATE

REPRESENTING RELIGION IN WORLD CINEMA
Copyright © S. Brent Plate, 2003.

All rights reserved. No part of this book may be used or reproduced in any manner whatsoever without written permission except in the case of brief quotations embodied in critical articles or reviews.

First published in 2003 by PALGRAVE MACMILLAN™
175 Fifth Avenue, New York, N.Y. 10010 and
Houndmills, Basingstoke, Hampshire, England RG21 6XS.
Companies and representatives throughout the world.

PALGRAVE MACMILLAN is the global academic imprint of the Palgrave Macmillan division of St. Martin's Press, LLC and of Palgrave Macmillan Ltd. Macmillan® is a registered trademark in the United States, United Kingdom and other countries. Palgrave is a registered trademark in the European Union and other countries.

ISBN 1–4039-6050-X hardback
ISBN 1–4039-6051-8 paperback

Library of Congress Cataloging-in-Publication Data

Representing religion in world cinema : filmmaking, mythmaking, culture making / edited
by S. Brent Plate.
    p. cm. — (Religion/culture/critique ; 2)
    Includes bibliographical references and index.
    ISBN 1–4039-6050-X —ISBN 1–4039-6051-8 (pbk.)
    1. Motion pictures—Religious aspects. 2. Religion in motion
pictures. I. Plate, S. Brent, 1966- II. Series.

PN1995.5.R47 2003
791.43'682—dc21   2003051179

A catalogue record for this book is available from the British Library.

First Palgrave Macmillan edition: December 2003
10 9 8 7 6 5 4 3 2 1

Printed in the United States of America.

CONTENTS

SERIES EDITOR PREFACE

RELIGION/CULTURE/CRITIQUE is a series devoted to publishing work that addresses religion's centrality to a wide range of settings and debates, both contemporary and historical, and that critically engages the category of "religion" itself. This series is conceived as a place where readers will be invited to explore how "religion"—whether embedded in texts, practices, communities, or ideologies—intersects with social and political interests, institutions, and identities.

Representing Religion in World Cinema: Filmmaking, Mythmaking, Culture Making poses the question of "religion" through the medium of cinema, looking for religion not only in the content of film but in the form and reception of cinematic representations. Both religion and film are forms of mediation, this anthology argues, and therefore can be read together to generate new theoretical insights about both what counts as "religion" and how cinema as a global form transforms our thinking about myth and culture. The essays in this collection challenge the reader to rethink all assumptions about "religion and film," interrupt the hegemony of both Christianity and Hollywood, and focus concentrated attention on different centers of religious life and cultural production. Feature films from Iran, South and East Asia, Europe, and the United States; locally produced video and documentaries from Ghana and Mexico; experimental genres from the Philippines, New Zealand, and Cuba—all of these forms of cinematic mediation emerge in a collection of essays commissioned for inclusion in this groundbreaking volume. As "religion and media" emerges as a leading edge in the interdisciplinary academic study of religion, S. Brent Plate's collection in this volume makes a critical contribution to this newly developing field. It is a great pleasure to include this anthology and its essays in this series.

Elizabeth A. Castelli
RELIGION/CULTURE/CRITIQUE Series Editor
New York City
April 2003

ILLUSTRATIONS

ACKNOWLEDGEMENTS

Conversations with many people in many places got this project off the ground, and I am grateful for the ongoing dialogue with colleagues around the world. Without them I would not be able to continue my own work. As always, Tel Mac supplied a heavy dose of the intellectual stimulus for this project. Chas Gay and Simon Halliday deserve credit for their supreme reviewing abilities. Practically speaking, I would like to thank Randy Scoggin for help with the images, Amanda Smith for help in the preparation of the manuscript, and Jen Simington for excellent copyediting. Finally, and most importantly, Melisa's contributions have been incalculable.

Introduction

Filmmaking, Mythmaking, Culture Making

S. Brent Plate

In the 2001 Australian national census, over 70,000 people marked "Jedi" as their religion. Responding to this religious/political movement, Chris Brennan, director of the Star Wars Appreciation Society of Australia, stated, "This was a way for people to say, 'I want to be part of a movie universe I love so much.'"[1]

In another place and time, devout viewers entered cinemas barefoot and performed *puja* in front of the goddess Santoshi Maa, who came to life on screen in the 1975 Indian film *Jai Santoshi Maa*. As a result of the film, a massive following of this previously obscure goddess erupted across northern India.

And at the liminal hour of midnight on any given Saturday, in just about any major metropolis in the United States, groups of people, dressed especially for the occasion, can be found attending a screening of *The Rocky Horror Picture Show*. Most of those in attendance have watched the film so often that they will sing along with all the songs.

If Fredric Jameson has discussed cinema in terms of a "geopolitical aesthetic," we might rephrase this for the purposes of the present volume to understand cinema as a "geo*religious* aesthetic." With the zealous speed of missionary outreach, in just one hundred years film has traveled across oceans and continents, infiltrating urban centers, small towns, and villages—a fact reflexively taken up in films such as *Cinema Paradiso* or *The Last Picture Show*, in which we see the role of cinema in establishing communal life, often usurping the role that religious traditions have had in previous times. As a georeligious aesthetic, cinema is bound to religion in a myriad of ways, and we aren't just speaking here of *The Ten Commandments* or *Jesus of Nazareth*. Films are not religious simply because of their *content* but become religious due to their *form* and *reception*. George Lucas may have borrowed from several religious traditions rich in myth for the *Star Wars* script, yet the Australian Jedis know that religion is much more than a set of words: Religion is imagistic, participatory, performative, and world-creating—and sometimes it is cinema that best provides these activities.

Thus, to study the relation between religion and film in a variety of cultural settings requires that contributors to *Representing Religion in World Cinema* walk an occasionally thin line between anthropology, media studies, cultural studies, film studies, and religious studies. For this reason, I scarcely need to suggest the interdisciplinary nature of this volume, though it probably should be hinted at that some of the articles fall more within one discipline or area of study than another; some articles may look familiar to an anthropologist and unfamiliar to a film studies scholar, while others will look familiar to scholars of film and barely register in the mind of a religious studies scholar; some pay more attention to film production, while others highlight film reception; some work with specific religious traditions, and others operate on comparative-theoretical levels of myth and ritual. Moreover, religion, film, and culture are not static categories, for as our subtitle intimates, there is a "making" component that must be considered: Filmmaking is related to culture making is related to mythmaking. Contributors explore the processual nature of these categories and how the creative activity of one impinges upon, and sometimes dominates, the others.

Religion Making Media Making Culture

The connections between film and religion should not be surprising, for looking at the formal structures of each we find some uncanny parallels. Compare, briefly, the following two sets of quotes:

> A ritual provides a frame. The marked off time or place alerts a special kind of expectancy, just as the oft-repeated "Once upon a time" creates a mood receptive to fantastic tales.[2]

> Whatever its shape, the [camera] frame makes the image finite. The film image is bounded, limited. From an implicitly continuous world, the frame selects a slice to show us. . . . Characters enter the image from somewhere and go off to another area—offscreen space.[3]

and

> Religious beliefs were responsible for substituting a different world for the world perceived by the senses.[4]

> If the ideal of art is to create an illusion of reality, the motion picture made it possible to achieve this ideal in an unprecedented way.[5]

The first quotes in each pair are by theorists of religion—the first by Mary Douglas, the second by Emile Durkheim. The second quotes are by film scholars—the first by Kristin Thompson and David Bordwell and the second by Gerald Mast, Marshall Cohen, and Leo Braudy. Film is perhaps the furthest thing from the religionists' minds when they write these phrases, and religious myth and ritual are likewise far from the film scholars' minds, yet the similarity of their phrasing is striking.[6] Starting out from these cursory descriptions, I would put forward the hypothesis that film and religion are analogous in the first instance due to their activities of taking the world-as-it-is, and inventing a new world through the dual processes of "framing" and "projecting."

To further the connection between these parallel processes of religion and film, we must understand the *mediated* nature of each. To begin, I take "media" in a neutral sense, meaning something "in the middle," "between," serving as a bridge to connect the space between two or more things, transmitting particular messages and information. Hence, oral speech is a medium, just as print is, just as film is, and just as are the various mass and electronic media. As mediations, the framing and projecting activities of religion-making and filmmaking take the world "out there" and bring it "in here," to our temple, to our table, to our theater. Through the medium of film, space and time are re-created by activities such as cinematography and editing, just as consecration rites and the mythological forces of religion reform the material "stuff" of the world, offering a new, ideal world, projected for a community's pleasure and, indeed, for their very survival. Film, like religious myth and ritual, offers windows onto other worlds. The attraction and, indeed, promise of cinema is the way it offers a glimpse of something beyond, "over the rainbow," even if only for 90 minutes at a time.

But at this point things get messy, and the nice and neat "two worlds" view breaks down, because media, as scholars from Marshall McLuhan to Elizabeth Eisenstein to Friedrich Kittler have pointed out, are not so neutral.[7] Specific media actually alter the very information being transmitted; there is no concrete, easily definable distinction between the medium and the message. James Carey's important essay "A Cultural Approach to Communication" offers a useful understanding of the power of media as he discusses the difference between the commonly held idea of a *transmission* view of communication—whereby information is "sent" or "imparted" and arrives relatively unaltered—in contrast to what he calls the *ritual* form:

> The model here is not that of information acquisition, though such acquisition occurs, but of dramatic action in which the reader joins a world of

contending forces as an observer at a play. We do not encounter questions about the effect of functions of messages as such, but the role of presentation and involvement in the structuring of the reader's life and time. . . . it is a presentation of reality that gives life an overall form, order, and tone.[8]

Media of communication are not hollow, empty receptacles that connect addresser and addressee. Rather, media are dynamic entities that actively shape and reshape the world. In other words, religions and cultures do not merely *use* media, but instead are *used by* media, and created by them.

This latter fact has stirred the anxieties of some contemporary sociologists, philosophers, and cultural critics concerned with the recent rise of multimediated electronic technologies and, more importantly, concerned with *who* has control of these media technologies. Manuel Castells, in part of his three-volume work, *The Information Society,* sounds a warning against what he calls "the culture of real virtuality," "in which appearances are not just on the screen through which experience is communicated, but they become the experience."[9] Yet, Castells is also careful to suggest that

reality, as experienced, has always been virtual because it is always perceived through symbols that frame practice with some meaning that escapes their strict semantic definition. . . . Thus, when critics of electronic media argue that the new symbolic environment does not represent "reality," they implicitly refer to an absurdly primitive notion of "uncoded" real experience that never existed. All realities are communicated through symbols. And in human, interactive communication, regardless of the medium, all symbols are somewhat displaced in relationship to their assigned semantic meaning. In a sense all reality is virtually perceived.[10]

We only exist insofar as we exist with others, and to be with others means we must communicate and do so through, and *in,* media; there is nothing outside media. Along these lines, media may always be a more effective tool with which to change the world than swords and missiles. So we cannot escape the ideological questions as to who has control of the media.

For our concerns here, we take film to be a particular audio-visual medium that frames and projects the world "out there." This means the contributors in the present volume are interested in a certain formal analysis of particular films and provide insights into questions such as: What happens in the plot of the film? What is the effect of the mise-en-scène or cinematography? Why did the production designer use one color and not another? How is a character transformed within the story of the film? And, more to the point, how are religious practices, myths, and symbols evoked within the film? How is religion represented, and thus mediated?

Yet to fully understand the medium of film we cannot stop there but must take some steps toward comprehending the place of the spectators and the role of participation, and enquiring about the social effects of a film upon those who engage with it. To claim film is "disembodied" or "voyeuristic" because viewers do not somehow interact with the characters on screen is to radically miss the point of the medium of film. Films do not merely appear on a screen; rather, they only exist in any real sense as far as they are watched, becoming part of the fabric of our lives. Film viewing is thus a social activity that alters our interactions in the world. Even if viewers do not know the people next to them in the movie house, their outlooks on the world, and thus also their social interactions, have been changed because of the film they have seen. They come away believing, variously, that romance really is possible in the most absurd situations, that all Arabs really are terrorists, or that Roman Catholic mothers are all rigid, intolerant, and their children are in dire need of liberation. While most cinemagoers rationally know the difference between the "screened world" and the "real world," and will readily reaffirm the split in exit polls, the veil between worlds is surprisingly transparent, and the "two worlds" thesis given above breaks down readily. Film, across the world, and in ways unthinkable even one hundred years ago, has changed our georeligiosity.

Film is not the only medium of concern in this volume, and it is necessary to approach religion itself, on the one hand, as always having been and always being mediated. On the other hand, religion is in itself a mediating activity. We get a whiff of this in Clifford Geertz's well-known definition of religion in his "Religion as a Cultural System" essay, where he argues how religion formulates "conceptions of a general order of existence." This is immediately followed up by his observation that these conceptions are "clothed" with an "aura of factuality," making them seem "uniquely realistic."[11] While he does not discuss media as such, Geertz's suggestive comments articulate the way in which "clothing" (what Geertz means primarily to be myth, ritual, and symbol) actually alters the "conceptions" (message), having a powerful effect in and on religious systems. In other words, religious traditions do not function unless they are "dressed up" in myths, rituals, and symbols.

One of the ways this is achieved by religions is by putting these conceptions into specific media (and by now it should be clear that the autonomy of these "conceptions" is in doubt). From cultures in which orality is the primary mode of communication, to highly literate book-bound cultures, to contemporary multimediated cultures, religion is morphed by, adapts to, and affects the media with which it is engaged. Indeed, myths, rituals, and symbols are only existent *as* media: A myth must be transmitted, whether by "word of mouth" or through the technologies of television; a ritual must be enacted, whether involving readings from sacred, printed texts or by processions through architectural space; a symbol must be shared, whether it is a colorful banner in a synagogue or a piece of bread. We thus must presume that religion—however oriented toward the "invisible," the "spiritual," the "wholly other," it may be—is nonetheless also always material and mediated. Through, and *as,* media, religion builds worlds.

And in its existence as media, religion must change in order to stay the same. That is, for religious traditions to continue through history they must be translated, or better, *transmediated,* put in a new form. As Lawrence Babb has suggested in a thoughtful introduction to the collection *Media and the Transformation of Religion in South Asia:* "nothing is truly fixed; time inevitably deposits new layers over previously stored materials, and each generation finds its own new ways of construing the deposits of the past. Therefore, as symbols circulate through such a system, the system as a whole is not only socially reproduced but also altered."[12] For the Torah to survive after the destruction of the Second Temple, the oral law had to be written down. Similarly, the spoken words of the Buddha had to eventually be written down, compiled, and edited to ensure the survival of his teachings, as well as for the cohesion of the communities who followed in his wake. And in each of these circumstances, the "message" itself (if ever there was such a singular thing) is changed. (And of course, each of these transmediazations simultaneously gives way to radical disagreements among adherents, and they are often the catalysts for great schisms in religious traditions. Then again, we may argue that religious traditions—just like political systems—also need debate to survive, and transmediazations bring these debates to a crescendo.) In the contemporary age, one of the most powerful media that both ensures the continuation of older myths, even as it alters them, is the medium of film: Films are one of the chief storytellers for the contemporary age.

Traditions are not only carried on and changed through chronological time via transmediality, they are also altered through *intermediality:* the interruption of one medium into the structures of another medium. By this I do not simply mean a borrowing of other media sources, a banal influencing, or even adaptation, for intermediality often entails a much more radical intrusion whereby the rogue medium infiltrates the patterns and assumptions of the given medium and causes a shift in perspective.[13] With intermediality we must account for the mixture of two or more media that are, on one level, each transformed into a new singular "medium," and, on another critical level, productively separated out and analyzed on their own terms. In this way, film is (or has become) an audio-visual medium that has built upon several pre-existent media—most prominently photography, oral speech, and music—just as it fuses those very media into one new medium. So when, for example, a still photographic image appears within the context of a "motion" picture, the apperception of the viewer is triggered at a particular level of what Pierre Bourdieu has called the *habitus*.[14] Viewers understand the function of a still photograph from their "real world" cultural interactions—the still photograph often has to do with a specific process of memorialization, pointing to a previous life experience now preserved in a mediated form—and the viewer brings this experience and practice into the space of the cinema (indeed, the practice of cinema is the practice of life; the two are inseparable). The still photograph has a great effect, as any good filmmaker knows, because it points beyond the confines of the 90-minute film and suggests there is an entire other world, with a before and after, unfolding on the other side of the screen. Characters appear to have a real history. In another direction, the intermediality of the extemporaneous speech within a feature film prompts a feeling of presence, of raw emotion, of a character who is genuine through and through—an effect that is nonetheless reliant on heavy-handed editing techniques. Such speech creates an implied "im-media-cy" that tends to erase its own mediated nature as a film. This is when media becomes most powerful (and most dangerous): when it seems to cease being media. And thus for critical viewers and producers, there is a necessity to break down the various components of media and show their always-mediated nature. This is as true for film as it is for religion.

I have previously used orality as an example several times and have done so purposely because I am hoping to reaffirm "media" as a plural noun that has a diversity of forms not wholly subsumed in the singular phrase "the media," by which is too often meant electronic and mass media. There are many critical reasons to understand media as a plurality that includes pre-electronic formats, and in light of the following contributions to this volume, such intermedial relations will play an important part. So, in approaching film as an audio-visual medium, we might be attentive to aspects of what Walter Ong called a "secondary orality" which, like primary orality, is participatory, invites communal relations, and concentrates on the present moment even as it is more self-conscious as a medium than is primary orality since it is understood through the media of writing and print.[15] Because film utilizes oral communication, a thorough analysis of the filmic medium might do well to think through the impact of orality. If we want to understand the primary processes of religion-making within the context of filmmaking, we will need to see how the older media are adapted in new forms. Several of the essays here do precisely this.

Even so, in the processes of intermediality and transmediality, there is a fine line between change and continuity. The new form must be familiar enough to the receptive audience to provide continuity, and thus comfort and a sense of belonging, but also unfamiliar enough to jar the audience to a new way of seeing. Successful films, like successful myths, offer a projection of another, sometimes ideal, world to which we can relate, but also stir us to renewed action, emotion, and thought.

One important outcome of the interface between religion and media is that we find how religion itself is altered by its media, and how media are continued or discontinued by the ways in which religious traditions conform to particular media. For example, if the printing press was an "agent of change," as Elizabeth Eisenstein suggests, we might also ask how religion (specifically, Christian Protestants) unwittingly and concomitantly promoted these very print technologies. Furthermore, we find how transmediality and intermediality push at the question of originality, for if everything changes with every new media permutation, then what did it all look like "in the beginning"? While there are many myths of origins, there is no original myth. Just as myths are always syncretic, media are always multimedia. As we look here specifically at the medium of film, we find that film actually changes the beliefs and practices, the myth and rituals, the symbols and structures, of religion.

Filmmaking and mythmaking do not occur in cultural vacuums but are deeply affected by the languages, customs, beliefs, and social lives of people living in specific geographic locations and specific times. And just as culture is encoded in media, so does its media of communication shape culture itself. Again, the question of *who* is controlling the media is vital, for as Ella Shohat and Robert Stam argue in their critical work, *Unthinking Eurocentrism*:

> The contemporary media shape identity; indeed, many argue that they now exist close to the very core of identity production. In a transnational world typified by the global circulation of images and sounds, goods and people, media spectatorship impacts complexly on national identity and communal belonging. By facilitating an engagement with distant peoples, the media "deterritorialize" the process of imagining communities. And while the media can destroy community and fashion solitude by turning spectators into atomized consumers or self-entertaining monads, they can also fashion community and alternative affiliations.[16]

Film (as well as video and other contemporary media) is certainly global in its range and functions to "deterritorialize" local cultures, yet has simultaneously enabled smaller group identities to be made visible on a global screen. Visibility, which film and video technologies allow, is a central component to identification.

So, among the issues to arise from the georeligious aesthetic of cinema are issues of ideology and power, and these are deeply tied to the mythmaking potential of film.[17] Framing and projecting are enacted by decisions made in the production of film. If a frame selects a slice of the world to show us, someone, somewhere (whether the director, the cinematographer, or the editor) has created that very frame and made choices about its boundaries. While this does not negate a resisting gaze of the viewers, at some level the ideologies of film production must be assessed.

The ideology of filmmaking is seen not only through the production of film but also through its distribution. The contributions here do not assume film aesthetics are value free, yet neither do they rely on the simplistic premise that Hollywood production overpowers all other modes of local production. There can be little doubt that the Hollywood film industry has had dramatic effects on many local cultures around the world, to the extent that even major film-producing countries (e.g., the U.K., France, Canada, India) have limited—sometimes through legislation—the number of U.S.-produced films in distribution in their nations. Nonetheless, new media developments always carry with them the promise of a more democratic representation. This was true for the invention of writing, for the invention of the printing press, and continues to hold true for newer film and video technologies. Not only do more people have access to *receiving* the new media, more people have access to *producing* with the new media.[18]

And as the articles here look around the globe, we find many examples of the confluence of cinema and religion as both products of culture and producers of culture. The essays gathered here do not amount to a comprehensive view—geographically, religiously, or culturally speaking—nor could they, but are instead bound by their interrogation of the links between culture making, filmmaking, and mythmaking.

This volume is situated at a nexus of already interdisciplinary fields of study—in particular, "religion and film" as it is found within religious studies, and "religion and media" as it is found in departments and societies of media studies, including those proceeding from an anthropological basis and those from the standpoint of communications. Religion and film is a rapidly expanding subfield within religious studies that contains some dynamic scholarship but remains beleaguered by both a Christian emphasis and a Hollywood emphasis—and it is not coincidental that these emphases go hand in hand. While the Hollywood-Christian myth of redemption/ resurrection/happy ending is a powerful one, it is not the only one. Thus, one of the reasons for assembling this volume on "world cinema" is to provide an alternative voice to the Hollywoodcentrism that resides within religion and film circles.[19]

Nonetheless, if religious studies biases popular Hollywood cinema, cultural studies and film studies are deficient when they turn a blind eye to religion. Malory Nye, in the editorial introduction that launched the journal *Culture and Religion* in 2001, rightly notes the absence of religion within cultural studies: "when religion is seen 'it' is usually subsumed within other frameworks: such as identity, sub-culture, class, or as a (relatively unimportant) form of cultural difference. . . . It seems that the majority of those working in cultural studies have yet to be convinced that religious studies scholars are not closet theologians."[20] While the skepticism toward "closet theologians" is not unfounded, the fear does not hold true for the totality of religious studies.

Which is interesting on a number of levels, not least of which is Rachel Moore's argument in *Savage Theory* that early filmmakers were deeply interested in a re-enchantment of the modern world and saw film as the tool with which to reinsert magic into life—even as they relied on an exoticized othering of the religious.[21] The omission is also glaring since there are simply so many films produced around the world, including Hollywood, that have overtly religious themes. With avant-gardists like Stan Brakhage and Maya Deren, auteurs like Krzysztof Kieslowski and Ingmar Bergman, and revampers of myth like George Lucas and Randall Wallace, all emphatically dealing with religious elements in their works, it is difficult to understand the reluctance of film and cultural studies to address the issue of religion in any broader and more critical way than they have.[22]

Contributions

For heuristic purposes, I have delineated this volume into three sections: "Re-mythologizing Cinema," "Re-presenting Religion," and "Making Films, Making Nations." While there are reasons to group the essays together in this way, there could easily be equal arguments for another arrangement, and I hope my structures are not strictures that detract from the quality of each of the individual contributions. Meanwhile, what will be readily apparent is that each section contains a multiplicity of perspectives on the theme of that section.

We start with four quite distinct essays, from quite distinct perspectives, written on films from quite distinct cultures, each critically exploring the interaction of filmmaking and mythmaking. To begin, Philip Lutgendorf offers an extended analysis of the Indian film mentioned in the opening paragraphs of this introduction, *Jai Santoshi Maa*, seeing it for the ways it continues the Indian genre of "mythological" film, which already pulls on ancient written and oral sources even as it borrows its imagery from more contemporary media such as poster art. Because of the intermedial nature of the film, as well as its merging of old and new stories and ideas, it became a fairly successful film in India in the 1970s, spawning a large cult following of the titular goddess. The second essay, by Judith Weisenfeld, on Julie Dash's *Daughters of the Dust,* shows how a film can transmediate older forms of mythmaking, bringing them up to date, even as such processes can remain distinct for a particular culture and inaccessible to others. Dash's work thus speaks both to a distinctly African American, women's experience (specifically that of the Gullah), as it shows other contemporary U.S. filmviewers what they are not. In the end, the medium of photography intrudes into the film, providing self-reflexive insights into questions concerning the mediated nature of culture, religion, and its representation. Linda C. Ehrlich explores the myth of Orpheus in a variety of cinematic adaptations in a variety of languages and cultures. She makes note of the malleability of myth, of the ways it adapts to new locations and new media. Of particular note is the "open ending" structure of each of the films, which allows for a continuation of myth: Myths never end, they are merely retold in new forms. Finally, Paul Nathanson follows up with some "theological notes" on Woody Allen's *Shadows and Fog,* which he sees as an intriguing combination of both myth and parable (a "parable" being an innovative and challenging mode of storytelling that disrupts the otherwise traditional stabilizing role of myth). The film, Nathanson suggests, represents a "Jewish way of thinking" as it attempts to find meaning in the modern world—even as it ostensibly portrays a mid-twentieth-century, central-European setting, it nonetheless points to the late-twentieth-century United States—an attempt to face death through art.

The next section provides four essays—also distinct from each other—on the ways in which religion is represented in film, on film, through film. Here, contributors pay attention to the ways the medium of film alters religion through its representational processes. Francisca Cho begins the section by examining two Korean, "Buddhist-themed" films *(Passage to Buddha* and *Beyond the Mountain).* She points out the transmediazations that take place from older East Asian storytelling forms into modern cinema, and the ways in which artistic engagement in any media can induce "significant life experiences" while remaining firmly within a traditional Buddhist worldview. Based on her field research in Ghana, Birgit Meyer offers an intriguing examination of the role of "video-films" in Ghanaian Pentecostal Christianity, showing how local religious groups understand the power of media. In the aftermath of democratization, and the concomitant rise of capitalism, competition in the marketplace is met by competition among religious denominations, and these video-films offer a religious product to a viewing public, producing newer worldviews. Lloyd Ridgeon's essay on Iranian director Mohsen Makhmalbaf argues for an implicit, hidden apocalyptic religious content in the film *A Moment of Innocence.*

Like the Sufi Islam found in Persia/Iran, Makhmalbaf seeks out a highly personal, interiorized apocalypse that, while in contrast to both political revolution and Shi'ite Muslim communal life, nonetheless contains transformative potential. Next, Luis A. Vivanco brings us to a ritual event during the spring equinox at Chichén Itzá, exploring questions raised by ethnographic filmmaking as to who is the insider, who is the outsider, and how the sacred is represented on film. Jeff Himpele and Quetzil Castañeda's video, *Incidents of Travel in Chichén Itzá*, allows for a self-reflexive style of filmmaking that nonetheless raises ever-new questions for its receptive audience about who exactly is the "savage other."

One of the primary modes of structuring the contemporary world is through the category of nationalism. As Faye Ginsburg, Lila Abu-Lughod, and Brian Larkin suggest, "Although many people consider themselves to belong to subnational or transnational communities, the nation is the primary context for the everyday lives and imaginations of most of the people who produce media and constitute its audiences."[23] Thus, the final section examines the role of mythic filmmaking in nation building, query-ing the role of religion in the midst of such constructions. First up, Antonio D. Sison re-views the 1976 Filipino film *Perfumed Nightmare,* seeing its avant-garde tactics as a way of struggling toward a postcolonial identity in the Philippines. By synthesizing techniques of "third cinema" with indige-nous Filipino religious practices and traditions, Sison suggests ways in which filmmaker Kidlat Tahimik reimagines a cultural identity. Also working with postcolonial issues, Janet Wilson thinks through several recent New Zealand films, noting some of the ways Maori culture has met with British Puritan culture. The clash is often a violent one, creating upheaval within the structures of gender and family. Several contemporary filmmakers take up the theme of identity disruption, even as they attempt to forge a new way of envisioning New Zealand identity. Next, Edna M. Rodríguez-Mangual takes up the challenge of postcolonial identification in Cuba, which is necessarily complicated by the Communist Revolution of 1959. The essay examines the visibility and invisibility of the Afro-Cuban religion, Santería, in the shaping of a national identity within Cuban cinema. While Santería, and Afro-Cubans in general, have rhetorically been included in the cultural history of the Cuban Revolution, they are often made invisible when it comes to actual cultural production such as film. Finally, Kris Jozajtis brings us to the United States and looks at the construction of its twentieth-century identity through D. W. Griffith's classic, albeit racist, *The Birth of a Nation*. The essay argues that the representation of religion in Hollywood has always been subordinate to the broader cultural process of U.S. nationhood, and the film both maintains and transforms what Robert Bellah famously described as the "American civil religion."[24]

Notes

1. See Stewart Taggart, "Bad Movie Hurts Jedi Down Under," *Wired News* (August 31, 2001). Available at http://www.wired.com/news/culture/0,1284, 54851,00.html.
2. Mary Douglas, *Purity and Danger* (London and New York: Routledge, 2000 [1966]), 64.
3. David Bordwell and Kristin Thompson, *Film Art: An Introduction*, 6th. ed. (New York: McGraw Hill, 2001), 216.
4. Emile Durkheim, *The Elementary Forms of the Religious Life*, excerpted in *Durkheim on Religion*, W. S. F. Pickering, ed. (London: Routledge and Kegan Paul, 1975), 140.
5. Gerald Mast, Marshall Cohen, and Leo Braudy, in the introduction to the section "Film and Reality," in *Film Theory and Criticism*, 4th. ed. (New York: Oxford University Press, 1992), 3.
6. Ronald Grimes is certainly correct to warn against *equating* ritual and media (and also against *segregating* them), for there are a number of fruitful ways of relating the realms in differing circumstances. See, among other places, his article "Ritual and the Media" in *Practicing Religion in the Age of Media*, Stewart M. Hoover and Lynn Schofield Clark, eds. (New York: Columbia University Press, 2002), 219–234. Herein, I am attempting to analogize religion and media, to see one in light of the other, and hope that the encounter might be a productive one that does not end with a nice, neat equation.
7. See McLuhan's classic and still relevant works, *The Gutenberg Galaxy* (Toronto: University of Toronto Press, 1962) and *Understanding Media: The Extensions of Man* (New York: McGraw-Hill, 1964). Also, see Elizabeth Eisenstein, *The Printing Press as Agent of Change*, 2 vols. (New York: Cambridge University Press, 1979); Friedrich Kittler, *Gramophone, Film, Typewriter* (Stanford: Stanford University Press, 1999). Still useful as an introductory work on the relation of religion and media is Walter Ong's *Orality and Literacy* (New York: Methuen, 1982).
8. James W. Carey, "A Cultural Approach to Communication," in his *Communication as Culture: Essays on Media and Society* (Boston: Unwin Hyman, 1989), 21.
9. Manuel Castells, *The Rise of the Network Society* (Malden, MA: Blackwell, 1996), 373. Although there are many intellectual writings sounding these warnings, one prominent work is Martin Heidegger's "The Question Concerning Technology," trans. William Lovitt and David Krell, *Basic Writings* (San Francisco: HarperCollins, 1993), 307–341.
10. Castells, *The Rise of Network Society*, 372–373.
11. Clifford Geertz, "Religion as a Cultural System," in his *Interpretation of Cultures* (New York: Basic Books, 1973), 87–125.
12. Lawrence Babb, "Introduction" to *Media and the Transformation of Religion in South Asia*, Lawrence Babb and Susan Wadley, eds. (Philadelphia: University of Pennsylvania Press, 1995), 2.

13. Thus, intermediality is cousin to the notion of "intertextuality," as given by Mikhail Bakhtin and taken up by Julia Kristeva, who suggests that it is "the passage from one sign system to another" that involves the "destruction of the old position and the formation of a new one" (Julia Kristeva, *Revolution in Poetic Language*, trans. Leon Roudiez [New York: Columbia University Press, 1984], 59).

14. See Pierre Bourdieu, "Structures, *Habitus*, Practices" and "Belief and the Body," in his *The Logic of Practice*, trans. Richard Nice (Cambridge: Polity Press, 1990), 52–65, 66–79.

15. Walter Ong, *Orality and Literacy*, 136.

16. Ella Shohat and Robert Stam, *Unthinking Eurocentrism: Multiculturalism and the Media* (London: Routledge, 1994), 7.

17. For more on the relation of myth and ideology, see the recent works: Robert Ellwood, *The Politics of Myth* (Albany: State University of New York Press, 1999); Bruce Lincoln, *Theorizing Myth* (Chicago: University of Chicago Press, 1999); and Robert Segal, *Theorizing About Myth* (Amherst: University of Massachusetts Press, 1999). The work that remains to be done in religious studies is to examine the ways in which myth functions as ideology and how this is tied to its media.

18. The work of Faye Ginsburg has been particularly strong on this point. See, for example, "Culture/Media: A (mild) polemic," *Anthropology Today* 10.2 (April 1994): 5–15; "Shooting Back: From Ethnographic Film to the Ethnography of Media," in *A Companion to Film Theory*, Toby Miller and Robert Stam, eds. (London: Blackwell, 1999), 295–322; and many of the essays in the volume she edited with Lila Abu-Lughod and Brian Larkin, *Media Worlds: Anthropology on New Terrain* (Berkeley: University of California Press, 2002).

19. See, for example: Peter Fraser, *Images of the Passion* (Westport, CT: Praeger, 1998); Robert K. Johnston, *Reel Spirituality* (Grand Rapids, MI: Baker, 2000); Clive Marsh and Gaye Ortiz, eds., *Explorations in Theology and Film* (Malden, MA: Blackwell, 1998); Joel W. Martin and Conrad Ostwalt, eds., *Screening the Sacred* (Boulder: Westview Press, 1995); Thomas M. Martin, *Images and the Imageless*, 2d. ed. (Lewisburg, PA: Bucknell University Press, 1991); John R. May, *Image & Likeness* (New York: Paulist, 1992); John R. May, ed., *New Image of Religious Film* (Kansas City, MO: Sheed and Ward); Margaret Miles, *Seeing and Believing* (Boston: Beacon Press, 1996); Bernard Brandon Scott, *Hollywood Dreams and Biblical Stories* (Minneapolis, MN: Fortress, 1994); Bryan P. Stone, *Faith and Film* (St. Louis: Chalice, 2000). There are many good, critical works here, but what is seen again and again are the equations: "film=Hollywood film" and/or "religion=Christian Theology." John Lyden's recent *Film as Religion* (New York: New York University Press, 2003) offers a good overview of many of these previous works, critiquing the Christian-centered nature of most and developing a methodology for religion and film via social scientific accounts (especially Geertz's), though Lyden, too, only works with Hollywood films. A volume I coedited with David Jasper (*Imag(in)ing Otherness: Filmic Visions of Living Together* [Atlanta: American Academy of Religion/Scholars Press, 1999]) explored a variety of religious

traditions in world cinema by specifically thinking through filmic depictions of otherness in a pluralistic world.

20. Malory Nye, "Culture and Religion," *Culture and Religion* 1.1 (May 2000): 7.
21. See Rachel Moore, *Savage Theory: Cinema as Modern Magic* (Durham: Duke University Press, 2000). In an intriguing way, Timothy K. Beal deals with similar topics in the chapter "Screening Monsters" in his *Religion and Its Monsters* (New York: Routledge, 2002). As Beal states in relation to Moore's work, "the cinematic event is envisioned as a return to modernity's repressed, a 'modern primitive' religious ritual" (ibid., 221 n.3).
22. For a useful overview of some of the ways "religion and media" are being studied together, see Lynn Schofield Clark's "Overview," in *Practicing Religion in the Age of Media,* Hoover and Clark, eds., 7–33. The work of Clark and Hoover at the University of Colorado, and the new Center for Religion and Media at New York University (run by Faye Ginsburg and Angela Zito), offer many strong approaches to the relation of religion and media, though film is only one of several media included.
23. Ginsburg, Abu-Lughod, and Larkin, "Introduction," *Media Worlds,* 11.
24. See Robert N. Bellah, *The Broken Covenant: American Civil Religion in a Time of Trial* (New York: Seaburg Press, 1975).

Section One

Re-mythologizing Cinema

Chapter One

Jai Santoshi Maa Revisited:

On Seeing a Hindu "Mythological" Film*

Philip Lutgendorf

Audiences were showering coins, flower petals and rice at the screen in appreciation of the film. They entered the cinema barefoot and set up a small temple outside. . . . In Bandra, where mythological films aren't shown, it ran for fifty weeks. It was a miracle.

—Anita Guha (actress who played the goddess Santoshi Ma)[1]

Genre, Film, and Phenomenon

Cecil B. DeMille's cynical adage, "God is box office," may be applied to Indian popular cinema, the output of the world's largest film industry, albeit with certain adjustments—one must pluralize and sometimes feminize the subject of the adage. The film genre known as "mythological" was present at the creation of the Indian feature film and has remained a hardy perennial of its vast output, yet it constitutes one of the least-studied aspects of this comparatively understudied cinema, cursorily dismissed (or more often ignored) by scholars and critics.[2] Yet DeMille's words also belie the fact that most mythologicals—like most commercial films of any genre— flop at the box office. The comparatively few that have enjoyed remarkable and sustained acclaim hence merit study both as religious expressions and as successful examples of popular art and entertainment.

Of the 475 Indian films released in 1975, 3 enjoyed enormous success. All were in Hindi, the lingua franca of the entertainment industry based in Bombay (a.k.a. Mumbai), lately dubbed "Bollywood," which (although it generates less than a quarter of national cinematic output) enjoys the largest audience throughout the subcontinent and beyond. *Sholay* (Flames) and *Deewar* (The wall), were both heavily-promoted "multistarrers" belonging to the genre sometimes referred to as the *masala* ("spicy") film: a multicourse cinematic banquet incorporating suspenseful drama, romance, comedy, violent action sequences, and song and dance. Both were expensive and slickly made by the standards of the industry, and both featured Amitabh Bachchan, the male superstar whose iconic portrayal of an "angry young man" would dominate the Hindi screen for the next decade. Female characters were marginal to both, and this was not surprising given that their target audience was young urban males.

The third "superhit" of 1975 could hardly have been more different, however, and came as a complete surprise to both the industry and the press. *Jai Santoshi Maa* (Hail to the mother of satisfaction)[3] was a low-budget film about a little-known Hindu goddess, featuring unknown actors, cheap sets, and crude special effects, and a plot and audience dominated by women. Yet it became a runaway, word-of-mouth hit, packing cinemas in major urban centers and smaller provincial towns. It also became something more: a phenomenon that gave a new and specifically Indian inflection to the American pop phrase "cult film," for audiences commonly engaged in ritual and devotional behavior during its screenings, and temples and shrines to its titular goddess soon began to appear in many parts of India. As the years passed, the film acquired the status of a cult classic, and was regularly revived, especially for women's matinees on Friday, the day associated with the *vrat* or ritual fast and worship of Santoshi Ma; by all accounts, hundreds of thousands and perhaps millions of women periodically participated in such worship. Media accounts of the sudden emergence of a "celluloid goddess" attracted the interest of scholars interested in the impact of film on religion and popular culture, and as a result *Jai Santoshi Maa* became unique among mythological films by becoming the subject of a modest scholarly literature.

Significantly, this literature reflects the work of sociologists, anthropologists, and historians of Indian art and religion, rather than of film scholars.[4] Although these authors provide much insight into the Santoshi Ma cult, I think it is fair to say that, broadly speaking, they are more interested in Hindu goddesses than in Hindi films. Two of the most substantive analyses (by Veena Das and Stanley Kurtz) explain the popularity of *Jai Santoshi Maa* in terms of factors that are unseen by and (in a conscious sense) unknown to most of its viewers. In this process of peering, as it were, beneath the surface of the film, that surface appears to have largely been overlooked—indeed, it is Kurtz's stated intent to "dissolve" the apparent specificity of Santoshi Ma into a generic Mother Goddess allegedly shaped by infantile experience.[5] Yet there are many aspects of *Jai*

Santoshi Maa that Indian viewers may be expected to "see" and understand quite readily, and that seek to engage them through reference to familiar beliefs, discourses, and practices. It is my conviction that a re-reading of the film in terms of such contextual elements will reveal *Jai Santoshi Maa* to be an intelligent and witty film that deserves the success it has enjoyed. I will argue that, within its aesthetic conventions of flatly painted backdrops and gaudily costumed gods who appear and disappear with a clash of cymbals, the film presents a well-crafted narrative abounding in references to folklore and mythology and offering trenchant commentary on social convention; it also develops a "visual theology" that is particularly relevant to female viewers. In addition, I will propose that Veena Das's pioneering and commendable effort to place the film in a sociohistorical perspective may now, more than two decades later, be reconsidered.[6]

From Katha to Camera

Whereas most mythological films of previous decades were either based on episodes in Sanskrit literature or on the legends of spiritual exemplars of the past, *Jai Santoshi Maa*, which has as its principal human character a village housewife living in (more or less) present-day India,[7] is based on a story drawn from a popular pamphlet belonging to the genre known as *vrat katha*. A *vrat* is a disciplined religious observance for a fixed period (usually a day), involving partial or complete fasting, the ritual worship of a deity, and the recitation or hearing of a relevant *katha* (story). Some *vrat* rituals may be undertaken at any time; others occur on fixed dates that recur at weekly, monthly, or annual intervals. Some have specified aims—often the protection and wellbeing of relatives, especially husbands, brothers, or sons—whereas others seek the fulfillment of wishes. Although Indian men sometimes perform *vrats*, women are far more inclined to this type of ritual, and many *vrats* are passed down within families through women's oral tradition.[8]

Long neglected by scholars of Hinduism, *vrat* rituals and stories have recently attracted interest as part of a broader recuperation of women's religious experience.[9] Scholarship encompasses both critiques of *vrats* as "rituals contributing to the subordination and disempowerment of women"—and indeed, *vrat* stories generally encode a patriarchal ideology, making a woman responsible, through correct ritual, for the health and success of her male kin—and accounts that stress women's perceptions of agency, creativity, and ritual empowerment through *vrat* performance, as well as the role of such observance (which may include group rituals done outside the home) in maintaining women's social networks.[10]

The worship of Santoshi Ma through a *vrat* observed on Fridays with the aim of fulfilling wishes had evidently been spreading among women in northern India for more than a decade prior to the making of the film. The latter incorporated both a modified enactment of the *vrat katha* narrative and a paradigmatic performance of the ritual. It may be assumed that many women who viewed it already knew the relevant story or would learn it through their own film-inspired performance of the ritual (which, as noted, always includes a reading of the story). For this reason, the intertextual relationship between the two versions of the tale must figure in an analysis of the film.

I must disagree with the scholars who claim that there is nothing new or special about Santoshi Ma, despite her physical resemblance to some other goddesses and her worshipers' insistence, in certain contexts, that "all Mothers are one."[11] Her distinctive features figure implicitly in both her *vrat* and her film and doubtless contributed to the success of both. In identifying these features, I want to expand on Veena Das's observation that Santoshi Ma appealed especially to lower-class urban women seeking relief from "the everyday tensions of existence" by invoking "a goddess who is gentle, benevolent and dependable."[12] Santoshi Ma is the daughter of Ganesh, god of favorable beginnings, who is worshiped to "remove obstacles" and insure success. His auspicious elephant head, generous paunch, and hand-held bowl of rounded laddus (his favorite rich sweet-meat) suggest his association with the achievement of this-worldly aims, as do the names of his wives, Riddhi and Siddhi—"prosperity" and "success" (sometimes collapsed into the hyphenated name of a single consort). Although references to Ganesh's family life (apart from his childhood relationship with his own parents, Shiva and Parvati) are rare in classical mythology, the revelation that he has a daughter named Santoshi seems not inappropriate. This word, connoting satisfaction, fulfillment, or content-ment, invokes the constellation of terms and practices associated with what John Cort calls the "realm of wellbeing"—the pursuit of "health, wealth, mental peace, emotional contentment, and satisfaction in one's worldly endeavors," rather than the attainment of spiritual liberation, salvation, or a more favorable future birth.[13] It is also important to note that, in the context of this goddess, the word alludes both to fulfillment in general and also to the fulfillment of specific requests made by the observer of her *vrat*. Unlike other popular *vrats* enjoined on women by their families, such as *Karva Chauth* (observed for the welfare of husbands) or *Bhaiyya Duj* (done for the benefit of brothers), the Santoshi Ma *vrat* is elective and open-ended in terms of its goal.

The simplicity of the *vrat* is striking: It is be observed on a series of Fridays (some pamphlets specify 16, a time span popularized by the film) by doing *puja* or ceremonial worship with flowers, incense, and an oil lamp before an image of Santoshi Ma and offering her a bowl of raw sugar and roasted chickpeas *(gur-chana)*.[14] These are simple, inexpensive foodstuffs, and the instructions require a very small quantity of each—in effect, a few pennies worth. That Santoshi Ma is satisfied with such offerings again underscores her benevolent character as well as her accessibility to poor devotees. The worshiper should take a bit of *gur-chana* in hand and recite or listen to the *katha*. Afterward, the offerings in the bowl may be fed to a cow, or distributed as the goddess's *prasad* (her divine "leftovers," substantializing her grace). The only other stricture is that the performer of the *vrat* should eat only one meal during the day and should not eat, or serve to anyone else, sour or bitter foods. When one's wish has been granted, one should serve a festive meal—likewise sans sour dishes—to eight boys; this ceremony of thanksgiving is known as *udyapan* or "bringing to conclusion." The *vrat* story may be summarized as follows:

> An old woman's seven sons were all hardworking except the youngest, who was irresponsible; hence his mother served him each night, without his knowledge, the leavings of his brothers' dinners—*jutha* or polluted food. His wife became aware of this and told him; horrified, he left home to seek his fortune. He found work with a wealthy merchant and became prosperous, but forgot about his wife. Years went by and the abandoned wife was abused by her in-laws, forced to cut wood in the forest, and given scant and wretched food. One day she saw a group of women worshiping Santoshi Ma; they told her about the sixteen-week *vrat* that fulfills wishes. The wife successfully performed it, wishing for her husband's return. As a result, Santoshi Ma appeared to him in a dream and told him of his wife's plight. By her grace, the husband quickly closed his business and returned home with great wealth. Angry at his wife's mistreatment, he set up his own household, where his wife conducted the *udyapan* ceremony. But his in-laws contrived to have sour food served to the eight boys, offending the goddess; as a result the husband was imprisoned for tax evasion. His wife prayed for forgiveness and performed the *vrat* and *udyapan* a second time, successfully. Her husband was released from prison and she soon gave birth to a handsome son. Later, Santoshi Ma paid a visit to the family, assuming a fearsome form. The couple's in-laws fled in terror, but the pious wife recognized her patron goddess and worshiped her. Her in-laws then begged for forgiveness, and the whole family received the goddess's blessing.[15]

Several features of the story merit comment. That its characters are nameless and generic—"an old woman," her "seventh son," and so on—is typical of what A. K. Ramanujan calls the most "interior" kind of folktales: those generally told by women within domestic space. When such tales move outside the home and are taken up by professional bards in public space, the characters acquire names and more complex personalities[16]—as will those in the movie. Secondly, the goddess in the story, though named, is not given a birth narrative; she simply is, although the heroine does not initially know about her. The third notable feature, common to the *vrat katha* genre, is the mechanistic nature of the divine response to human ritual action: When an error occurs through no fault of the heroine's, an evil result befalls her automatically, which can only be remedied through her corrected ritual performance. All of these features would be significantly altered in the transformation of this minimal narrative—comprising but a few pages in most published versions—into a 2-hour and 20-minute feature film.

Jai Santoshi Maa Re-Viewed

The story opens in what is obviously *dev-lok*—the world of the gods—a setting immediately recognizable to anyone who has seen a mythological film. The basic elements of this heavenly realm, imagined as lying above the clouds, are decorated walls and plinths that rise out of a drifting, dry ice–generated fog. Ganesh and his family are seen celebrating the autumn festival of Rakhi (a.k.a. *raksha bandhan,* the "tying of protection"), when sisters tie string bracelets on the wrists of their brothers and receive from them sweets, gifts, and the promise of protection. Ganesh is receiving a bracelet from his sister Manasa, but his two little sons are distressed because they have no sister to likewise honor them. The divine sage Narada appears, immediately recognizable by his costume and stringed instrument as well as by his cry, "Narayan, Narayan!" (a name of Vishnu, of whom he is a devotee). In Hindu lore, Narada is a mischievous busybody who flits about the worlds eavesdropping and stirring up trouble. He takes up the children's nagging of Ganesh ("Daddy, bring us a sister!"), piously announcing that the god "who fulfills everyone's wishes" must not disappoint his own sons. Ganesh is visibly annoyed by this demand that he sire another child, and his two wives appear embarrassed and downcast. But after additional pleading, Ganesh becomes thoughtful and raises his right hand in the boon-granting gesture. Tiny flames emerge from his wives' breasts and move through space to a lotus-shaped dais, where they form into a little girl, upon whom flower petals rain down. Riddhi and Siddhi are overjoyed. Crying, "Our daughter!" and "Oh, my little queen!" they embrace her affectionately and lead her to her brothers for the tying of the rakhi bracelet. The girl then faces the camera and bows slightly with palms joined while Narada extols her: "This mind-born daughter of Lord Ganesh will always fulfill everyone's desires, will cause the Ganges of gratification to flow and known by the name of 'Mother of Satisfaction,' will promote the wellbeing of the whole world. Hail Santoshi Ma!"

Through this charming scene—which assumes that gods celebrate holidays just as human beings do, and that they may similarly be pestered by their children—the responsibility for Santoshi Ma's birth is diffused over numerous agents: the nagging boys and busybody sage, the wives, Ganesh's sister, and, of course, Ganesh himself. This collective agency of divine figures, acting out of apparently human motives albeit with superhuman powers, and displaying no evidence of omniscience or even of much forethought, will characterize the portrayal of all but one of them throughout the film. It is a style of representation that is entirely "traditional"—attested to by centuries of oral and written narrative, visual and performance art, and now in several decades of mythological films. Whereas the praising of deities in worship or in philosophical discourse may emphasize their "otherness" to the human—their being eternal, all-powerful, all-knowing, etc.—the praising of deities through stories about their "acts" *(charitra)* or "play" *(lila)* stresses their humanlike qualities, which are vividly evoked. For the majority of Hindus, such divergent discourses coexist unproblematically in their respective contexts.[17]

It is clear that Ganesh is reluctant to create a daughter; he yields only to placate his sister, sons, and wives. As Kurtz notes (drawing on Lynn Bennett's research), Santoshi Ma is thus established as a "sister-daughter" goddess, filling a role that, in the context of north Indian patriarchy, connotes both auspiciousness and liability.[18] A daughter gives joy to her brothers and female relatives—and the maternal affection of Riddhi and Siddhi is especially evident—but is a worry to her father, who must ultimately provide her dowry, guarantee her chastity, and oversee her transfer to another family. As we witness the "birth" of the little girl-child whom Narada paradoxically hails as a "Mother" of fulfilled wishes, we may recognize the ambivalent welcome she receives—a cooing embrace from her mothers, a somber stare from her father—as representative of the emotions that sometimes attend the birth of a daughter in India.

The scene shifts abruptly to earth, where we witness the fulfillment of Narada's benediction through the joyous worship of Santoshi Ma by a group of singing and dancing women, led by the maiden Satyavati (Kanan Kaushal). The setting is another mythological film staple: a pastel-colored, neoclassical temple enshrining in its sanctum a brightly painted image, here equipped with a glittering motorized halo. Everyone looks well fed and prosperous, bedecked in bright costumes that suggest a nonspecific north-Indian rural setting. The women's choreographed ensemble dancing is unlike anything one would see in a real temple (where worship is normally individual and idiosyncratic)—again, this is standard cinematic convention. Satyavati stands in the center of the whirling dancers and leads them in the first of the film's three catchy *bhajans* or devotional hymns, *Main to arti utaru* (I perform Mother Santoshi's arti)—referring to ceremonial worship with a tray bearing lamps, flowers, and incense. The emphasis throughout this scene is on the experience of *darshan*: of "seeing" and being seen by the goddess—the reciprocal act of "visual communion" that is central to Hindu worship.[19] [Figs. 1.1, 1.2, 1.3.] The camera repeatedly zooms in on Satyavati's face and eyes, then offers a comparable point-of-view zoom shot of the goddess as Satyavati sees her. Finally, it offers a shot-reverse shot from a position just over the goddess's shoulder, thus approximating (though not directly assuming) Santoshi Ma's perspective and closing the *darshanic* loop by showing us Satyavati and the other worshipers more or less as Santoshi Ma sees them. Each shot in this repeated sequence (which is intercut with the dancing women, musicians, etc.) is held for several seconds, establishing an ocular dialogue further emphasized by the lyrics.

Satyavati: There is great affection, great love in Mother's eyes.
Chorus: . . . In Mother's eyes!
Sstyavati: There is great mercy, power, and love in Mother's eyes.
Chorus: . . . In Mother's eyes!
Satyavati: Why shouldn't I gaze, again and again, into Mother's eyes?
    Behold, at every moment, a whole new world in Mother's eyes!
Chorus: . . . In Mother's eyes!

Such *darshan* sequences contribute to an aesthetic of "frontality" often noted in popular cinema, especially in mythologicals, which often consciously recapitulate the conventions of poster art.[20] But their ubiquity should not obscure their significance: The camera's movements invite the viewer to assume, as it were, both positions in the act of *darshanic* intercourse, thus closing an experiential loop that ultimately moves (as most Hindu loops do) toward an underlying unity. Indeed, the face of Santoshi Ma seen in the sanctum is of a young woman who resembles Satyavati.

When the song ends we see Satyavati and her girlfriends leaving the temple, chatting about their requests to the goddess. When asked about hers, Satyavati becomes embarrassed, lowers her eyes, and quietly says, "Mother's pearl." Initially puzzled, the girls quickly divine that by this allusion (the masculine noun *moti* or "pearl" connoting something of great value), Satyavati is expressing concern over her marriage prospects. A friend reassures her that "Just as Sita found Rama, so you too will get a bridegroom who pleases your heart." As the now-blushing Satyavati runs away from her friends, she collides with a handsome young man, Birju (Ashish Kumar), and their eyes meet. A quick sequence of shot-reverse and point-of-view shots recapitulates, in the context of worldly love, the *darshanic* dialogue in the temple, and Satyavati's girlfriends giggle that the Mother seems to have responded quickly to her request.

Figures 1.1, 1.2, 1.3 "The emphasis throughout this scene is on the experience of *darshan*: of 'seeing' and being seen by the goddess—the reciprocal act of 'visual commun-ion' that is central to Hindu worship. The camera repeatedly zooms in on Satyavati's face and eyes, then offers a comparable point-of-view zoom shot of the goddess as Satyavati sees her. Finally, it offers a shot-reverse shot from a position just over the goddess's shoulder, thus approximating Santoshi Ma's perspective and closing the *darshanic* loop by showing us Satyavati and the other worshipers more or less as Santoshi Ma sees them."

This scene, with its epic reference (to Sita and Rama's romantic first encounter in a flower garden, in the Hindi Ramcaritmanas of Tulsidas), is also the first of several instances in which the heroine invokes Santoshi Ma while obliquely asserting her own desire. The next follows immediately, when she returns home to find her father, a pious brahman widower, reciting a Ramcaritmanas verse in which the goddess Parvati assures Sita that she will obtain her desired bridegroom (*Ramcaritmanas* 1.236.7). He, too, is preoccupied with his daughter's marriage, but when he speaks to her and finds her lost in thought, he remarks in mock exasperation, "You are really amazing!" Satyavati, still in her reverie, replies "Oh no, he is amazing!" When her father, taken aback, asks "He? Who is 'he'?," she is pulled out of her daydream to confront the embarrassment of having made a confession of love in front of her father—another traditionally unacceptable expression of agency. Glancing at the *prasad* still in her hands, Satyavati rescues herself by changing the meaning of "he" to "it" (since Hindi pronouns are gender free): "I mean . . . I mean, it is amazing! Santoshi Ma's *prasad!*" Again, the goddess here serves to deflect attention from Satyavati's budding desire, which is nevertheless clear to viewers.

The next scene rapidly introduces Birju's prosperous family through allusions to the mythology of Krishna, for Birju (whose name is an epithet of the flute-playing god) is, like Krishna, the youngest of many sons and an artistic and restless soul, plays a bamboo flute, and is doted on by his eldest brother Daya Ram ("compassionate Ram"), a hefty farmer whom Birju himself likens to Krishna's elder brother Balaram. We also meet Birju's six sisters-in-law, of whom two are singled out: Durga and Maya, both named for powerful goddesses and clearly shrewish and annoyed with their still-unmarried and unemployed junior brother-in-law, whom they regard as lazy. The anonymous family of the *vrat katha* is thus rapidly transformed into a set of named individuals with distinct personalities and relationships to the hero. Further, it becomes plain to viewers familiar with the printed story that the mistreatment of the junior son (and later of his wife) will here be perpetrated not by his sweet-looking widowed mother (played by Leela Mishra, who made a career of such benign, white-saried roles) but by his scowling sisters-in-law. This obeys (and instructs new viewers in) what Rosie Thomas identifies as "one of the most tenacious rules of Hindi cinema," namely, "that it is 'impossible' to make a film in which a protagonist's real mother is villainous or even semivillainous. . . . "[21]

Another rule of Hindi cinema is that there must be a fight, usually over a woman's honor, and this is provided by introducing another character unknown to the *katha*: a villain (signaled by his mustache and swarthy looks) named Banke ("twisted") who tries to rape Satyavati when she is coming home late one night from another temple festival. Birju hears her cries and, with the aid of his comical sidekick Tota Ram (Ram the parrot), beats off Banke and his henchmen, even forcing the villain to grovel at Satyavati's feet. In the process, Birju sustains a head wound, which permits Satyavati to bring him home and introduce him to her father, signaling demurely that this heroic figure is the man she loves. Later, at their lamp-lit gate, Birju too declares his love for her. The delighted pandit gives his blessing to his daughter's choice and soon proceeds to arrange the marriage, though only after Satyavati has returned alone to Santoshi Ma's temple and asked for this boon, promising a pilgrimage of thanksgiving to all the Mother's shrines. Once again, Satyavati's assumption of agency is couched within the language of self-effacing devotion.

The marriage ceremony is presented through a sequence of vignettes that recapitulate its key moments—and also its prototypical representation in such famous films as *Mother India* (1957): the circumambulation of the sacred fire, the daughter's tearful leave-taking of her childhood home, and her first steps into the household in which she will spend the rest of her life. These scenes effectively evoke the protocols of a rural Indian wedding, with special sensitivity to the viewpoint of the *bahu* or new bride: as the men and women in Birju's family repair to separate sections of the compound, Satyavati is left with her new sisters-in-law. Durga and Maya simmer with jealousy at seeing their "worthless" brother-in-law achieve a love match with a young woman whose beauty is praised by all. They contrive a frighteningly inauspicious welcome at the gate of the house, then complain within earshot of Satyavati that she has "stolen" their own wedding ornaments. Satyavati's vulnerability and fear is painfully apparent throughout this sequence. Though the women's malice is exaggerated, the types of teasing depicted (including booby trapping the decorated nuptial bed) and the anxiety aroused are common enough to resonate with female viewers.

In the next scene, Birju's brothers force him to join them in the fields while Satyavati grinds wheat at home. Overcome by desire for his bride, Birju runs home and, despite the women's taunts at his "shameless" behavior, pulls Satyavati into their bedroom.[22] His wife's response suggests both her pleasure at his attention and her worry over her in-laws' disapproval, the brunt of which she will have to bear. As Birju romances her, she surprises him by invoking their patron deity.

Birju: It's only you whom my eyes behold, here, there, everywhere!
Satyavati: Me?
Birju: Yes.
Satyavati: (coyly shaking her head) No, there's but one form everywhere.
Birju: What form?
Satyavati: Like you sang that day: "Here, there, everywhere, why ask
    where She is . . . our Santoshi Ma!"

Birju: (taken aback) Santoshi Ma?
Satyavati: Yes, before our marriage I made a vow at Mother's feet.
Birju: Vow? What vow?
Satyavati: That after obtaining you, I would take Mother's *darshan* in her temples.
Birju: (smiling) Oh, is this your vow?

Despite its pious language, the scene maintains a coyly amorous tone: Satyavati is revealing an intimate secret to her beloved, and it pleases them both. This is underscored by what immediately follows: a reprise of a *bhajan* previously sung by Birju (*Apni Santoshi Ma* [Our Santoshi Ma]), now accompanying footage of the couple on pilgrimage, taking *darshan* at five temples located in three different states. This type of musical sequence, displaying exotic geography and suggesting, through changes of costume, both lapse of time and material abundance, is common in Hindi films. Its associations are normally with romance, not devotion, but it is here skillfully used to convey both. The refrain of Birju's song, heard while the couple walk along the riverbank at a pilgrimage place, "She's here, there, everywhere—don't ask where she is!—our Santoshi Ma!" now seems less a theological assertion than an invocation of the joy and freedom of travel—which for many Indians, combines equal measures of pilgrimage and tourism. Whereas big-budget *masala* films may whisk their lovers off to Kashmir or Switzerland, director Vijay Sharma sticks closer to home but achieves the same purpose. Satyavati appears in different saris at successive temples, and she and Birju gaze reverently at each image of the Mother, then turn to look adoringly at one another. They are plainly on an extended, private vacation. Once again, by invoking her goddess, Satyavati has achieved what many a young Indian wife would most like (and many middle-class women increasingly enjoy, as "honeymoons" have come into fashion): time alone with her new husband, free from the oversight of his family members.

This rapturous interlude is followed by a return to the world of the gods, and the introduction of a dramatic plot twist unknown to the *katha* pamphlets: Narada inciting the jealously of Lakshmi, Parvati, and Brahmani—the wives of the so-called "Hindu trinity" of Vishnu, Shiva, and Brahma—toward Santoshi Ma, and anger at her devotee.[23] The setting is Vaikunth Lok, the heaven of Vishnu, imagined as an opulent celestial home strewn with couches and pillows. The goddesses are heavily adorned housewives, and their dialogue is deliciously witty.

Lakshmi: (to maidservant, after noticing empty throne couch) Where has the Master of Vaikunth gone?

Maidservant: Don't know.
Parvati: (entering through doorway and looking around tentatively) Sister
    Lakshmi . . . ?
Lakshmi: (visibly pleased) Parvati! Come in, Sister. (Parvati approaches.)
    Today you've come from Kailash [Shiva's heaven] after a long time.
Parvati: What can I do, Lakshmi? I'm kept so busy serving Bholenath
    [Shiva], I don't get any leisure. Today he went out somewhere, so I
    came right over! But I don't see your Narayan around either.
Lakshmi: (petulantly) Yes, he also took off early this morning, without
    saying anything.
Brahmani: (entering through doorway) Men are all the same! Brahma-ji
    also took off without so much as a word to me.
Parvati: Never mind, Brahmani. (smiling) This gives us all an excuse to
    get together.

At this point Narada enters. After praising the three goddesses, he notes
with mock dismay that people on earth no longer seem interested in
worshiping them—they have found "some other" goddess. Here again, the
film plays on viewers' awareness of the relative novelty of Santoshi Ma's
cult, for the goddesses have clearly never heard of her. Their angry response
indicates that they consider her to be an upstart [fig.1.4]. When Narada
adds that Satyavati, a faithful wife, is the "exemplary devotee" of the
goddess and tirelessly serves holy men, the three are further enraged.

The scene cuts to the door of Birju's house, where three sadhus are
calling for alms. They are angrily sent away by Durga and Maya, but
Satyavati surreptitiously calls them back and humbly offers them the
prasad of Santoshi Ma. Though initially surprised by the poor offering,
they note Satyavati's devotion and accept it, loudly acclaiming her patron
goddess. Back in heaven, the same mendicants appear before the goddesses,
who are still fuming at Narada's tidings. When the sadhus, too, acclaim
Santoshi Ma, the goddesses' rage erupts afresh and they begin to push them
out the door. The three then transform into Vishnu, Shiva, and Brahma,
much to the embarrassment of their wives. But they continue to praise
Santoshi Ma, and offer their wives her prasad. "Gur-chana—you call that
prasad?" asks Parvati disdainfully, and Lakshmi adds, "We don't eat that!"
After the men leave, their wives continue to fume: "Who is goddess
Santoshi compared to us?" Soon they hatch a plot: By ruining Satyavati's
happiness, they will reveal to mortals the futility of worshiping Santoshi Ma.

These scenes evoke complex associations. Satyavati's recall of the
sadhus underscores the folk belief that, although many in mendicant garb
are merely lazy drifters, sadhus should never be turned away empty handed,
for they may be enlightened souls or (as here) gods in disguise. Class
distinctions are also suggested in the goddesses' disdainful refusal of the

humble *prasad* brought from earth by their husbands. Their initial response to the three sadhus—calling them "beggars" and pushing them away—mirrors that of Satyavati's sisters-in-law and underscores the goddesses affinity with them as "established" figures in their respective families, human and divine. Similarly, Satyavati's own affinity with Santoshi Ma—both are young newcomers in their respective realms—is likewise affirmed. The stage is now set for the goddesses' persecution of Satyavati/Santoshi Ma, which will unfold through the young bride's female in-laws.[24]

There ensues a series of worsening tribulations, beginning with Birju's abandoning the household after learning that he has been served the leavings of his brothers' meals. Although this incident parallels the printed *vrat katha*, it introduces psychological and emotional complexity. The happy-go-lucky Birju, who has until now been oddly oblivious of his family's disapproval of his ways and hostility toward his wife, becomes incensed when he learns of the tainted food he has been eating. But whereas he can think only of the insult to his honor, we see, in Satyavati's terrified pleading to be taken with him, her awareness of the fate she will suffer in his absence. Birju, of course, ignores her pleas and makes a dramatic exit, leaving her at the mercy of his family. The goddesses, watching on high, are delighted, and promise Narada still worse to come.

Figure 1.4 "Here again, the film plays on viewers' awareness of the relative novelty of Santoshi Ma's cult, for the goddesses have clearly never heard of her. Their angry response indicates that they consider her to be an upstart. When Narada adds that Satyavati, a faithful wife, is the 'exemplary devotee' of the goddess and tirelessly serves holy men, the three are further enraged."

As Birju takes a ferry across a lake, they generate a tempest and attempt to drown him, but Satyavati's prayers to Santoshi Ma are answered: The goddess (now in a youthful, adult form, portrayed by Anita Guha) appears on earth and rescues him, showing herself to Birju as a young ascetic woman. Apparently unaware of this, the jealous goddesses come as village women to inform Birju's family of his death. Though Satyavati refuses to believe this (since the Mother cannot have ignored her prayers) and the compassionate Daya Ram rushes out to search for his brother, the sisters-in-law now treat Satyavati as an inauspicious widow and domestic menial. Further trials ensue: finding Satyavati alone cutting wood in the forest, the rogue Banke attempts revenge for his earlier humiliation. Before fainting, Satyavati calls on Santoshi Ma, who again manifests, transforming her trident into a cobra that chases Banke to the edge of a cliff from which he falls to his death.

Birju, meanwhile, enjoys excellent fortune. Hired by a gem merchant, he learns to assay precious stones and receives the attentions of the old man's voluptuous only daughter, Geeta. Unlike the hero of the printed story, who simply forgets his wife when abroad, Birju suffers amnesia induced by the three jealous goddesses, allowing viewers to voyeuristically savor his budding love affair. This too offers education in Hindi Film 101, since the hero with two loves—one domestic and virtuous, the other exotic and risqué—is one of Bombay cinema's enduring tropes. Geeta wears skimpy, glittering saris and beehive hairdos, and Birju sports a rakish mustache and plays his flute during their frolics in her mansion and nearby flower garden. This is intercut with pathetic scenes of Satyavati's worsening condition, and a sung commentary on this by a male singer, "Mat ro" ("Don't cry") that introduces nationalist discourse about the moral fortitude of "the Indian woman." But the horrible taunts of her sisters-in-law, who eventually confine her to a corner of the courtyard and beat and starve her, even as they force her to scour pots and chop firewood, drives Birju's wife to attempt suicide. She is stopped by Narada, in his sole appearance in the film's world of mortals, who comforts her and tells her to perform the sixteen-Fridays fast for Santoshi Ma. Narada's intervention here is notable, replacing the anonymous group of women in the written *katha*. The whimsical sage served as agent provocateur in Santoshi Ma's birth and again intervened to stir up the senior goddesses' jealousy against her. Now he further incites Satyavati to defeat them. His presence in fact accentuates the parallelism of the two narratives—for just as Satyavati is being tested by her in-laws, so Santoshi Ma, through Narada's machinations, is being tested by the (diffused, collective) will of the gods.

Satyavati's devotion is now given a ritual framework and a specific goal. The enactment of the rite is dramatized by another *bhajan, Karti hum tumhara vrat* (I perform your *vrat*), which shows the passage of time through the increasing number of lamps on Satyavati's tray and the darkening circles under her eyes, dramatically intercut with scenes of Birju and Geeta in love. Unlike the earlier hymns with their celebratory tone, this one is a plaintive cry of distress, with the refrain: "You are my only mooring in midstream, / Mother, carry me safely across!" As the climax of the fast approaches, the tricky Narada again warns the three goddesses that their plan may go awry, and they contrive to make it impossible for Satyavati to obtain even a scant cup of *gur-chana* for her sixteenth Friday. Taking the form of a white-haired, gap-toothed old woman, Santoshi Ma magically causes the needed supplies to fly out of an astonished merchant's shop and onto Satyavati's tray; she offers them, completes her *vrat,* and finally verbalizes her request: that her husband not forget her.

Santoshi Ma immediately restores Birju's memory and, for good measure, performs a miracle to smooth things out with his employer and Geeta, so that they send him off with good wishes and bulging coffers. She also causes Geeta to meet Daya Ram, wandering in search of his lost brother, and to direct him, too, homeward. As in the printed story, Birju is horrified to discover his wife's plight, and though his family members (eyeing his wealth) proffer their love, he rejects them and proceeds to build a grand mansion, complete with its own ornate temple to Santoshi Ma. Satyavati, now restored to health and richly dressed, plans a lavish *udyapan* ceremony and, harboring no grudge, begs her husband to forgive his kin, whom she invites to the festivities. These are depicted through a reprise of the first *bhajan,* but with a striking visual difference. The dancing women waving *arti* trays are now no longer rustic belles in mirrorwork skirts, dancing in a village temple, but middle-class matrons in fashionable silk and georgette saris, dancing in a party setting redolent of bourgeois comfort. The transformation encodes not merely Satyavati's own odyssey but the desired journey of many an Indian family.

Durga and Maya (inspired by the three goddesses who have yet to concede defeat) squeeze lime juice into one of the milk dishes for the ceremonial meal. The results are literally volcanic (Santoshi Ma's angry face is intercut with stock footage of a lava-spewing eruption), but unlike the written story, the film does not direct the goddess's ire at Satyavati and Birju. Instead, the two sisters-in-law are stricken, their limbs twisted and faces blackened, and their sons who have eaten the tainted food fall dead. Moreover, the earthquake that rocks Birju's new house also shakes the worlds of the three goddesses, causing their divine husbands to faint. Although Birju's kin accuse Satyavati of poisoning the children and threaten to kill both him and her, the senior brother, Daya Ram, appears and defends Satyavati, declaring, "She is not a sinner; she is a paragon of truth and virtue. She is not a woman, she is a goddess." When the angry accusations continue, Satyavati runs to the temple and offers a final, anguished plea in the form of the song *Madad karo Santoshi Mata* (Help me, Mother Santoshi): "Today, don't let infamy stain, O Mother / The fair name of our bond." This invocation of their *nata* (intimate "bond," "connection," or "relationship") brings the goddess herself to the scene, to rectify all wrongs, reversing, at Satyavati's request, the deformity of Durga and Maya and restoring all the children to life. As all errant parties confess the wrongs done to Satyavati, the Mother blesses the family and disappears amid loud acclamation.

A brief parallel coda ensues in heaven, where Narada leads the three repentant goddesses to "take shelter at the feet" of Santoshi Ma. Looking embarrassed, they state that they always knew who she was (Parvati remarks, "She is my granddaughter") but were merely testing the depth of Satyavati's devotion.[25] The camera then cuts to Santoshi Ma's face; she appears coolly triumphant, neither needing nor caring for the defeated goddesses' endorsement.

Their spouses now materialize, along with Ganesh, to form a tableau: Santoshi Ma in the center on her lotus throne, with rays of light emanating from her, flanked by gods and goddesses—a family photo, but also a court scene, with its most important personage centrally placed—as Narada solicits a final benediction that explicitly confirms a "new" deity's incorporation into the pantheon: "Now all of you give a blessing to Goddess Santoshi so that her name too, like yours, will live eternally."

Getting "Satisfaction"

Several scholars of Hindi cinema have argued that significant thematic changes occurred in commercial films during the mid-1970s. M. Madhava Prasad has noted the decline, after several decades of dominance, of the type of "social" film that he calls the "feudal family romance," and its replacement by a "populist cinema of mobilization" that attempts to address (and, according to Prasad, to co-opt) the rising expectations of lower-class groups "agitating for the realization of the new nation's professed democratic and socialist ideals."[26] Similarly Kajri Jain notes the shift in leading men from the "soft, romantic" heroes of earlier decades to the unquestioned megastar of the 1970s and 1980s, Amitabh Bachchan, whose lithe and sinewy physique contributed to his effective portrayal, in numerous films, of a "goal-driven, instrumentalized" subaltern hero, a working class "angry young man."[27] Significantly, the major action hits of 1975, *Deewar* and *Sholay,* figure as key texts in both scholars' analyses.

1975 was also, of course, the year when nearly three decades of Congress Party rule suffered its most significant challenge. Amid exposés of widespread bureaucratic corruption and a court decision against the prime minister, activist Jayaprakash Narayan called for a "total revolution," and massive strikes threatened to cripple the country's nationalized infrastructure. Indira Gandhi responded in June by declaring a state of national emergency, suspending constitutional liberties and freedom of the press, and jailing thousands of her opponents. This desperate measure would eventually further weaken the Congress mandate, leading to Gandhi's massive defeat at the polls in 1977 and, in the longer term, to the rise of opposition parties that mobilized religious and local caste- and class-based identities. Though the changes that ensued certainly stopped short of "total revolution," they nevertheless eroded the authority of the elite that had been ruling the nation since Independence and contributed to the political awakening and rising expectations of formerly disenfranchised groups: "scheduled" and "backward castes" and lower-middle-class laborers, artisans, and merchants.

Rather than categorize *Jai Santoshi Maa* as an anomalously successful mythological in a year of violent "mobilization" films, I propose that it too represents part of a larger picture of nonelite assertiveness and agency, but with specific relevance to an audience unaddressed by films like *Deewar* and *Sholay*: an audience mainly consisting of lower-middle-class women. The adaptation of a popular *vrat-katha* to the screen—skillfully preserving key features of its written version while also invoking and in fact demonstrating the representational and narrative conventions of mainstream cinema—helped to incorporate this new audience into the "public culture" of the period. Evoking a rural and lower-class ethos through its setting and themes, and full of clever intertextual references accessible (and hence satisfying) to its audience, this is a film that addresses viewers' aspirations in several ways.

Above all, it concerns the life experience that is typically the most traumatic for an Indian woman: that of being wrenched from her *mayka* or maternal home and forced to adjust to a new household in which she is often treated as an outsider who must be tested and disciplined, sometimes harshly, before she can be integrated into the family. Satyavati's relationship with Santoshi Ma enables her to endure the sufferings inflicted on her by her sisters-in-law and to triumph over them, but it also accomplishes more. It insures that Satyavati's life consistently departs from the script that patriarchal society writes for a girl of her status: She marries a man of her own choosing, enjoys a companionate relationship (and independent travel) with her husband, and ultimately acquires a home of her own, out of reach of her in-laws.

Moreover, viewers can enjoy her achievement of all this because it is presented as the "Mother's grace," bestowed on a humble, submissive woman who overtly asks little for herself. While appearing to adhere to the code of a conservative extended family (the systemic abuses of which it dramatically highlights), the film quietly endorses goals, shared by many women, that subvert this code. This oblique assertiveness has a class dimension as well. The three goddesses are shown to be "established" both religiously and materially: They preside over plush celestial homes and expect expensive offerings. Santoshi Ma, who is happy with *gur-chana* and is in fact associated with less-educated, and less-advantaged people, is in their view a poor new-comer threatening to usurp their status. They intend to nip her "upward mobility" in the bud, yet in the end must concede defeat and bestow their (reluctant?) blessing on the *nouvelle arrivée*. The sociodomestic aspect of the film (goddesses as senior in-laws, oppressing a young bride) thus parallels its socioeconomic aspect (goddesses as established bourgeois matrons, looking scornfully at the aspirations of poorer women).

Satyavati's relationship to Santoshi Ma, established through the parallel story of the goddesses, suggests that there is more agency involved here than at first appears to be the case—though it is again the diffused, depersonal-ized agency favored in Hindu narrative. Satyavati's successful integration into Birju's family, indeed her emergence as its most prosperous female member, parallels Santoshi Ma's acceptance in her divine clan and revela-tion as its most potent *shakti*. In both cases this happens without the intervention, so standard in Hindi cinema, of a male hero, for there are no exemplary male figures in the film. Birju is a pleasant but clueless hunk who escapes disaster only through the timely intervention of his wife. In heaven, the tridev are likewise amiable gentlemen, yet evidently in control neither of their wives nor of the cosmos. If there is a presiding divine figure (apart from the quixotic prankster, Narada, who pushes the plot forward through whimsical and even malicious interventions) it is the serene and self-possessed "mother of satisfaction," Santoshi Ma.

Yet through its visual treatment of the reciprocal gaze of *darshan* and its use of parallel narratives, the film also suggests that Santoshi Ma and Satyavati—deity and devotee—are, in fact, one, a truth finally declared, at film's end, by the wise and compassionate Daya Ram. As in the ideology of tantric ritual (or the conventions of "superhero" narrative in the West), the "mild-mannered" and submissive Satyavati merges, through devotion and sheer endurance, with her ideal and alter ego, the cosmic superpower Santoshi Ma. Similarly (and only apparently paradoxically), the latter's ultimate incorporation into the "established" pantheon comes about pre-cisely through the persistent agency of her long-suffering earthly counter-part. This is in fact consistent with the relationship between divine and human realms found in much Hindu lore, which reverses the standard Christian formula to present an ultimately human-centered theology that unfolds, so to speak, "in heaven as it is on earth."

Figure 1.5 "Appearing as a little girl at the film's beginning, as a self-confident young woman in her manifestations throughout most of the story, and as a grandmotherly crone on the final Friday of Satyavati's fast, Santoshi Ma makes herself available to viewers as an embodiment of the female life cycle and conveys the quietly mobilizing message that it is reasonable for every woman to expect, within that cycle, her own measure of 'satisfaction' in the form of love, comfort, and respect."

In a further theovisual argument, the film proposes that not only is Santoshi Ma available to all women through her *vrat* ritual but that she is, in fact, all women. Appearing as a little girl at the film's beginning, as a self-confident young woman in her manifestations throughout most of the story, and as a grandmotherly crone on the final Friday of Satyavati's fast [fig. 1.5], Santoshi Ma makes herself available to viewers as an embodiment of the female life cycle, and conveys the quietly mobilizing message that it is reasonable for every woman to expect, within that cycle her own measure of "satisfaction" in the form of love, comfort, and respect.

Notes

*I am grateful to Madhu Kishwar and Brent Plate, both of whom encouraged me to turn my longstanding interest in *Jai Santoshi Maa* into an essay. A longer version of this essay (including additional discussion of the history of Indian "mythological" films and their neglect by scholars) appeared in the journal *Manushi* 131 (2002), as a two-part article entitled "A Superhit Goddess" and "A 'Made to Satisfaction' Goddess" (10–16, 24–37). I also thank my colleague in cinema studies, Corey Creekmur, for his useful comments on an earlier draft.

1. Nasreen Munni Kabir, *Bollywood, The Indian Cinema Story* (London: Channel 4 Books, 2001).
2. For more on this, see Lutgendorf, "A Superhit Goddess," *Manushi* 131 (2002): 10–16.
3. I use the Romanized spelling of the title given in the film credits. Elsewhere I spell the goddess's name as Santoshi Ma.
4. Sociologist Veena Das's 1980 essay on the film includes a synopsis of its plot but quickly moves to an ambitious typology of mother goddesses within which she situates Santoshi Ma; she then speculates on the socioreligious concerns of the film's primary fans, whom she identifies as lower-class urban women. However, Das offers two penetrating and related observations on the film, concerning the relative centrality of its human heroine: "It seems to me that in an important sense one may justifiably ask whether the true subject of this story is not Santoshi Ma, but Satyavati" (Das, "The Mythological Film and Its Framework of Meaning: An Analysis of *Jai Santoshi Ma*," in *India International Centre Quarterly* 8.1 [1980]: 49), and the parallel structure of its two narratives, divine and human: "Every significant chain of events relating to Satyavati points to a successive movement in the evolution of Santoshi Ma. . . . " (ibid.). Surprisingly, neither of these insights seems to have been pursued in subsequent scholarship, but I will return to them shortly.

In a panel on "Santoshi Ma, the Film Goddess" at the annual meeting of the American Academy of Religion in 1984, art historian Michael Brand traced the history of the goddess's worship to the early 1960s, when five temples to Santoshi Ma were dedicated at widely separated sites in northern India. He also showed how the iconography of the goddess rapidly became standardized through poster images. Brand's paper indicated that the cult of Santoshi Ma was already spreading among women—through word of mouth, pamphlet literature, and poster art—well before the making of the film.

In the course of fieldwork on the Santoshi Ma cult, anthropologist Stanley Kurtz concluded that Santoshi Ma was not perceived by devotees as distinctive or new, and was in fact often confused with other popular goddesses (Kurtz, *All the Mothers Are One: Hindu India and the Cultural Reshaping of Psychoanalysis* [New York: Columbia University Press, 1992], 2–4, 15–16). Like Das, he became principally interested in creating a comprehensive typology of female deities, but in the service of a yet more ambitious agenda: a reworking of Freudian theory to account for the different cultural aims of Hindu childrearing. His book, *All the Mothers Are One* includes an extended discussion of both the printed and cinematic narratives of Santoshi Ma, focusing on the tension Kurtz identifies between an Indian child's "natural" and "in-law" mothers (the women of its father's family, who play a key role in childrearing) (ibid., 111–131). Kurtz's critique of the cultural biases inherent in earlier psychological studies of Indian childhood is often fascinating, yet his use of Freud's theory of infantile sexuality to explain the multiplicity of Hindu goddesses (as reflecting unconscious memories of early experiences with multiple female caregivers) is certainly open to question.

Kathleen Erndl's *Victory to the Mother,* on goddess cults of the Punjab hills, includes a chapter on "The Goddess and Popular Culture" that devotes a section to Santoshi Ma, who "has taken all of northern India by storm." However, Erndl says little about the film, beyond noting its massive popularity (*Victory to the Mother: The Hindu Goddess of India in Myth, Ritual, and Symbol* [New York: Oxford University Press, 1993], 141–152). She summarizes Santoshi Ma's story based on written sources and identifies the goddess with the lion-riding Sheranvali popular in northwestern India, an unmarried goddess who is both virgin and mother (ibid., 3–6). Like Kurtz, Erndl argues that there is nothing particularly "new" about Santoshi Ma, apart from her unusually rapid diffusion through the media of print, film, and radio (ibid., 144).

5. Kurtz, *All the Mothers,* 13–28.

6. I am considerably assisted by having access, as previous scholars did not, to a good-quality copy of the film in DVD format (Mishra 1975, distributed by Worldwide Entertainment Group), which greatly facilitates analysis of its scenes. The DVD also offers optional English subtitles.

7. The film's earthly sets create a rustic milieu that (as in many Hindi films with rural settings) is intentionally vague as to locale or chronology; though there are no specific details to suggest the late twentieth century, neither are there any that would signal a particular period in the past, and the pilgrimage sites visited by the heroine and her husband are obviously contemporary, with asphalt streets and overhead electrical wires visible in some shots.

8. Anne Mackenzie Pearson, *Because It Gives Me Peace of Mind: Ritual Fasts in the Religious Lives of Hindu Women* (Albany, NY: State University of the New York Press, 1996), 3–11.

9. Ibid., xv–xvi.

10. Ibid., 8–9.

11. Kurtz's repeated references to "an everchanging array of goddesses" who "replicate, expand, merge, and contract in number and type" (Kurtz, *All the Mothers,* 98), and to an "ongoing, kaleidoscopic process wherein new goddesses are generated and recombined" (ibid., 121) reflect the perceptions of an outside observer. To an individual Hindu worshiper, there is no "everchanging array of goddesses" but rather a limited number of divine Mothers who are approached for the specific needs at which they specialize. Though worshipers, if pressed, will often articulate the idea that all such goddesses are ultimately manifestations of a single divine feminine power or *shakti,* they nevertheless take the goddesses' individual personalities and functions for granted in their dealings with them.

12. Das, "The Mythological Film," 54.

13. John E. Cort, *Jains in the World: Religious Values and Ideology in India* (New York: Oxford University Press, 2001), 187–200.

14. My description of the ritual and story is based on Vidyavindhu Simha and Yamuna Agnihotri, *Din-din parva, bharatiya vrat, parva evam tyohar* (New Delhi: National Publishing House, 2000), 338–339. This massive compen-

dium of hundreds of *vrat*s includes a version of the story that closely corresponds to the pamphlet versions cited by other scholars; indeed Das noted in
1980 that such standardization seemed to be the outcome of print-media
transmission (Das, "The Mythological Film," 55.)

15. Simha and Agnihotri, *Din-din parva,* 338–339.

16. A. K. Ramanujan, "Two Realms of Kannada Folklore," in *Another Harmony:
    New Essays on the Folklore of India,* Stuart H. Blackburn and A. K. Ramanujan,
    eds. (Berkeley and Los Angeles: University of California Press, 1986), 43–46.

17. A. K. Ramanujan labels such representation of deities "domestication" and
    attributes it especially to "folk" retellings of their deeds (ibid., 66–67).
    However, although one can cite (as he does) specific instances in which a
    distinction between relatively more dignified and more domesticized represen-
    tations are found in respectively "elite" and "folk" versions of stories (e.g., the
    treatment of the Rama story in the classical Tamil epic *Iramavataram* of
    Kampan versus the same epic's raucous and often ribald exposition and staging
    by shadow puppeteers) (Stuart Blackburn, *Inside the Drama House: Rama
    Stories and Shadow Puppets in South India* [Berkeley and Los Angeles:
    University of California Press, 1996], 22–54), domesticized portrayals are not
    uncommon in elite texts (e.g., the Sanskrit *purana*s). Such representation is
    found even in the ultra-orthodox Srivaishnava tradition of South India: For
    example, that sect's largest annual festival includes a publicly staged episode in
    which Lakshmi quarrels with her husband Vishnu (the Supreme Being of the
    Srivaishnavas) and locks him out of the house (his principal temple at
    Srirangam) after he has been away all day, because she suspects him of having
    an affair (Vasudha Narayanan, *The Vernacular Veda: Revelation, Recitation,
    and Ritual* (Columbia, SC: University of South Carolina Press, 1994), 129–130).
    The "elite" versus "folk" distinction is only of limited utility here, and the
    cultural sense of the appropriateness of such portrayals would seem to depend
    heavily on the context of performance (cf. Ramanujan's argument in another
    essay that Indian discourse is characteristically "context-sensitive" and tends
    to avoid the absolutes and universals favored in Western ideology; Ramanujan,
    "Two Realms," 47–50).

18. Kurtz, *All the Mothers,* 21–25; Lynn Bennett, *Dangerous Wives and Sacred
    Sisters: Social and Symbolic Roles of High-Caste Women in Nepal* (New York:
    Columbia University Press, 1983).

19. Diana Eck, *Darsan: Seeing the Divine Image in India* (Chambersburg, PA:
    Anima Books, 1981).

20. Geeta Kapur, "Mythic Material in Indian Cinema," *Journal of Arts and Ideas*
    (1987): 80; Anuradha Kapur, "The Repression of Gods and Heroes: Parsi
    Mythological Drama of the Early Twentieth Century," *Journal of Arts and
    Ideas* (1993): 92.

21. Rosie Thomas, "Melodrama and the Negotiation of Morality in Mainstream
    Hindi Film," in *Consuming Modernity: Public Culture in a South Asian World,*
    Carol A. Breckenridge, ed. (Minneapolis: University of Minnesota Press,
    1995), 164.

22. Like the wedding ritual, this scene recapitulates one between Raj Kumar and
    Nargis in *Mother India.*

23. Brahma's wife is also known as Sarasvati and is worshiped as the patron of art and learning. The name change here is indicative of the film's disinterest in the usual attributes of these goddesses, and its stress instead on their wifely roles as established matrons of divine households.

24. This scene and ensuing ones in which the goddesses gleefully watch the havoc they wreak are discussed by Kurtz, who notes the apparent discrepancy between theater audiences' enthusiastic reception of such scenes—which were "particularly relished" during screenings—and the disapproval expressed by some of his interviewees for what they claimed were innovations inspired by the "commercial motives" of the filmmaker (Kurtz, *All the Mothers*, 14). Kurtz accounts for this paradoxical reaction through his reworked psychoanalytic theory: The goddesses' anger represents the child's subconscious memory of the unequal relationship between his natural mother and her female in-laws, which is enacted in a "more explicit and more exciting" manner in the film than in the written story (ibid., 116). Kurtz further argues that "the commercial nature of the mythological film," of which the audience is aware, permits it to take "unorthodox" liberties with the story (ibid., 269 n.2). Although I agree with Kurtz that the dynamics of joint family households are being invoked here, I am unconvinced by his reorientation of the plot around suppressed memories of (male) childhood. Its central character is patently Satyavati and its conflict centers on *her* mistreatment by her in-laws, reflecting domestic tension that is hardly an unconscious memory but rather a daily experience for many women. Further, as I have already noted, the supposed problem of cinematic "unorthodoxy" ignores the ubiquity of this kind of "domestication" of deities and its ready acceptance by most Hindus in a narrative context. However, it is understandable that in a more analytical context—as under a foreign re-searcher's "close questioning" about the religious meaning of a film scene (ibid., 14)— some interviewees might indeed feel compelled to object to it.

25. This kind of "excuse-ex-machina" is also found in brahmanical narrative, where it is inserted to preclude the (impossible) admission of injustice commit-ted by male exemplars. Two famous examples are Rama's bland assertion, following Sita's successful completion of a fire ordeal, that he never actually doubted her virtue (*Ramayana* 6:121), and King Dushyanta's similar dis-claimer to Shakuntala (in the *Mahabharata* version of the Shakuntala story, in which the king never loses his memory but lies about his liason with the girl; *Mahabharata* 1.7.69). In both cases, the preceding powerful speeches by the women, and the awareness of the injustice they have suffered, has tended to make a stronger impression on audiences than the face-saving coda.

26. M. Madhava Prasad, *Ideology of the Hindi Film: A Historical Construction* (Delhi: Oxford University Press, 1998), 138–159.

27. Kajri Jain, "Muscularity and its Ramifications: Mimetic Male Bodies in Indian Mass Culture," *South Asia* 24 (2001): 216–221.

Chapter Two

"My Story Begins Before I Was Born":

Myth, History, and Power in Julie Dash's *Daughters of the Dust**

Judith Weisenfeld

In her 1991 film, *Daughters of the Dust,* director Julie Dash seeks to derive both a narrative structure and a cinematic style from the West and Central African[1] religious traditions that inform the cultural sensibilities of the Gullah people who form the center of her story.[2] In taking this approach, Dash requires that viewers enter Gullah culture fully from the outset, and she provides little context for her American audience to translate the characters or the story into the more familiar classical Hollywood style.[3] Translation, the film insists, damages the integrity of the unique cultural and social experience of the Gullah people, and, as viewers, we are called upon to take the difficult road of letting go of ingrained expectations for what a film about the consequences of slavery *should* look like, how characters in such a story *should* behave, and what the function of religion in the community *should* be. Dash is so keen on disrupting what American audiences had been conditioned to anticipate concerning how African Americans—and black women in particular—should appear on film that she sought to set the atmosphere of a "foreign" film from the start, beginning with the voice of one of the narrators speaking in Gullah without providing subtitles.[4] In this film, which is so much about opening oneself to West and Central African ways of apprehending the world, Dash requires that we engage these possibilities along with the characters in the film, even as we might find the task of doing so confounding or discomfiting. From the opening shots of the beach of Ibo Landing—of the images of Bilal Muhammad (Umar Abdurrahamn) praying near the water at sunrise, and the first glimpse of the family's matriarch Nana Peazant (Cora Lee Day) fully clothed and washing herself in the ocean like a "salt water Negro"[5]—we are asked to take a religious journey entirely in the terms of this extended Gullah family, especially from the perspective of the women. The first feature-length film by an African American woman to gain theatrical release in the United States, *Daughters of the Dust* became a flashpoint for discussions of the meaning of diaspora for black women, the quality and concerns of African American film in the 1990s, black aesthetics, and the burden of representing African American history.[6] Examining the West and Central African and "New World" religious groundings of the film's narrative and thematic concerns, this essay explores Dash's engagement of both myth and history in order to make sense of the varied and heated responses to this religious film that positions black women at the center of its vision.

The two modes that help to structure *Daughters of the Dust*—attention to historical detail with a focus on the specificity of Gullah culture and a cyclical structure that relies heavily on a central myth of origin and on archetypal characters—do not coexist without tension, but, for Dash, the tension derives from the very constitution of the African diaspora. The dislocation that produces diaspora and the struggle to make a home and construct individual and collective identity in the "New World" has necessitated that people of African descent rely on a complicated and ever-evolving combination of various African ways of being and sensibilities encountered and transformed in the diaspora.[7] The Gullah people provide a particularly rich case for Dash's investigation, but her concerns move beyond this particular community and are aimed at exploring the ways in which the cultures of people of African descent in the diaspora are fundamentally *of* the diaspora. Cultural critic Greg Tate writes, "Praised for its photographic sculpturing, *Daughters* is also a powerful piece of African American psychological modeling and portraiture. . . . It is, finally, slavery that transformed African people into American products, enforcing a cultural amnesia that scraped away details without obliterating the core. We remain in a middle passage, living out an identity that is neither African nor American, though we crave for both shores to claim us. It is *Daughters'* achievement to represent this double alienation as an issue for the community as a whole, and as personal and interpersonal issues for the film's principal characters."[8] Tate's assessment links Dash's work to W. E. B. Du Bois's notion of "double-consciousness," which Dash uses in a way that resists a rigid separation between African and American and seeks a fluid and dynamic combination of potential African diaspora identities.

Daughters of the Dust is steeped in detail. Dash and her crew lovingly and painstakingly constructed sets and settings using ethnographic photographs from the early 1900s, adorned the characters in a variety of African hairstyles, and filled the frame with objects that speak of the African sources of Gullah culture in order to locate the characters in a rich and vibrant historical setting.[9] Historical accuracy is an important element of Dash's goals for the film as she feels deeply the responsibility of representing attentively the history, culture, and lives of the Gullah people from whom she descends. At the same time, she does not understand her film project to be an ethnographic one—that is, she does not want the film to provide only empirical documentation of historical data. Myth, symbol, and archetype are equally important structures for conveying the information she wishes her audience to have. Dash noted when responding to a question about the film's relationship to history, "I think I felt I had to bring a basic integrity of the historical events and issues, but I had to be free to be able to create some drama, to create some symbolism. . . . "[10] It is not symbolism invented for the world of the film on which she draws, however, but on symbols with roots deep in the varied cultural streams that contribute to the cultures of the African diaspora. The film treats us to some of the visual symbolism of West and Central African religious traditions and to visual and oral accounts of a New World African myth of community origins, and presents us with characters constructed around archetypes from Yoruba religion.

In many interviews and in commentaries on the film, Dash explained that the film's narrative structure was inspired by the African *griot* tradition in which a family or community history is recounted in vignettes rather than through a linear narrative of causality. So while the film's events are deeply rooted in the year 1902, the story sometimes flashes forward or backward in time in ways that are not clearly marked in typical Hollywood fashion. Indeed, Dash argued at one point that the entire film could be read as a flash forward from the period of slavery.[11] Many viewers and reviewers of the film identified what they understood to be a conflict between the film's deep commitment to historical accuracy (read as ethnography) on the one hand, and the nonlinear approach to narrative, the use of myth, and the presentation of characters as archetypes on the other (read as confusing at best and as historically irresponsible at worst).[12] Some reviewers felt challenged to locate "the story" in the midst of the details and had difficulty ascribing meaning to the symbolic images upon which the camera lingers, an indication of the perceived conflict between Dash's use of myth and history in the film. In Dash's version of the Gullah world, however, historical detail, symbol, elements of character and place, etc., appear in relation to one another and in an order that creates a composite over the course of the film, requiring viewers to engage mythic time that brings together past, present, and future and historically located events at the same moment.

Sources of Power

The Turn in the Path

Daughters of the Dust focuses on the Peazant family, whose members have lived on one of the Sea Islands at a place called Ibo Landing since slavery. On the August day in 1902 during which most of the action takes place, some members of the family prepare to migrate to the mainland and north. They gather for a picnic on the beach to have their photographs taken and to share a meal before the departure. Nana Peazant, the eldest Peazant, sees no need to leave and, in fact, feels that she and her family's history are both so connected to the place of Ibo Landing that she cannot leave. As some of the Peazants prepare for their journey, two members who have been gone for some time return home to see them off. We meet Viola (Cheryl Lynn Bruce), who lives on the mainland and has become a Christian missionary, and Yellow Mary (Barbara O), who had been a wet nurse to a white American family in Cuba but who is on her way to Nova Scotia with Trula (Trula Hoosier). Tensions around the departure and about the family's future become located in a crisis moment in which Eula Peazant (Alva Rogers), who married Eli (Adisa Anderson) and into the family, finds herself. She has been raped by a white man and is pregnant, and Eli is unsure whether the child is his. The uncertainty about the relationship of the child to the family mirrors the uncertainty about the family's future up north. The Unborn Child (Kai-Lynn Warren), embodied as a little girl whom the audience sees at various points in the film, has been sent by the old souls on a mission to convince Eli that she is, indeed, his child. In the end, Eli, Eula, and Yellow Mary stay with Nana, and the child is born and raised on Ibo Landing.

This conclusion allows Nana, "the last of the old," and the child, "the first of the new," to meet and experience each other and speaks to the film's interest in traditional West and Central African understandings of the power of time. Tradition and recapitulation, not linear notions of progress, are prime values in this community, and the appearance of the child sent by the ancestors completes the circle, ensuring the future of family and community. A Kongo cross inscribed on the back of a turtle and seen briefly during a ceremony honoring the eldest members of the family and "the old souls," or ancestors, signals the importance of this religious sensibility for the world of the film [fig. 2.1]. The cross is a map of the cosmos, with each point representing a moment in the life cycle, including time in the world of the dead. The horizontal line divides the living from the dead. The point at the center is especially potent as past, present, and future meet there. As Robert Farris Thompson notes, "The 'turn in the path,' i.e., the crossroads, remains an indelible concept in the Kongo-Atlantic world, as the point of intersection between the ancestors and the living."[13] The continual counterclockwise movement around the circle and the power that the crossroads affords ensures that the living and the dead continue to interact and that traditions are protected and preserved. Nana and the Unborn Child in fact serve as the film's narrators, both often speaking about the power of time, particularly when one knows how to gain access to past, present, and future at the "turn in the path."

Although the future of the Peazant family as a whole is of concern in the film, the social and religious power of women is of particular interest to Dash, as the combination of voiceover and image indicates in the opening frame. In a series of shots—of dust in Nana's hands, of Nana bathing herself in the water while dressed in an indigo dress, of Eula in bed, and of Yellow Mary traveling in a small boat down the river—Dash introduces the audience to the three central female characters. At the same time, we hear a voiceover in which Yellow Mary recites:

I am the first and the last
I am the honored one and the scorned one
I am the whore and the holy one
I am the wife and the virgin

Figure 2.1 "A Kongo cross inscribed on the back of a turtle and seen briefly during a ceremony honoring the eldest members of the family and 'the old souls,' or ancestors, signals the importance of this religious sensibility for the world of the film. The cross is a map of the cosmos, with each point representing a moment in the life cycle, including time in the world of the dead. The horizontal line divides the living from the dead."

I am the barren one, and many are my daughters
I am the silence that you cannot understand
I am the utterance of my name.[14]

In the only instance in which she looks outside the scope of African and African diaspora cultures for sources for the film, Dash turns here to the Gnostic text "The Thunder, Perfect Mind" to speak to the sources of her female characters' power. In this opening frame, the film asserts that women derive spiritual power from the ancestors and from engaging the wisdom the ancestors' example provides.

"The Thunder, Perfect Mind" was likely a liturgical text in its original context and in the film's opening moments Dash uses it in a similar way, as an invocation of a transcendent power but, perhaps more important, as a means to call on an ancestral power that is also manifest in the persons of these three women.[15] In emphasizing the activity of the ancestors, whose presence is felt profoundly by Nana and Eula and to whose care Yellow Mary eventually submits, Dash grounds her work in West and Central African worldviews that understand the ancestors as providing a critical link between humans and the divine. The ancestors function as guardians of tradition and protectors of the family, an involvement that requires humans to be attentive to the needs and concerns of the dead. In an crucial scene early in the film, Nana tries to convince Eli how important paying attention to the ancestors is for the family's future. Eli finds his great-grandmother sitting quietly in the graveyard, the set for which was clearly modeled on photographs taken in the 1930s of Kongo-influenced graveyards on the Sea Islands and coastal Georgia.[16] Nana sits before her husband's grave and tells Eli, "I visit with old Peazant every day since the day he died. It's up to the living to keep in touch with the dead, Eli. Man's power doesn't end with death. We just move on to a new place, a place where we watch over our living family. . . . " For Nana, the spiritual power of the members of the living family lies in acknowledging the presence and potency of the ancestors and in accepting the obligation to take on the same responsibility once one has died.

Such a commitment makes Viola, who has discarded African-inspired family traditions in favor of those of Christianity, deeply uncomfortable. "Old folks supposed to die!" she insists. "It's not right! We're supposed to die and go to heaven!"[17] Like Viola, Hagar rejects the old ways and looks forward to the modern life of the mainland, as well as to the identity and social transformations she imagines that individual choice outside the bounds of ancestral tradition will provide.[18] At the same time, she acknowledges the power of the ancestors but believes they can only have an impact on her life in Ibo Landing. In a parting gesture, Hagar stands before

Nana's bottle tree—a protective device—and bellows to the ancestors, "As God is my witness. . . . When I leave this place, never again will I live in your domain." In allowing Viola's and Hagar's negative perspectives on ancestral obligations to be part of the film's story, Dash emphasizes diversity of religious sensibility among African Americans, even while making clear that she values "the old ways" and fears the consequences of linking Christianity and the mainland with progress, as some of her characters propose.

It is not surprising that Hagar understands *place* to be a source of power for the ancestors. Dash spends a great deal of time in the film tracing the geography that sits at the center of the religious sensibility and spiritual power of the black women in her story. Ibo Landing, the Peazant family's home, appears as a fully drawn character as a result of the strikingly beautiful tracking shots that sweep the viewer across the beach, and follow human characters as they move through the cemetery, the fields, and along the beach. Through repeated attention to trees and to water, we become familiar with the natural landscape and its spiritual implications. Large trees become players in significant exchanges between human characters, as Dash draws out the Kongo-inspired understanding of trees as conduits to the world of the dead. They also appear as part of the humanly constructed landscape, as in the case of Nana Peazant's chair, which has branches and twigs attached to it and reminds us of her deep connection to the ancestors.[19] Although early in the film Dash presents a visual survey of the living space of some of the Peazants and we later see the barn where Eli works as a blacksmith, the built environment—houses, public buildings—does not connect the people of Ibo Landing in the ways that the natural environment does. The Peazants are of Ibo Landing, for all that implies with regard both to the spiritual, cultural, and emotional devastation of the slave trade and the power that the presence of their ancestors in the ground affords.

The Peazants' commitment to their ancestors goes beyond rhetorical acknowledgment of their existence as they find ways to encounter them, often at crossroads moments. In the scene in which Nana attempts to guide Eli out of the spiritual crisis brought on by the rape of his wife, Dash cuts back and forth between the conversation in the graveyard and a group of girls from the Peazant family playing uniquely diasporic ring games. As Nana implores Eli to "call on those old Africans," Dash presents the girls and slows the motion in the frame, a technique she uses to bring past, present, and future together for her viewers.[20] Nana assures Eli, "They'll come to you when you least expect them. They'll hug you up quick and soft like the warm sweet wind. Let those old souls come into your heart, Eli. Let them touch you with the hands of time. Let them feed your head with wisdom that ain't from this day and time." While Nana reiterates the central element of the mythic sensibility of the film, the girls become possessed, making clear the proximity of the ancestors and their involve-ment in all aspects of daily life. The girls, Iona (Bahni Turpin), whose name is most often pronounced "I own her," and Myown (Eartha Robinson), are completely at ease in this transition between child's play and possession, seem joyous at the appearance of these spiritual forces, and readily submit to this experience that, like their names, binds them to the family.[21]

Myths of Origin

Eula, who has become connected to the Peazants by marriage, realizes the importance of honoring the ancestors, and her character also provides the opportunity for Dash to explore the power the ancestors provide in ways that reach beyond the blood kin of the Peazant family to every descendant of enslaved Africans in the Americas. Eula performs the critical task of telling the story of the Ibo. Dash incorporated into her script a well-known story in African American folklore about a group of Ibo brought by ship directly from Africa to St. Simons Island. Refusing to submit themselves or their descendants to slavery, the Ibo are said to have walked over water or to have taken flight home to Africa. Various sources preserve these stories, and many of the Gullah people interviewed for the fieldwork study *Drums and Shadows,* produced in 1940 by the Savannah Unit of the Works Progress Administration's (WPA) Georgia Writers Project, related tales of flying Africans that they had heard from parents and grandparents.[22] Jack Tattnall of Wilmington Island, for example, told an interviewer (who attempted to render Gullah speech in the transcription):

> Long as I kin membuh, missus, I been heahin bout dat. Lots uh slabes wut wuz brung obuh frum Africa could fly. Deah wuz a crowd ub um wukin in duh fiel. Dey dohn lak it heah an dey tink dey go back tuh Africa. One by one dey fly up in duh eah an all fly off an gone back tuh Africa.[23]

At least one of Dash's characters, Bilal Muhammad, does not believe that the Ibo made it back, a view represented by some of the Gullah people in *Drums and Shadows:*

> Heahd bout duh Ibo's Landing? Das duh place weah dey bring duh Ibos obuh in a slabe ship and wen dey git yuh, dey ain lak it an so dey all staht singin an dey mahch right down in duh ribbuh tuh mahch back tuh Africa, but dey ain able tuh git deah. Dey gits drown.[24]

And Yellow Mary scoffs when Eula recalls a girl whose owner drowned her in the water nearby, asking "Oh, I thought this was *Ibo* Landing . . . ?" Eula responds, "That doesn't mean you can't drown here."[25] But the truth or falsity of the story is not of concern to Dash, nor to us here. Rather, the question of how the myth has functioned for Gullah people to construct a collective identity and of how Dash uses it to bring non-Gullah African Americans into that identity and history is central.[26] Literary critic Stacy I. Morgan has noted of these tales, "From at least the early twentieth century to the present, [they] have enabled Sea Islanders to claim slave ancestry as a component of their collective identity while exerting a prerogative to (re)construct this history through their own matrix of symbols and narrative devices."[27] For her telling of the tale, Dash relied on Paule Marshall's fictionalized version in her 1983 novel, *Praisesong for the Widow*. In the book, about an African American woman reconnecting with the West African elements of her cultural heritage, the story of the Ibos plays a central part.[28]

Dash's handling of Eula's account of the story establishes African diaspora cultures and beliefs as normative and uses Eula, not blood kin to the Peazants, to draw the viewer into these beliefs and history. Just before she begins to tell the story, Eula stands near the water at Ibo Landing looking out at the floating wooden figure of a shackled African man, discarded from a ship's prow, and we see the Unborn Child run toward her and enter her body. The child, who narrates the beginning of the scene in a voiceover, characterizes the experience of entering her mother as "the journey home." Here Dash slows the motion again to bring the past, present, and future together in the frame at the same time that the child enters Eula. Eula speaks to the child within her, telling her about the Ibo who stepped off the boat "and took a look around . . . not saying a word, just studying the place real good. And they saw things that day that you and I don't have the power to see. Well, they saw just about everything that was to happen around here. . . . The slavery time, the war my grandmother always talks about . . . those Ibo didn't miss a thing. They even saw you and I standing here talking." As Eula relates this story of how "those old Africans" walked across the water and back home, Eli enters the scene, having just emerged from a moment of deep connection with the ancestors in the cemetery behind them. In an extremely emotional and affecting moment, he walks on the water, out to the floating wooden figure, kneels down next to it, and pours a libation into its mouth [fig. 2.2]. Sending the figure out onto the river, Eli returns to shore and embraces Eula, the experience of recapitulating the actions of the Ibo and of feeling the power of the ancestors having convinced him, as Nana had insisted, that the "ancestor and the womb are the same thing" and that the child is his.

Dash offers the story of the Ibo as a myth of origin for the Peazants, the people of Ibo Landing, and for African diaspora people generally. In some

ways, it seems an unlikely story to cast as a myth of origin, whether one
believes that the Ibo walked or flew back to Africa or that they drowned,
because, unlike most traditional cosmogonic myths, this one can be located
in historical time, in a time not unlike our own. Clearly, it is not a story of
the beginning of time but one in which, in the act of defying the construction of their identity and that of their descendants as slaves, the Ibo's
"walk" marks the production of a new diaspora identity. Because the film's
story relies so heavily on the sensibility captured in the Kongo cosmogram,
one that sees past, present, and future meeting at once and that values
ongoing interaction between the living and the dead, it is not necessary to
return to the beginning of time or even to Africa to find the origins of
African diaspora people. When Eli expresses his outrage to Nana about
Eula's rape and questions the efficacy of the African diaspora worldview to
which she subscribes, he also casts doubt on the utility of a myth of origin
located exclusively in Africa. "What're we supposed to remember, Nana?"
he cries out. "How, at one time, we were able to protect those we loved?
How, in Africa world, we were kings and queens and built great big cities?"
The significance of the story in the context of the film lies neither solely in
the fact that the Ibo came from Africa, nor in the belief of some that they
returned there. For *Daughters*, what is most important are the lessons the

Figure 2.2 "In an extremely emotional and affecting moment, he walks on the water,
out to the floating wooden figure, kneels down next to it, and pours a libation into its
mouth. Sending the figure out onto the river, Eli returns to shore and embraces Eula, the
experience of recapitulating the actions of the Ibo and of feeling the power of the ancestors
having convinced him, as Nana had insisted, that the 'ancestor and the womb are the same
thing' and that the child is his."

story provides about the emergence of African diaspora identities and the contributions of African cultures to those identities, not simply a valorization of a pure African past. Nana tells Eli that what she desires to leave him with is an understanding of the value of memory—"of who we are and how far we've come." In this configuration, Nana emphasizes both origins in Africa and the cultures and communities of the diaspora experience as equally important.

For Nana, remembering is not simply an intellectual enterprise but a project that taps and mobilizes profound spiritual forces. In the opening explanatory titles and in the voice of the Unborn Child at a number of points in the film, we are told that members of the community "recall, remember, and recollect." The tripling in this phrase may appear excessive but, understood in context of both the worldview set out in the Kongo cosmogram and the concerns elaborated in the myth of origin on which Dash relies, there is no redundancy. The phrase emphasizes the connection that those in the present have to the past (recall), the importance of each member of the community owning their own experience (remember), and the difficulties of the critical project of retaining family and community histories despite the disruption that produces diaspora (recollect), all in an effort to move the community into the future.

Nana and Eula understand the spiritual power of memory and seek to put it into effect in their lives in various ways. Eula feels the presence of the ancestors and knows how to contact them, in one case communing with her dead mother by placing a letter under a glass of water. Even Nana, "the last of the old," learns from Eula's close ties to the ancestors. In a voiceover, Nana proudly asserts, "Eula said we the bridge what they cross over on. We the tie between then and now, between the past and the story what to come."[29] As we hear Nana say this, we see Eula walking up a hill on the beach and, again Dash uses the speed aperture computer to slow her motion just as Nana speaks of the bridge, signaling the convergence of past, present, and future. What Nana offers the family at the film's end is a "hand," or protective device and a mechanism for keeping in constant contact with the ancestors, regardless of the individual's proximity to the land in which the dead are buried. Derived from the Kongo *nkisi,* these small charm bags contain "medicines and a soul, combined to give [them] life and power. The medicines themselves are spirit-embodying and spirit-directing."[30] The "hand" that Nana constructs contains some of the "scraps of memories" she keeps in a tin can, most importantly a piece of her mother's hair and one from her own head. In a "root revival of love"[31] ceremony that takes place under a large tree, which functions as a conduit to the next world, she asks her children, grandchildren and great-grand children to kiss the hand.

As with the story of the Ibo, Nana's "hand" does not ask the family, or the broader community that includes the viewers, to locate themselves exclusively in the African past but looks to the complicated cultural blends that the diaspora experience has produced. As she sits in her chair under the tree at Ibo Landing, Nana takes the "hand," a bundle to which she has attached the St. Christopher medal that Yellow Mary had worn around her neck, and places it on top of Viola's Bible, insisting that "we've taken old Gods and given them new names." While this formulation emphasizes the essential continuity from African to African diaspora traditions and places ultimate value on the African source, it also allows for multiple perspectives on and expressions of religious belief. Some characters resist this formulation in favor of a rigid binary. Hagar refuses to kiss the "hand," calling it Hoodoo and blaming the community's poverty and lack of opportunity on these beliefs while Trula, Yellow Mary's lover, runs from the ceremony, disturbed by it strangeness and fearful that she has lost her lover to Yellow Mary's family. At the same time, Nana's presentation of the "hand" and the Bible together makes it possible for Viola to reaffirm her commitment to the family and the ancestors and for Mr. Snead, an outsider, to choose to participate in the ceremony. At once affirming of African sources of black spirituality in the New World, the myth of Ibo Landing and the Peazant family "hand" also open out to broader constructions of community and religious identity. And, while the entirety of the community is of concern in the film, it places black women at the center as the pivotal transmitters of cultures and caretakers of the concerns of the ancestors.

Cleanliness and Ruin

The use of "The Thunder, Perfect Mind" as the opening frame for the film, with its liturgical invocation, locates the source of the spiritual power of the female characters firmly with the power of the ancestors. As Dash traces this power throughout the film, she uses strategies like slowed motion and the figure of the unborn narrator to place the viewer in a mythic time where past, present, and future meet. Even as she uses themes from "The Thunder, Perfect Mind" to amplify the power of the crossroads, Dash also uses it to set out another set of gendered concerns that are located firmly in historical time. In introducing the characters of Nana, Eula, and Yellow Mary with the paradoxical assertions of "Thunder," Dash begins the process of describing the power that derives from the charged historical experiences of black women in America that renders them whore and holy one, wife and virgin, silence and profound utterance.

As Robert Farris Thompson has noted, cleanliness is a central theme in *Daughters of the Dust*, with all of the characters appearing "starched up" in white to have their photographs taken, wearing the color of death and, therefore, of the ancestors and their wisdom.[32] At the same time, we become well aware of the strong theme of ruin, in the language of the characters—especially as brought about through sexual assault—running throughout the film. Ultimately, the film asserts that black women's religious power is not diminished by these potentially devastating experiences in historical time. In the paradox of being simultaneously whore and holy one, and *in the mean between them,* lies power. Dash's new mythic narrative of African diaspora identity embraces this element of black women's power.

Two of the main characters in *Daughters of the Dust* struggle with finding the mean between the poles set out in "Thunder," and Dash resolves their dilemmas in different ways. We learn early on in the film that Yellow Mary has likely been a prostitute, prompting Hagar to chastise her for coming home to "put her shame on Mother Peazant." Just as Yellow Mary has become disconnected from her identity as formed in the context of the Peazant family and Ibo Landing in her time away, so Viola, having left the island for the mainland, has put aside her past. Viola's rejection of the old ways and of her old self is enabled by her new religious identity as a Christian. She understands Christianity as asking her to accede to a set of standards that provides access to hidden truth and will bring her new life. She tells the children, "When I left these islands, I was a sinner and I didn't even know it. But I left these islands, touched that mainland, and fell into the arms of the Lord." In her search for cleanliness and in her acceptance of Protestant perspectives on the self and on time, Viola relinquishes the closeness of the ancestors. She denies them authority over the land in which they are buried and accepts a linear and progressive view of time. She reads to the children, "The earth, O Lord, is swelling with fruitage and reminds us that this is the seed time of life. That not today, and not tomorrow shall come the true reaping of the deeds we do, but in some far-veiled and mighty harvest." Truth, for Viola, is veiled and distant, not ever-present, as is connection to the ancestors.

In Dash's characterization, Viola's search for a self that can function on the mainland has led her to deny the balance between cleanliness and ruin that is valued in the community. She brings this excessive concern with a particular understanding of cleanliness to her religious instruction of the children and to her etiquette lessons for some of the older girls. Nana's presentation of the "hand" seeks to make a place for varied religious expressions, as long as the ancestors are acknowledged and cared for, and Viola makes the decision to participate in the ceremony. Although she focuses on the Bible and barely touches the "hand," her participation, nevertheless, signals her willingness to construct a well-rounded self that acknowledges her personal and family history.

Where Viola, in her focus on being unspotted, has lost the sense of balance and power in the mean between cleanliness and ruin, Yellow Mary has lived with and accommodated herself to her status of being ruined. Dash uses ruin in two senses in relation to Yellow Mary. First, we learn that, after giving birth to a stillborn baby, she left the island to become a wet nurse to a wealthy white family that took her to Cuba. She eventually became so desperate to get away from her employer's sexual abuse that she "fixed" her breasts to ensure that she could no longer nurse.[33] Hagar and a number of the women also make clear their belief that Yellow Mary has worked as a prostitute and she does not deny it, emphasizing instead her ability to provide for herself and contribute financially to the Peazants on Ibo Landing. Like Viola's, Yellow Mary's experiences in the world across the water have caused her to become disconnected from her identity as a Peazant and from the family's history. In a brief scene that was cut from the final version of the film, Viola asks Yellow Mary, "Lord, girl, where have you been all these years, what happened to you?" and Yellow Mary answers, "Pick a story,"[34] intimating that she has no clear story of her own while away from Ibo Landing. After she reconnects with Nana and Eula, Yellow Mary comes to believe that the price she has paid for her independence has been too great and that she has lost too much of herself in allowing ruin to define her. Setting aside her plan to go to Nova Scotia with Trula, Yellow Mary tells Nana, "You know I'm not like the other women here. But I need to know that I can come home, . . . to hold on to what I come from. I need to know that the people here know my name." And to her family, she shouts, claiming the balance between cleanliness and ruin, "I'm Yellow Mary Peazant! And I'm a proud woman, not a hard woman." It is significant that this utterance takes place after we see Yellow Mary sitting in Nana's chair, a symbol of connection to the ancestors.

At the film's climax, Eula addresses the ways in which ruination has shaped the women's individual and collective identities:

"As far as this place is concerned, we never was a pure woman. Deep inside, we believe they ruined our mothers, and their mothers who have come before them. And we live our lives always expecting the worst because we feel we don't deserve no better. Deep inside we believe that even God can't heal the wounds of our past or protect us from the world that put shackles on our feet. . . . Even though you're going up North, you're going to think about being ruined too. You think you can cross over to the mainland and run away from it? You're going to be sorry, sorry if you don't change your way of thinking before you leave this place."

With Eula's insistence that black women need to love themselves and each other in spite of and because of the legacy of ruin, Yellow Mary embraces her need for connection to the family. Eula counsels the women to "live [their] lives without living in the fold of old wounds" and not to be afraid to follow the paths of their desire. When she first returned to Ibo Landing, Yellow Mary had insisted that she could not remain in any one place for too long and needed new places and faces, but, at the film's conclusion, she embraces the possibilities of the return home.

Ethnographic Expectations and the Empowered Eye[35]

The home to which Yellow Mary recommits herself is, indeed, connected to Ibo Landing and to the ancestors buried there but is also largely located within the more abstract construction of individual and community identity that Dash allows her characters to develop. In this way, Dash opens up the possibility of people of African descent fashioning a home for themselves in the diaspora, regardless of their particular community connections of geographical location. Despite the fact that this is not a story that audiences should understand as limited to the Gullah people, many viewers responded to the film by charging that it promoted a narrow vision.[36] This kind of response to the film points to the expectation on the part of some viewers that, because they could not find a recognizable Hollywood story in *Daughters* and because it focused on African Americans, the film must therefore meet the requirements of a certain kind of realism. Many critics determined the contours of such a recognizable story in the context of black films produced in the late 1980s and early 1990s. *Daughters of the Dust* was released in the midst of a "realist" wave of black films about black male urban experiences that met with both critical and popular acclaim.[37]

While many critics found Dash's goals and the film itself compelling, many others evaluated it as not a "realistic" product because it did not adhere to the template set by the directors of the urban black male genre of the 1990s. Castigating film critics who argued that the beauty of the film made it inherently unbelievable as an accounting of any version of African American life, B. Ruby Rich wrote, "People of color are expected to produce films of victimization, films that trace the oppression that their peoples have suffered, be they the Middle Passage, internment camps, or border crossings. They are supposed to make films about their pain and anguish, full of anger—exorcisms of emotional distress for their communities of origin and occasions of guilt and remonstrance for mainstream audiences."[38] In short, critics of this sort require a particular version of history in which myth, poetry, and beauty are out of the question.

This response that finds *Daughters of the Dust* fundamentally unrealistic relies on two assumptions that have made interpretation by many film critics of Dash's concern with the spiritual power of black women so difficult. The first grounding assumption is that, because the film does not conform to the standards of the gritty urban realism of black male cinema of the late 1980s and early 1990s, it must, therefore, be a documentary and function as an ethnography of the Gullah people. But confusion arises in this approach because the ethnographic tradition has generally positioned the ethnographic filmmaker outside the group whose story he chronicles. In writing about race and early ethnographic film, Fatimah Tobing Rony asserts, "The term [ethnography], however, although at times used by anthropologists as a synonym for the objective description of a people, instead is a category which describes a relationship between a spectator posited as Western, white, urbanized, and a subject people portrayed as being somewhere nearer to the beginning on the spectrum of human evolution."[39] For Rony, ethnographic films have traditionally been expected to present the Other to Western, white cultures as primitive, exotic, and historyless and to empower white viewers through the assertion of objectivity in the cataloguing of these cultures.

Dash's deep concern with historical accuracy has easily led many viewers to expect the qualities of ethnography from the film, but she insists that it cannot be read simply as ethnography. Dash effectively rejects these racialized traditions of ethnographic film by advocating on behalf of black women, placing them at the center of the film, and privileging them as the empowered viewers. While she argues that she hoped that the film would be accessible to every viewer, she also asserts that, "I wanted black women first, the black community second, white women third. That's who I was trying to privilege with this film. And everyone else after that." This commitment and the various strategies that she used to locate black women and their concerns at the film's core also insist that white viewers cannot engage *Daughters of the Dust* with distanced, objective, innocent eyes.[40] Dash understood the power of this move, as well as the disruptive nature of her film's perspective, noting, "I've said, often, that I think a lot of people are severely disturbed by the film because they're not used to spending two hours as a black person, as a black woman. . . . "[41]

The second assumption that has led to an assessment by some viewers that *Daughters of the Dust* is unrealistic derives from the discomfort with Dash's use of nonlinear narrative and myth as elements that are as equally important as historical detail. Todd Carr, of *Variety*, in his stinging review asserted, "[F]or a work so heavily into its own ethnicity, one is left with any number of unanswered questions relating to Gullah history. . . . Regardless of the extent of research, [the film] refuses to satisfy on a documentary level."[42] But the questions the film poses and attempts to answer are not ethnographic or documentary questions. Rather, they have to do with the imaginative ways in which the spiritual resources available to peoples of the African diaspora—in the form of a myth of origin or the embrace of the ancestors—help to shape individual and community identity and to aid in cultural survival and resistance.

These concerns with myth and spiritual power determine the contours of the film, rather than simply convey an interest in a body of historical information about the Gullah people. Dash eschewed the character-driven, cause-and-effect structure of the classical Hollywood cinema in favor of a structure derived from the storytelling approach of African *griots*, keepers of family and community history in oral form. As we noted earlier, for Dash, the *griot's* use of vignettes, rather than a linear narrative trajectory, shapes the story to a large degree, requiring viewers to embrace a certain measure of uncertainty as they process the "scraps of memories" that Dash sets before them. Just as she refused to rely on traditional Hollywood structures for the film, Dash also constructed her characters around archetypes from Yoruba deities, making them, perhaps, less fully drawn than in conventional films yet enabling them to speak profoundly to the film's central concerns.[43] It is difficult to imagine a place for such archetypes in either Hollywood films or in ethnographic traditions.

Finally, Dash presents a critique of ethnographic conventions in relation to people of African descent through the character of Mr. Snead. Viola brings Snead, an elite, educated outsider, to Ibo Landing to photograph the family at what is likely their last time together. Snead is a man of science and deeply invested in Western ways of knowing, something viewers learn when he first appears and demonstrates the kaleidoscope for Viola, Trula, and Yellow Mary. Equipped with his camera, he dutifully photographs the Peazants and, at first, attempts to debunk their myths and make light of "the old ways." For Dash, Snead functions as a stand-in for the viewer in his desire "to take pictures of these very, very primitive people and go back and have a showing of what he's photographed. . . . "[44] Eventually, Snead finds the Gullah traditions and the members of the Peazant family so compelling, however, that he leaves aside the camera as an intermediary between himself and the people he has met and begins to speak with them and to engage fully their sense of myth and history from their perspective.

In addition to standing in for the audience, Snead can be understood to stand in for Dash herself, as part of her project entails reclaiming the camera for black female spectators and finding ways for the religious sensibilities of African diaspora peoples to be represented.[45] In the course of the film, none of the adults of the Peazant family sees the Unborn Child, who moves among them as a spiritual force attempting to complete her mission and make clear that she was sent by the ancestors. At a critical juncture in the film, someone does see the Unborn Child and, at this moment, Dash underscores the power inherent in controlling the camera. As Mr. Snead prepares to photograph the Peazant men, he peers through his camera lens and is shocked to see a little girl standing next to a crouching Eli, her hand resting on his shoulder [fig. 2.3]. Jumping away from the camera and looking at the group of men standing before him, Snead no longer sees the Unborn Child and clearly considers that it must have been conjured by the heat and his imagination. It is significant that Dash equips Snead with the modern technology of the camera and makes it the avenue to his increasing openness to the ways of knowing and seeing embraced by the people of Ibo Landing. In doing so, she refuses to understand the camera as necessarily a tool of the ethnographic gaze that has been so problematic for people of African descent or entirely wedded to a particular sensibility that denies voice to the religious sensibility of the range of black women *Daughters of the Dust* presents to us. She leaves us, instead, with a heartening and challenging attempt to reimagine the possibilities of representing myth, history, and power from the perspective of black women.

Figure 2.3 "As Mr. Snead prepares to photograph the Peazant men, he peers through his camera lens and is shocked to see a little girl standing next to a crouching Eli, her hand resting on his shoulder. . . . It is significant that Dash equips Snead with the modern technology of the camera and makes it the avenue to his increasing openness to the ways of knowing and seeing embraced by the people of Ibo Landing. In doing so, she refuses to understand the camera as necessarily a tool of the ethnographic gaze that has been so problematic for people of African descent or entirely wedded to a particular sensibility that denies voice to the religious sensibility of the range of black women *Daughters of the Dust* presents to us."

Notes

*I would like to thank Lisa Gail Collins, Margaret Leeming, Brent Plate, and Timea Szell for their careful and thoughtful readings of drafts of this article and Jeffrey Stout for his insights and generosity in our conversations about the film. I presented an earlier version of this piece at a "Lounge Seminar" in the Department of Religion at Princeton University and am grateful to the faculty and students who attended and engaged in a lively discussion of the film.

1. *Daughters of the Dust,* dir. Julie Dash (Geechee Girls Productions, 1992). While there is considerable variety among West and Central African peoples with regard to religious beliefs and practices, it is possible to identify a number of general characteristics held in common across ethnic groups, some of which will be addressed in the course of this essay. For a broad discussion of these general characteristics as they relate to African diaspora cultures, see Mechal Sobel, *Trabelin' On: The Slave's Journey to an Afro-Baptist Faith* (Westport, CT: Greenwood Press, 1979) and Robert Farris Thompson, *Flash of the Spirit: African and Afro-American Art and Philosophy* (New York: Random House, 1983).

2. Gullah culture developed among the enslaved Africans who worked to produce cotton, indigo, and rice on the Sea Islands off the coast of South Carolina, Georgia, and Florida. Isolated by virtue of their location on islands and allowed more cultural freedom because white slaveholders were often absent from these plantations, Gullah people developed distinctive religious and social practices grounded in West African traditions. The term "Geechee" refers to African American slaves on the Georgia coast who are culturally similar to Gullah people. The word "Gullah" is generally thought to be derived from the name "Angola," but Margaret Washington Creel suggests that it may have originally referred to the Gola people of Liberia and that "Geechee" may derive from the neighboring Gizzi people. This would mean that Upper Guinea is the primary source for Gullah and Geechee cultures rather than the widely accepted Kongo-Angola origin. See Margaret Washington Creel, *"A Peculiar People": Slave Religion and Community Culture Among the Gullahs* (New York: New York University Press, 1988).

3. The classical Hollywood cinema is defined both by stylistic markers and particular practices of production and exhibition. Although the boundaries of the period can be set in a variety of ways, David Bordwell, Kristin Thompson, and Janet Staiger argue that the classical Hollywood system was in place from 1917 until 1960. They assert that the system involved a particular style of narrative that emphasizes character and motivation, causation, and the creation of a coherent world in the use of space, composition, sound, and editing and that the style emphasizes a realistic presentation of the narrative. In addition, the vertically integrated studio system in which studios controlled production, distribution, and exhibition of films prevailed. See David Bordwell, Kristin Thompson, and Janet Staiger, *The Classical Hollywood Cinema: Film*

Style and Mode of Production to 1960 (New York: Columbia University Press, 1985).

4. When the film was shown on PBS's American Playhouse in 1992, the dialogue in Gullah was subtitled. Dash originally wanted the film to be silent, but the producers from American Playhouse were concerned that it would not be accessible and so she wrote a script with dialogue. Julie Dash, audio commentary to the preliminary footage (DVD, Kino International, 1999).

5. Referring to enslaved Africans who were born in Africa, captured into slavery, and brought to the United States by sea.

6. Dash was unable to get the support of a major studio during the fundraising period and relied, instead, on other funding sources, including the nonprofit American Playhouse series, the National Endowment for the Arts, and various southern arts foundations, prompting her to comment that, "One of the ongoing struggles of African American filmmakers is the fight against being pushed, through financial and social pressures, into telling only one kind of story. African Americans have stories as varied as any other people in American society. . . . Our lives, our history, our present reality is no more limited to 'ghetto' stories, than Italian Americans are to the Mafia, or Jewish Americans are to the Holocaust. We have so many, many stories to tell." Without a distributor, Dash took *Daughters* to festivals in 1991, including the Sundance Film Festival, where it won the award for cinematography. Eventually, Kino International, a distributor specializing in foreign-language films, agreed to take on *Daughters* and arranged for it to open at the Film Forum in New York City in January of 1992, where it sold out for every show with African American women expressing particular interest. See Julie Dash, *Daughters of the Dust: The Making of an African American Woman's Film* (New York: The New Press, 1992), 7–26, for a discussion of the production and distribution process.

7. For a useful discussion of the historical processes involved in the production of African diaspora cultures, see Sidney W. Mintz and Richard Price, *The Birth of African American Culture: An Anthropological Perspective* (Boston: Beacon Press, 1992). My use of the term "New World" follows Dash's in her various commentaries on the film.

8. Dash, *Daughters,* 70–71.

9. *Drums and Shadows: Survival Studies Among the Georgia Coastal Negroes,* produced by the Savannah Unit of the Georgia Writers' Project under the Works Progress Administration, and first published in 1940, was clearly an important source for Dash's work in setting the historical context. In oral history interviews and photographs, the contributors attempted to document the unique culture of the Sea Islands and to demonstrate connections to African languages and cultural practices. Dash was also influenced by the photography of James VanDerZee.

10. Houston Baker, "Not Without My Daughters," *Transition* 57 (1992): 164.

11. Julie Dash, audio commentary (DVD, Kino International, 1999).

12. In an otherwise favorable review in the *Denver Post,* for example, Howie Movshovitz wrote, "I can't think of a movie where the story matters less. It's not that the story is inconsequential, although it has something of an uncritical

Sunday-schoolish attitude toward the past. What gets you in this film are the images of the island, the almost constant sound of breakers rolling onto shore and the rhythms of island life" (*Denver Post,* 20 March 1992). Writing in the *Houston Chronicle,* film critic Jeff Milar posed a series of questions and mocking answers to his readers in his largely unfavorable review, asking, "Do you feel that any 10 minutes of it could be exchanged with any other 10 minutes of it? Well, obviously, you have arrived with preconceptions of linearity, and 'Daughters of the Dust' is not linear. . . . Do you think that the film is composed of arbitrary images, arbitrarily sequenced, which never quite settles down to practical textual work? Well, you just don't 'get' it. I didn't get it" (*Houston Chronicle,* 13 March 1992). *USA Today*'s reviewer for "Movies in Brief" dubbed the film a "structural shambles" (*USA Today,* 1 April 1992).

13. Thompson, *Flash of the Spirit,* 109.

14. All dialogue, except where indicated, is taken from Julie Dash, *Daughters of the Dust.* The script is written in English, but the actors spoke the dialogue in Gullah. The published script includes an example of the translation.

15. See George W. MacRae, "The Thunder, Perfect Mind," in *The Nag Hammadi Library,* James M. Robinson, ed. (New York: Harper and Row, 1978). Dash made a modification to the text, substituting daughters for sons. I thank Lynn LiDonnici for her assistance in thinking about "Thunder."

16. See the photographs by Muriel and Malcolm Bell, Jr., in *Drums and Shadows,* for example.

17. Dash, *Daughters,* 161.

18. I thank Lisa Gail Collins for pointing out to me that, while Hagar invests heavily in reconstructing her identity as modern, progressive, and of the mainland, her gestures indicate how deeply ingrained are African-derived sensibilities.

19. For a similar use of chairs and trees, see Lonnie Holley's 1994 piece, "Him and Her Hold the Root," in Paul Arnett and William Arnett, eds., *Souls Grown Deep: African American Vernacular Art of the South* (Atlanta: Tinwood Books in association with the Schomburg Center for Research in Black Culture, 2000).

20. Dash and Arthur Jafa, the cinematographer, used a speed aperture computer to vary the speed during the shot and achieve this effect. On the possibilities of varied speed in black film, Arthur Jafa has written, "But I'm trying to figure out how to make Black films that have the power to allow the enunciative desires of people of African descent to manifest themselves. . . . I'm developing an idea that I call Black visual intonation (BVI). What it consists of is the use of irregular, non-tempered (nonmetronomic) camera rates and frame replication to prompt filmic movement to function in a manner that approximates Black vocal intonation. . . . The hand-cranked camera, for example, is a more appropriate instrument with which to create movement that replicates the tendency in Black music to 'worry the note'—to treat notes as indeterminate, inherently unstable sonic frequencies rather than the standard Western treatment of notes as fixed phenomena" (Arthur Jafa, "Black Visual Intonation," in *The Jazz Cadence of American Culture,* Robert G. O'Meally, ed. [New York: Columbia University Press, 1998], 267).

21. See Lisa Gail Collins, *The Art of History: African American Women Artists Engage the Past* (New Brunswick, NJ: Rutgers University Press, 2002) for a discussion of this scene as indicative of Dash's interest in showing black girls as both bearers and transformers of culture.

22. Savannah Unit, Georgia Writers' Project, Works Progress Administration, *Drums and Shadows: Survival Studies Among the Coastal Georgia Negroes* (Athens: University of Georgia, 1940)

23. *Drums and Shadows*, 108. At least a dozen of the people interviewed by the workers in the Georgia Writers' Project recount a version of this story.

24. *Drums and Shadows*, 185.

25. Dash, *Daughters*, 119.

26. In her chapter "Visible Roots and Visual Routes," in *The Art of History*, Lisa Gail Collins traces visual representations of elements of Sea Island cultures, including the story of Ibo Landing, in the work of contemporary black female artists also engaged in similar enterprises.

27. Stacy I. Morgan, "Dust Tracks Untrampled by the Dinosaur of History: The Ibo's Landing and Flying Africans Narratives as Mythic Counter-Memory," *Sycamore: A Journal of American Culture* 1.1 (spring 1997): 7. Available at http://www.unc.edu/sycamore/97.1/dusttracks.html (October 26, 2002).

28. Paule Marshall, *Praisesong for the Widow* (New York: Plume, 1983). Marshall's main character, Avey Johnson, an upper-middle-class suburbanite, becomes culturally and emotionally rejuvenated on the Caribbean island of Carriacau and comes to understand and value her family's history and traditions in the South. Avey, whose full name is Avatara, learns the importance of acknowledging that she is the embodiment of her ancestors, a truth she had resisted in her suburban life. When she was a child, Avey's Aunt Cuney told her the story of the Ibo in an attempt to help her construct a strong identity using this communal myth as a grounding. In her engagement with Avey around the story, Aunt Cuney seeks, as Stacey I. Morgan argues, to destabilize "the privileging of Western/Christian narratives and strictly 'scientific' perceptions of reality" by comparing the myth of the Ibo to events in the Christian scriptures. Young Avey questions the truth of the story. "Did it say Jesus drowned when he went walking on the water in that Sunday School book your momma always sends with you?" Aunt Cuney asks (Morgan, "Dust Tracks," 10). One of the Sea Islanders interviewed for *Drums and Shadows* links the power of these Africans to Jewish and Christian understandings of God's powers, pointing to the magic that Moses used. "Dat happen in Africa duh Bible say. Ain dat show dat Africa wuz a lan uh magic powuh since duh beginnin uh histry? Well den, duh descendants ub Africans hab duh same gif tuh do unnatchul ting. Ise heahd duh story uh duh flyin Africans an I sho belieb it happen" (*Drums and Shadows*, 28).

29. This is my own transcription from the film. The published script for this section reads: "Eula said I was the bridge that they crossed over on. I was the bridge between then and now. Between the past and the story that was to come" (Dash, *Daughters*, 107).

30. Thompson, *Flash of the Spirit*, 117. See also Wyatt Macgaffey, *Astonishment and Power: Kongo Minkisi and the Art of Renee Stout* (Washington, DC:

Published for the National Museum of African Art by the Smithsonian Institution Press, 1993).

31. Dash was perhaps influenced by Carolyn Rodgers's 1975 poem, "Some of Me Beauty" in *How I Got Ovah: New and Selected Poems* (New York: Anchor Press, 1975), 53, in which she rejects her former revolutionary persona in favor of what she felt was a more loving and universal sense of self and relation to others. Rodgers here speaks of the "spiritual transformation / a root revival of love."

32. An interview with Robert Farris Thompson, *Daughters of the Dust* (DVD, Kino International, 1999).

33. Because of budgetary restrictions, Dash was unable to film planned scenes of a flashback to Cuba that showed Yellow Mary's white employer molesting her and of her "fixing" her breast with conjure to end lactation. The implication of the "fix," a term for conjuring, without the images is that she mutilated herself.

34. Dash, *Daughters,* 108.

35. With credit to Toni Cade Bambara, "Reading the Signs, Empowering the Eye: Daughters of the Dust and the Black Independent Cinema Movement," in *Black American Cinema,* Manthia Diawara, ed. (London: Routledge, 1993).

36. In a review written in 1992 for an Internet newsgroup, a viewer who had recently seen *Daughters of the Dust* warned others, "If you decide to see this film, don't expect a film but think of it as a documentary. . . . Enjoy the beautiful photography and gain some insights into the culture of one of the African tribes" (Manish Malhotra, review of *Daughters of the Dust,* rec.arts.movies.reviews newsgroup, 1992).

37. These include Spike Lee's *Do the Right Thing* (1989), Matty Rich's *Straight Out of Brooklyn* (1991), John Singleton's *Boyz in the Hood* (1991), Mario Van Peebles's *New Jack City* (1991), Joseph Vasquez's *Hangin' With the Homeboys* (1991), and Ernest Dickerson's *Juice* (1992). See Paula J. Massood, *Black City Cinema: African American Urban Experiences in Film* (Philadelphia: Temple University Press, 2003) and Wahneema Lubiano, "But Compared to What? Reading Realism, Representation, and Essentialism in *School Daze, Do the Right Thing,* and the Spike Lee Discourse," in *Representing Blackness: Issues in Film and Video,* Valerie Smith, ed. (New Brunswick, NJ: Rutgers University Press, 1997).

38. B. Ruby Rich, "In the Eyes of the Beholder," *Village Voice,* 28 January 1992.

39. Fatima Tobing Rony, *The Third Eye: Race, Cinema and Ethnographic Spectacle* (Durham: Duke University Press, 1996), 8.

40. Of these strategies, Dash said, "But it's not just how the scenes are set up. We could get more specific and say it's the way the cameras are placed. Where the camera is placed, the closeness. Being inside the group, rather than outside, as a spectator, outside looking in. We're inside; we're right there. We're listening to intimate conversation between the women, while usually it's the men we hear talking and the women kind of walk by in the background. This time we overhear the women. So it's all from the point of view of a woman—about the women—and the men are kind of just on the periphery" (Dash, *Daughters,* 33).

41. Dash, *Daughters,* 40.

42. Quoted in Dash, *Daughters*, 39.
43. Dash envisioned Nana as connected to Obatala and the qualities of peace and harmony; Yellow Mary with Yemaja, mother of the sea; Eli with Oggún, the god of iron and a protector; the Unborn Child with Elegba, the owner of the crossroads; and Eula with Oya, "The Spirit of the Winds of Change." See Dash's notes in the margins of the published script in Dash, *Daughters*.
44. Dash, *Daughters*, 38.
45. Joel R. Brouwer also makes this argument in "Repositioning: Center and Margin in Julie Dash's *Daughters of the Dust*," *African American Review* 29.1 (1995): 5–16.

Chapter Three

Orpheus on Screen:

Open and Closed Forms

Linda C. Ehrlich

In his *Mythologies,* Roland Barthes wrote: "Myth doesn't deny things; on the contrary its function is to talk about them. It purifies them, gives them a natural and eternal justification."[1] The cinema—itself a spinner of myths— offers us adaptations of the myth of Orpheus through such distinctive cinematic interpretations as Jean Cocteau's *Orphée* (1950), Marcel Camus's *Orfeu negro* (*Black Orpheus*, 1958), Carlos Diegues's *Orfeu* (2000), and Sidney Lumet's *The Fugitive Kind* (1960), based on the Tennessee Williams play *Orpheus Descending.* Through these adaptations, Orpheus—that harmonizer of opposites and trickster of death—travels through the centuries and across borders. Since the actual recitation of a myth can be considered important, even necessary, to its vitality, we can imagine the cinematic adaptations of the story of Orpheus as a modern means of this recitation.

In our examination of cinematic adaptations of the Orpheus myth, we can extend our gaze to other films that display a *katabasis* narrative pattern (from the Greek word *katabasis* meaning "a going down, a descent").[2] In this category, we can find such works as Kenji Mizoguchi's *Ugetsu* (1953) from Japan, Alfred Hitchcock's *Vertigo* (1958) from the United States, and Carlos Saura's *El amor brujo* (*Love the Magician,* 1986) from Spain, all structured around a pattern of the protagonist's descent into an unknown world, his or her contact with death (often embodied in human form), and subsequent return to the phenomenological world. The sacral quality of the experience is revealed as much through the protagonists' return as through their encounters with otherworldly elements. In films like *Ugetsu, Orfeu Negro,* and *El amor brujo,* contradictions between the mythopoeic time and the current time are reconciled in the evocative panning shots of the landscapes at the films' closings.

The endings of the Orpheus films mentioned above could be considered examples of the "open-discourse film," one of the four possible strategies for narrative film endings outlined by Richard Neupert in his book *The End: Narrative Closure and the Cinema*.[3] The open-discourse film is described as that rare film in which the story is resolved but the narrative discourse avoids strict closure. The open-discourse category corresponds with the following view of mythology set forth by Barthes: "In general, myth prefers to work with poor, incomplete images, where the meaning is already relieved of its fat, and ready for signification."[4] In exploring the possible religious elements of films like *Ugetsu, Orfeu negro, Vertigo,* and *El amor brujo,* I will concentrate on images of dance and fire, and on the open nature of the films' endings. Perhaps the original myth's ambiguous ending allowed directors to feel free in their decisions to bring their films to this kind of "unfinished" ending.

The Myth of Orpheus

Before looking at specific adaptations, it would be good to reacquaint ourselves with the outline of the story of Orpheus. In antiquity, the character of Orpheus fit into the ancient Greek view of the hero as an intermediary between man and the gods, thus never completely immortal. In the myth, Orpheus is the son of a Muse (probably Calliope) and either the Thracian river god Oiagros or—in some accounts—the god Apollo. When Orpheus's wife, the dryad Eurydice, is killed by a snakebite, the great singer takes his musical instrument, a lyre, and enters the underworld in search of her. His beautiful music calms Cerebos, the fierce three-headed dog who guards the underworld, and helps persuade Pluto to allow Eurydice to return. Unable to resist the temptation to look back at her before reaching the open air (and thus disobeying the divine injunction of Pluto's wife Persephone), Orpheus loses Eurydice a second time. (In this, Orpheus is responding to the doubt that Pluto might have tricked him, since—unknown to Orpheus—Eurydice had been instructed not to speak until she reached the rim of Hades.)

At this point, there are several major differences in the ending of the myth. Some claim that Orpheus becomes the victim of Thracian women known as the Maenads who tear him apart in a Bacchic frenzy, and that it was Dionysos who sent those women to punish Orpheus for worshiping Apollo. Many claim that his head and lyre were thrown into the river Hebros; his head was subsequently buried in the shrine of Dionysos on the island of Lesbos (where it served as a speaker of oracles for a while), and his lyre was placed in the temple of Apollo. Others say that Zeus tossed

Orpheus's lyre in the heavens (where Orpheus and Eurydice were reunited) as a constellation, while yet others claim that the Muses gathered his limbs together and put them to rest in a tomb at the foot of Mount Olympus.

In antiquity, Orpheus became the center of an ascetic cult that grew in conjunction with the cult of Dionysus. There is no extant classical play of the myth, but the Roman version—the one that stresses an unhappy ending—was seen in the writings of Virgil *(The Georgics)* and Ovid *(Metamorphosis)*. In some medieval allegorical works, Orpheus was identified with Christ, while, in the Renaissance (with its retrospective gaze at the classical period), Orpheus was seen as the archetypal poet whose singing ushered in cosmic harmony. During this period, he also became the patron saint of opera, notably Claudio Monteverdi's *La favola di Orpheo* (1607) and Chistoph Gluck's *Orfeo ed Euridice* (1762). Comedy entered into the Orpheus myth with light operas like Jacques Offenbach's *Orpheus in the Underworld* (1858) with its notorious can-can finale.

While the Romantics stressed Orpheus's esoteric, magical aspect, in the twentieth century the mythic figure increasingly came to represent the flawed artist. Psychosexual themes came to the forefront, either in the sense of woman as obstacle to the artist, or in the need of the artist to fuse masculine and feminine aspects in order to achieve creativity. In this sense, in the modern period, Orpheus has been viewed as a powerful symbol of metamorphosis. Judith Bernstock stresses how artists like Delaunay, Zadkine, and Klee saw in Orpheus a humanitarian spirit who had to flee from harsher aspects of this world to find harmony in Nature:

> The anguish of Orpheus is that of modern man divided against himself, but unified by his art, his song. Orpheus embodies the opposition and union of Apollonian and Dionysian, intellect and instinct, passive and aggressive, the craving for truth and its substitution by illusion.[5]

In her extensive study of literary references to Orpheus, Elizabeth Sewall divides the Orpheus story into three parts: (1) explications of his musical skill, (2) the journey into the underworld, and (3) the aftermath of this journey. She notes that "the myth of Orpheus is a statement, question, and method, at one and the same time."[6]

Cinematic Adaptations

As symbols that can be read and contemplated, but never definitively deciphered, myth points toward a primordial language, and films based on myths are attempts at translation. As we turn now to look at specific adaptations of the draws on the Orpheus myth, it is important to keep in mind that each one is the result of the historical and cultural milieu in which the film was made. As film scholar Dudley Andrew reminds: "Adaptation is a peculiar form of discourse but not an unthinkable one. Let us use it not to fight battles over the essence of the media or the inviolability of individual art works. Let us use it as we use all cultural practices: to understand the world from which it comes and the one toward which it points."[7]

Turning to the specific filmic adaptations, we find how Cocteau's Orpheus draws on French memories of the horrors of World War II as he turns Orpheus into a handsome poet whose overarching ambition hardens him to the damage he is inflicting on others. In *Orfeu negro*, the spirit of Carnival and exorcistic ceremonies enters as Orpheus becomes a flirtatious tram conductor and a singer of ballads that inspire children. (Diegues's *Orfeu*, from the same general cultural background, is an updated rap singer and skillful peacemaker.) In *Ugetsu*, Mizoguchi turns to the rhythms and profundities of the *nō* theatre as he transforms the Orpheus figure into an unschooled rural potter whose creations deepen in quality over time, after considerable hardships and many missteps. In *Vertigo*, Jimmy Stewart's Orpheus-like character obsessively tries to recreate the woman he loved (and believed lost to death), extending Hollywood's meditations on human mortality. In *El amor brujo*, the Orpheus figure, expressed primarily through his role as a flamenco dancer, becomes an important force in the revival of Spanish traditional artistic forms.

We are accustomed to think of the journey as a movement forward, if not always upward, past obstacles toward the completion of a goal. In contrast, the journey downward seems to imply defeat, regression. With these cinematic versions, however, the descent into the world of the dead instigates the forward movement. It is impossible to think of one without the other. In these cinematic adaptations of the Orpheus myth, dance and song offer a space for transcendence, and movement through fire offers a space for purification.

Cocteau's Orpheus

In 1926, Cocteau (poet, novelist, playwright) wrote a play, *Orphée*, followed by his Orphic film trilogy (*Le sang d'un poete* [*Blood of a Poet*, 1930], *Orphée* [1950], and *Le testament d'Orphée* [*Testament of Orpheus*, 1959]).[8] Cocteau's Orpheus (Jean Marais) is a self-obsessed poet, aware of the possibility of failure ("My life has passed its peak") who turns away from his family and the familiar in an obsessive search for increased fame. When this Orpheus hears another's poems filtering through his car radio, he remains outside of the home, his ear glued to those evocative words of an unknown author. Later, it will be exactly this car's rearview mirror that reveals to him the image of the (resurrected) Eurydice (Marie Déa), thus sending her back to the underworld. For this Orpheus, the underworld becomes the world beneath Paris, a world of concrete surfaces and harsh shadows. In his *Cineaste* tribute to the director, Morty Schiff writes: "Early on in the film, the poet hero, an expression of perpetual terror on his face, passes through a mirror to reach the forebodingly secret recesses of his creative imagination."[9] Death (Maria Casarès), personified as a beautiful woman, also enters and exits the world through a seemingly liquid mirror that allows us to see the lack of set borders between reality and dream. As if to show the relative powerlessness of all the main figures, Cocteau frequently captures them through high-angle shots, as when Death enters Orpheus's bedroom to gaze on him while he sleeps. Death's assistant, Heurtebise, leads Orpheus through a "no-man's land" made up of memories and the ruins of beliefs, just as the Paris of this 1950 film contains traces of a Nazi invasion, with its bland judges and black-clad motorcyclists who roam the street.

Orpheus's eventual return to his family is described by Eurydice as "a recovery from a nightmare." In Cocteau's interpretation, forbidden love becomes not the love of Orpheus for his deceased wife but rather the forbidden love of Death and her messenger for the two humans. At the close of the (now mundane) human tale, Cocteau leaves Death and Heurtebise progressing through the shadows of the underworld to an uncertain fate. The song of the poet is renewed, freed from the automatic writings inspired by death.

Orfeu negro (1958)

Orfeu negro (*Black Orpheus*, 1958), directed by Marcel Camus, was adapted from Vinicius de Moraes's play *Orfeu Negro da Conceiçao: Tragedia Carioca* (1956), but it was not well received in Brazil.[10] It is reported that the playwright was so unhappy with the film that he asked for his name to be taken off the screenplay. As Jared Banks concludes in his article in the *Canadian Review of Comparative Literature*, "*Orfeu Negro* is a film of great vivacity and technical genius, but it fails to adapt some of the darkest elements of the play and instead balances between the fabula from the play and what may be called a documentary of samba, *macumba*, and the slums of Rio de Janeiro."[11]

Orfeu negro was one of the first films to draw the world's attention to the richness of the Brazilian film industry, although technically it is a coproduction that falls outside the more innovative indigenous film industry known as the Cinema Novo. *Orfeu negro* won the Golden Palm for Best

Film at the Cannes Film Festival (winning over two more experimental films, Truffaut's *Les 400 coups* [400 Blows] and Resnais's *Hiroshima Mon Amour)*, the New York Critics Circle Award, and the Best Foreign Film at the 1960 Academy Awards. The haunting music, composed by Luis Bonfa and Antonio Carlos Jobim has established a worldwide reputation of its own, almost independent of the film.

Camus's film begins when Orpheus (performed by soccer player Breno Mello), a streetcar conductor, sees Euridice (played by former Katherine Dunham dancer Marpessa Dawn). Euridice has fled to Rio to escape a mysterious man she believes is trying to kill her. Euridice stays with her cousin in one of the *favela* in the Morro area of Rio and innocently attracts Orpheus's attention away from his more flamboyant fiancé, Mira (Lourdes de Oliveira). After the mysterious man succeeds in killing Euridice, Orpheus searches for her in this film's representations of hell, the thirteenth floor of the Missing Persons' Bureau and the morgue in Rio. He also attends a *candomblé* ceremony where he turns and sees his young lover's voice emerging from a gray-haired woman, calling out the young man's name.[12]

In her extensive, and firsthand, study of the samba, Barbara Browning notes that a quality of "emptiness" is essential for a successful *candomblé* ceremony, which is, in essence, "a request for the granting of meaningfulness . . . it is not meant to be read. It is not meant to suggest. We are the suggestion of divinity."[13] According to Browning, this evocative sense of openness becomes more legible, and more indicative of the individuality of the divinity, when the *candomblé* rhythms are taken into the street in the Carnival.

Browning notes how this dance tradition is largely entrusted to women. While Euridice must ascend the hill at the beginning of the film to find her cousin and share her first moment of recognition with Orpheus, it is her descent into the exuberant tumult of the Carnival that both announces her union with Orpheus and leaves her vulnerable to the man in the skeleton costume (Adhemar de Silva), who, as one of the little boys tagging after Orpheus perceptively observes, is not a man in a costume at all but Death itself. Orpheus is convinced, however, that he can out-trick Death and that his love will make him the victor. Central to this film is what Mikhail Bakhtin describes as "the carnival sense of the world"—life drawn out of its usual rut, "the trope of the world upside down."[14] While praising the film as avoiding some of the Hollywood clichés about Brazil, film scholar Robert Stam notes that *Orfeu negro* fails to link carnival to Afro-Brazilian mythology: "Rather than create a synthesis or a counterpoint, it simply superimposes one set of cultural references over another."[15]

At the end of *Orfeu negro,* Orpheus holds the limp body of Euridice, which he has retrieved from the morgue. He ascends the hill, speaking softly to the inert form. "You are guiding me like a child," he whispers. Gone is the concern for looking back, or not looking back. At the summit of the hill they encounter the hysterically jealous Mira and other screaming women—this film's version of the Maenads. When Mira hurls a rock at Orpheus, she sends him and Euridice pummeling down the hillside until the two unconscious bodies come to rest against an outgrowth in the rock. Having ascended together, they now descend the Morro, bodies intertwined. Camus adds a coda of several of the *favela* children dancing and playing the guitar to bring up the dawn, thus carrying on the Orphic tradition. This rather artificial coda becomes a nod toward the sense of "openness" in the myth itself.

Orfeu (2000)

Camus's version of this myth is not the only one to come out of a Brazilian setting. Carlos Diegues's more recent rendering of the Vinicius De Moraes play, entitled *Orfeu,* is set in the Rio of the end of the twentieth century, a world far more turbulent than the Rio of the 1950s of *Orfeu negro.*[16] Diegues clearly embraces the ideals of the Brazilian Cinema Novo, which he defined as a movement with "no official theoreticians, no popes or idols, no masters or guiding lights. . . . Cinema Novo is only part of a larger process transforming Brazilian society and reaching, at long last, the cinema."[17]

Diegues's Orpheus (Toni Garrido) is a sexy yet vulnerable young composer. As the unofficial guardian saint of the *favela* community "O Morro de Carioca," he is frequently dressed in white (in contrast to the more sinister character Luchinho, who prefers black). This long-haired Orpheus is somewhat larger than life: He is the object of desire of Euridice (Patricia França); of Carmen, Euridice's middle-aged aunt; of Mira, his Playboy-cover self-proclaimed fiancé; of Luchinho, a former boyhood friend turned cold-blooded drug gang leader; and even, it seems, of his mother Conceiçao, who cautions him not to tie himself down to one woman.[18] He moves in a space that is uniquely his own. Later, when he goes in search of Euridice's body, none of the gang's machine-gun bullets can penetrate his skin. He will die only when he himself wills it.

In the Diegues adaptation, children still wake Orpheus to "play in" the dawn. They still fly kites over the breathtaking Rio skyline. But Diegues's Orpheus composes his songs on a laptop computer and plays them on his electric guitar, while the local gang lord Luchinho watches a broadcast of the Carioca Samba School on a neighbor's television. According to the director, one reason he made *Orfeu* was to show how, in contemporary Brazil, "despair walks hand-in-hand with wealth, the archaic with the modern, violence with creativity, tragedy with *joie de vivre* . . . establishing an unending dialectic between heaven and hell."[19]

The belief in indigenous gods that characterizes Orpheus's otherwise pragmatic mother contrasts with his born-again Christian father who looks askance (but with some hidden delight) at the samba performances. Yet it is the father who takes up the drum beat, like a grieving tribal elder, to announce the death of his son. At the end of this film, the music continues as a lament, a call to attention. The two dead lovers lie side by side while the living encircle them. Even the police stand in tribute over the two young bodies. The street boy with green hair, who has named himself after Michael Jackson, turns and turns, screaming hysterically. Will this tragedy signal a change in the climate of gang violence that has strangled the poor community of the Morro? The equivalents of the Maenads—frighteningly sexy women in black fishnet stockings and heels—hurry away as Death takes up the main theme.

Unlike Camus's romanticized view of poverty, Diegues's Morro is a place where young boys sell cocaine on the streets and women without a future gaze out windows. Euridice, who is from the rural area of Acre, recognizes this immediately and resolves to leave even as she has just arrived. There is no costumed Death pursuing her here—only the same evils that drag so many others in that community down. This Euridice cannot dance the samba and Orpheus himself mostly carries out a kind of rollicking rap as the elaborately jewelled students of the samba school, Los Unidos de Carioca, perform intricate choreographies at the Sambadrome. Although Euridice does not actually participate in the Carnival, she is dressed by Orpheus's mother in a flowing gown of pale pink, like Lady Guinivere in a medieval ballad.

Mirror imagery plays a role in this adaptation, as it did in Cocteau's film. Deeply in love, Orpheus proclaims that "Orpheus and Euridice are the same." When he realizes he has lost her to Death, he sees her image superimposed over his own in the mirror. Overjoyed, he reaches to go through the mirror to her (surely a reference to Cocteau's film), but the glass shatters around him.

Diegues's Orpheus does descend into hell—the side of the overgrown slope where half-decomposing bodies and other abandoned objects are discarded—in his attempt to find Euridice. After he discovers her body where it has landed, draped over a tree, he himself descends into madness. But even the living morgue on the hill becomes transformed into a paradise as the camera pans from darkness to dawn, to close-ups of dew on green leaves and red birds of paradise (a transformation from the blood red of the earlier scene).

Unlike Cocteau's adaptation, there is no hope of reviving Euridice in this version. The most Orpheus can do is to ascend the familiar hill again with the body of Euridice in his arms, pleading with Mira or Carmen to help him out of his misery. Mira embraces him while simultaneously stabbing him, and he falls with Euridice in his arms. The coda ending of the film offers a moment of breath, if not of redemption. A high-angle shot of the Carnival shows an imagined scene of a costumed Orfeu and Euridice dancing and embracing, with their faces illuminating the nighttime scene. This wishful scene reminds us of all that could have been, and—like the ritual stomping of the mourners gathered around the corpses in the previous scene— reinforces the "open discourse" aspect of this retelling of the myth.

Ugetsu (1953)

Based on ghost stories by eighteenth-century Japanese writer Ueda Akinari (1734–1809), and on a short story by French writer Guy de Maupassant, this tale of a sixteenth-century potter and his encounter with a beautiful ghost won the Silver Lion at the Venice Film Festival of 1953 and is often cited by critics as one of the ten greatest films ever made.[20] Set in the tumultuous period of internecine fighting in twelfth-century Japan, this is the tale of a potter, Genjūrō, who leaves his loyal wife Miyagi and their son in order to live in apparent luxury with a beautiful noble woman, Lady Wakasa, only to discover that she is actually a ghost. When he is finally freed of her spell and able to return to his village, a sadder but wiser man, he thinks he sees his wife Miyagi there, only to find out that she is a spirit as well. (Miyagi had been killed by vagrant soldiers during the war.) With his deceased wife's spiritual help, Genjūrō rededicates himself to his work, his pottery, and to the care of their son.

The journey motif is undertaken by each of the four characters of Ugetsu to varying degrees. The circular journey motif is established first in Genjūrō and Tobei's marketing forays into the city and back, and then repeated in the pattern of the wake of the boat in the Lake Biwa scene. In this sense, Genjūrō's journey (which could also be called both Orphic and Dantean) takes a living man to a kingdom of death—a journey involving a painful passage through fire, and a final purification, with a woman (Beatrice/ Miyagi) as a guide. Genjūrō's journey, like that of Odysseus, with its pattern of embarkation, return, and renewal, is associated with the working through of a metaphysical problem concerning the nature of desire. The journey moves toward desire, to loss, to a partial restitution of what is lost—from the marketplace of the world back to a present enriched by memory.

Ugetsu takes the protagonist on a journey of purification downward, through violence and self-destruction, and then returns him home, a new kind of man. Genjūrō returns not only to his home and village but also to himself, in a new and more humble encounter (in Japanese, deai) with the true nature of his story. Like many heroes, he assumes a greater leadership role in his community. Dudley Andrew has pointed out how Mizoguchi's later films, like *Ugetsu,* produce a sense of "full emptiness," an intermediary state "between the borders of identification [when the text gives the illusion of plentitude], and interpretation." Andrew states that, in viewing a Mizoguchi film, we are "captive neither of artwork (traditional illusionism) nor of our own constructions (modernism)."[21]

In Western tragic drama, a character's fall from grace is often brought on by his or her sense of hubris. The Japanese downward and upward pattern is not without its concern for hubris, but it is also tied into Buddhist teachings of rebirth. For example, in one type of *mugen nō* performance, the ghost's descent to the human world is often followed by release from painful attachments and then ascent to the Western Paradise of the Amida Buddha. As Japanologist Arthur Thornhill explains, the ascent aspect is connected with a view of transcendence and salvation found in the newer sects of Buddhism, such as the Pure Land sect.[22] The physical structure of the *nō* theater itself incorporates the sense of a journey found in the structure of the *hashigakari* (an entranceway for the *shite* [protagonist]) who often reveals himself or herself to be a spirit from the dead returned to avenge some wrong or, in some other way, to work through entanglements or unfulfilled desires that took place while the *shite* was alive.[23] The reserved yet powerful vocal and movement *kata* (patterns) point to the central themes of the plays: Life as a dream and the desire to be liberated from the world of illusion. Komparu Kunio reminds that "the unfinished quality of *nō* signifies quite clearly that the shared experience born of the encounter between actor and audience is not limited to the duration of the performance."[24]

At one point Lady Wakasa sings, and the song's message is that of *mujō* (the evanescence of all things), pointing to the underlying philosophical framework and dignity that Mizoguchi, the director, and Yoda Yoshikata, the screenwriter, gave to all of the characters of this ghost story. As figures of the fantastic, the ghostly Lady Wakasa and the deceased Miyagi are like great directors who serve as representations of the imagination of the artist. Genjūrō's fate is sealed by the pivotal moment of Lady Wakasa's *nō* dance during his first night at her "palace" (which is actually a broken-down ghost house, transformed through supernatural means and skillful lighting). Wakasa's dance leads to the sudden ghostly chanting by her deceased father (whose voice is heard through his armor on display in the room), and then to her overt seduction of the now puppetlike potter.

Mizoguchi's exquisite unscrolling opening and closing panoramas, and his use of the diagonal (both in interior and exterior scenes), lead the eye outward to what might lie outside of the frame of the screen, connecting the inner with the outer world. In a similar fashion, in the ending of two other celebrated Mizoguchi films from the 1950s—*The Life of Oharu (Saikaku ichidai onna,* 1952) and *Sansho the Bailiff* (*Sanshō dayū,* 1954)—the camera assumes a distinctive kind of movement that heightens the theme of return. In the ending of these three late Mizoguchi films (including *Ugetsu*), we can see how the restless camera movements that precede the ending sequences are slowed down—not gradually, but suddenly. The central figure who had been surrounded by a large cast of characters is suddenly left alone in the frame. This is a moment of moral elevation, yet it is also a moment of realized lost. As Kenneth Johnson wrote in terms of the point of view of this kind of wandering camera:

> it is the wandering camera only that reveals the monstrator [i.e., the camera] moving in a time and space that has no logical place in the story. The more the monstration [i.e, the movement of the camera] is revealed, the further away we get from the "effaced" discourse of classical cinema, where point of view is meant to occur primarily through character.[25]

Like the *emakimono* (horizontal scroll) nature of many sequences of Mizoguchi's films, the viewer is made aware of the continuation of the story beyond the last frame. What we reach at the end of a Mizoguchi film from the later period is a point of stillness. Is it a moment of transcendence? Yes and no. Even more, it is a moment of return to what had previously been seen as inadequate. Desire for wealth is silenced; status is disregarded. All that is left in this kind of open ending is a begging bowl, pots baking inside a kiln, and an anonymous man collecting seaweed on a deserted beach.

Vertigo (1958)

Hitchcock's *Vertigo* lends itself to the modern psychosexual interpretation of the Orpheus myth, yet it is so much more. [Fig. 3.1.] As the characters in this film spy on each other, an elaborate dance with deception and reality develops. In the first part of the film, the retired detective Scottie (Jimmy Stewart) is manipulated by his deceitful "friend" Gavin and his accomplice Judy (Kim Novak) in order to make Scottie an unwilling accomplice to the murder of Gavin's wife Madeleine. In the second half of the film, Scottie himself becomes the manipulator of Judy as he tries to remodel her into the image of the Madeleine he remembers.

Following Madeleine's death, Scottie's life itself becomes a dance with death—for Judy (who had been disguised as Madeleine) in essence dies and becomes the false creation Scottie envisions.[26] An idealized love that requires one woman to transform herself into another leads to an ending in which a distraught Judy, startled by the sudden appearance of a nun in the bell tower, jumps to her death.

Figure 3.1   "Hitchcock's *Vertigo* lends itself to the modern psychosexual interpretation of the Orpheus myth, yet it is so much more. As the characters in this film spy on each other, an elaborate dance with deception and reality develops." (© 1958 Alfred J. Hitchcock Productions/Paramount Pictures Corporation. Photo courtesy the Cleveland Public Library)

In the first part of the film, Madeleine (as impersonated by Judy) is surrounded with a seeming mystery as she leads Scottie to "little pockets of silence and solitude, another world."[27] Yet, about two-thirds of the way through the film, Hitchcock reveals the nature of the murder of the original "Madeleine," a startling move that Robin Wood describes as "one of cinema's most daring alienation effects."[28]

There is an important moment in the film, close to the ending, that fuses past and present in the mind of the now totally obsessed Scottie and that illustrates his mental instability. Having convinced Judy to transform herself once again into Madeleine, the two lovers kiss and are filmed in a bold 360-degree tracking shot.[29] For a brief moment, the background is transformed, through the use of process footage, into the livery stable on the San Juan Bautista estate where, in the first part of the film, the couple had spent their last few moments together. The instability of their stance in the 360-degree shot reveals Scottie's instability at this moment and fore-shadows the film's inexorable rush toward its tragic ending. At the close, after dragging Judy up the bell tower, Scottie is freed of his crippling vertigo but not of his memories. He stands on a ledge, facing outward toward— what? While the immediate story has ended, the discourse is so open that it is impossible to predict what the rest of Scottie's existence will be. This is a bold step for a director working in a Hollywood milieu where films without a (relatively) neat sense of closure tend to be scorned. In comparing Scottie to Orpheus, Royal Brown refers to him as "a character forever 'wandering' between the Apollonian and the Dionysian," and notes, "not content to love Judy (or even Judy/Madeleine on a sexual, human level), Scottie is compelled to 'look' at her, i.e. to discover her secret and lay it bare, and in so doing loses her forever."[30]

El amor brujo (1986)

El amor brujo, the third film in Saura's dance trilogy, starring the formidable dancer Antonio Gades, is based on the two-act flamenco ballet of the same name by Mañuel de Falla (composed in 1914–15). [Fig. 3.2.] In this story, two fathers arrange for their children (Candela and José) to marry when they have reached a more mature age—an arranged marriage that benefits the families without any regard for the childrens' feelings.

In Saura's film, the protagonist, Carmelo (Antonio Gades)—a kind of Orpheus figure—descends into hell, this time *with* his beloved, Candela (Cristina Hoyos), in order to restore life to her. The true lovers—Carmelo and Candela—can only be reunited through an exorcistic dance with Death, a dance that calls Candela's deceased husband José (Juan Antonio Jiménez) back into being. The dance expresses Candela's longings for revenge against José, even if it will result (as we suspect) in the death of José's lover Lucia (Laura del Sol), though in the end we never quite know for certain if she dies. Spanish film scholar Marvin D'Lugo refers to this as a duality of "entrapment/liberation": entrapment within the confines of community tradition and liberation as the true lover frees his love from the emotional constraints that have bound her.[31]

At the end of *El amor brujo*, the two lovers are reunited, arm in arm, without threats from the dead. As they turn to face the dawn, the camera pans up and beyond the stage set of the gypsy encampment that we had grown to think of as a real locale, and not as the stage set in the old Samuel Bronston studio in Madrid (which we are shown at the beginning of the film). Harmony has been restored as the human figures grow smaller, as in a landscape painting where the human forms and setting merge. As Brent Plate wrote in an essay in *Literature and Theology*: "Transcendence does not come by an escape from the body, and in the visual arts it does not come through a disembodied vision, but it comes precisely *through* the material and the body."[32] It is precisely through the human form, perfectly embodied in the dancers, that the narrative will continue.

D'Lugo notes how *El amor brujo* (along with Saura's earlier film *Blood Wedding* (*Boda de sangre*, 1980) helps to universalize the marginalized

Figure 3.2 "In this 'transcendental aestheticism' of the flamenco . . . we as audience members become involved as well, waiting to catch those special moments of authentic flamenco *cante* and dance." (© 1986 Orion Pictures)

gypsy culture both within and outside of Spain through a "sustained narrative form."[33] The universalization enriched by the works of García Lorca and De Falla (inspirations for Saura's "dance films") moved away from the kind of *nacionalflamenquismo* imposed by Franco during his dictatorship as a way to support a flagging sense of Spanish identity.

In this "transcendental aestheticism" of the flamenco (to quote writer Luis Rosales), we as audience members become involved as well, waiting to catch those special moments of authentic flamenco *cante* and dance.

Purification through Fire

The *katabasis* pattern provides a mechanism for the purification of the protagonists in the Orpheus films—frequently it is a purification through smoke and fire. In *Ugetsu,* Genjūrō is warned by a wandering priest that the woman he had thought desirable is really nothing but a ghostly hag. Appalled by this realization, he slashes out at the phantom as she retreats through the equally empty rooms of her "mansion." One sword thrust overturns a candle, and the wooden structure quickly catches flame. After Genjūrō awakens in a field surrounded by the charred ruins of imagined splendor, the officials who find him tell him that the only reason he will not be arrested for stealing the sword—the one valuable object remaining from his journey into hell—is the fact that the castle has burned down. Purified by his journey through flame and smoke, Genjūrō can now return home a renewed man, the embodiment of the hero who must return home "humbled rather than elevated, wary rather than brash, the saved rather than the savior."[34]

In *El Amor Brujo,* the protagonists who must confront Death strengthen themselves through a ritual dance around fire, which reunites them with the community through the help of the village sorceress Tía Rosa (although the dance does not completely free Candela of José's spell). In contrast, in *The Fugitive Kind* (1960), Sidney Lumet's version of the Orpheus myth based on Tennessee Williams's play *Orpheus Descending,* fire appears not as purifying and uniting but as a means of annihilating Orpheus along with his song. The film and play, set in an unnamed Southern town, focuses on Lady (Anna Magnani), the Italian American wife of a cruel American shop owner, Jabe (an invalid).[35] Into her shop walks Val (Marlon Brando), a seductive drifter who claims that he wants to settle down. He is the guitar-playing Orpheus figure who speaks lyrically of a bird with no legs that can sleep on the wind.

As in *Orfeu negro,* the upper and lower dynamics of *The Fugitive Kind* are the reverse of those of the myth, with the lower realm representing relative safety and the upper world, danger. Movement along the staircase in Lady's house is a central visual motif. At the top of the stairs is Jabe, her husband and torment. In the shop on the lower level, Lady and Val find a brief haven for their love, a place where they can flourish like the once-barren fig tree Lady recalls from her youth. All of the outsiders in the film— Lady, Val, the promiscuous "bad girl" Carol (Joanne Woodward), the Sheriff's wife Vee (Maureen Stapleton), and the conjure man—adapt strategies for survival in the face of the overwhelming complacency and bigotry of the town.

When Lady recreates her father's wine cellar behind the shop, the outdoor space around it becomes a fantasy world of hanging lights and leaves. This is the space where Lady and Val retreat to embrace, after hearing that she is pregnant with his child. Here, for a moment, this claustrophobic film "breathes." But it soon becomes a hellish site as Jeb, from his sickroom above, throws a flaming torch into the wine cellar on its opening day and then shoots his wife as she starts to ascend the stairs. The racist local police drive Val back into the burning room with their police hoses, ensuring that there would be no restoration of harmony in this retelling of the Orpheus myth, and no continuation of the narrative.[36]

Contemporary Variations

The films described above do not exhaust the possibilities of films that recall the myth of Orpheus.[37] For example, there is the rather awful Vincent Ward film *What Dreams May Come* (which *Rolling Stone* described as "a skin-crawling nightmare of New Age clichés"[38]). The Orpheus figure in the story, Chris Nielsen (Robin Williams), resolves to remain in hell to try to save his wife Annie (Annabella Sciorra). Based on a 1978 novel of the same name by Richard Matheson, this film incorporates South Asian mythological ideas of *lila* (the play of the divine realm) onto a "visual palette composed entirely of Western romantic artwork."[39] Particularly striking in this otherwise unremarkable film is the role given to the imagination in creating one's own afterlife, and the way Orpheus *must* look back in order to save his wife.

Moving even deeper into the mainstream Hollywood milieu, we could look to the sci-fi thriller *Matrix* (directed by the Wachowski Brothers, 1999), with its pointedly named character Morpheus (Laurence Fishburne)— alternatively a cult leader, terrorist, or freedom fighter—who discovers a savior in the character Neo, a software expert (played by Keanu Reeves). What specifically ties into (but inverts) the Orpheus myth in this film is the fact that the sane world of Zion resides *beneath*, while Hell is the everyday world above. The katabasis pattern is reversed; instead we find the trope of an ordinary life disguised as something sinister.

These kinds of films can be seen as (in the words of Mircea Eliade) "swarming with half-forgotten myths, decaying hierophanies, and secularized symbols."[40] With our contemporary analytic distance from myth, we can view them as magic, as literary entertainment, as a stage all cultures must pass through, as superstition. Or we can view myth as cosmogonies describing the way the world came into being, or as "hierophanies"—spontaneous eruptions of the sacred into everyday life. Very few of us in modern society could speak as confidently as French professor of comparative poetics Yves Bonnefoy, who wrote:

> this primordial sacred history, formed by the body of significant myths, is fundamental for it explains and justifies at the same time the existence of the world, of man, and of society. This is why myth is considered both a *true story* . . . and the exemplary model and justification for the activities of man.[41]

Perhaps it is our discomfort with the idea that myth could have any objective validity that leads us to prefer the ambiguous ending. "It is this constant game of hide-and-seek between the meaning and the form which defines myth. . . . We constantly drift between the object and its demystication," writes Barthes, "powerless to render its wholeness."[42]

Final Landscapes

Only in the landscape are the ambiguities of the ending brought to some sense of harmony. In *Ugetsu,* the camera itself makes the final ascent in a sweeping pan that rises up from the mother's grave to encompass the entire village. As viewers, we assume the position of the camera as it places human activities in scale, like a Sung-period Chinese landscape dotted with examples of human livelihood (fishing, studying, and so on). In *Orfeu negro,* the camera leaves the children dancing on the summit of the Morro and pans over the striking skyline of Rio de Janeiro. *Vertigo* ends with the image of James Stewart as a point in an unclear vista. In *El amor brujo,* the dance entraps and then frees the disoriented Orpheus figure.

Along with the landscape, the struggles of art offer a possible resolution to the open ending. To Maurice Blanchot, Eurydice is "the limit of what art can attain," yet Orpheus's turning away is his only possible means of approaching her.[43] This paradoxical stance—desiring yet losing, working within an awareness of the futility of work—is what Blanchot defines as "inspiration," which is both the necessary condition and the indication of a

dangerous impatience. "Orpheus' gaze unties [order, rectitude, law], de-
stroys its limits . . . [it] is the extreme moment of freedom . . . [it] frees the
sacred contained in the work, *gives* the sacred to itself. . . . "[44] Blanchot
calls this contradictory state the only condition in which writing is possible,
when the artist enters what he calls "the *other* night," a kind of endless
death that opens onto a great depth.[45]

These different interpretations of the Orpheus myth show how the
cinema "transcends reality (quasi-magically) while maintaining a close
connection to the pictorial accuracy often associated with reality."[46] They
also point to the ways an ancient myth can be made contemporary and
culturally specific. Now we await new versions of the Orpheus myth on
screen, as we continue to explore the resonance of myth in our own time.

Notes

1. Roland Barthes, *Mythologies,* Annette Lavers, trans. (New York: Hill and
   Wang, 1972), 137.
2. The *katabasis* pattern might sound familiar because of its role in certain film
   genres like the Western, the war story, and science fiction, where the descent
   into the underworld is often replaced with a journey into equivalent hells, such
   as a hostile wilderness or enemy territory. The hero is frequently aided by a
   guide figure. Heroes who return from this kind of journey often assume roles of
   greater responsibility, as teachers or rulers. One could say that the journey,
   death, and resurrection aspects of the life of Christ form a *katabasis* pattern as well.
3. The other three ending strategies are: (1) the classical closed-text film (where
   the story is resolved and the narrative discourse is closed, as in John Ford's *The
   Quiet Man*), (2) the open-story film (where the story is left unresolved but the
   narrative discourse is closed, as in Truffaut's *400 Blows* and de Sica's Neorealist
   classic *The Bicycle Thief*), and finally (3) the open text film (where both
   narrative levels are left open, as in Godard's New Wave film *Weekend*). While
   Neupert fails to find any film that completely fits the third category, he does
   cite the metaphoric ending of Claude Chabrol's *Les bonnes femmes* (1960) as
   one possible example. See *The End: Narrative Closure and the Cinema*
   (Detroit: Wayne State University Press, 1995).
4. Barthes, *Mythologies,* 127.
5. Judith E. Bernstock, *Under the Spell of Orpheus: The Persistence of a Myth in
   Twentieth Century Art* (Carbondale: Southern Illinois University Press,
   1991), 179.
6. Elizabeth Sewall, *The Orphic Voice, Poetry and Natural History* (London:
   Routledge and Kegan Paul, 1961), 4.
7. Dudley Andrew, "The Well-Worn Muse: Adaptation in Film History and
   Theory," in *Narrative Strategies: Original Essays in Film and Prose Fiction,*

Sydney M. Conger and Janice R. Welsh, eds. (Macomb, IL: Western Illinois University Press, 1980), 16.

8. Writing about Cocteau's 1926 play, Walter A. Strauss observed: "when you streamline a well-known tragic theme, you come dangerously close to parody." "Jean Cocteau: The Difficulty of Being Orpheus," in *Reviewing Orpheus: Essays on the Cinema and Art of Jean Cocteau*, Cornelia A. Tsakiridou, ed. (Lewisburg: Bucknell University Press: 1977), 31.

9. Morty Schiff, "Jean Cocteau: Poet of the Cinema," *Cineaste* 20.3 (1994): 60.

10. Camus draws on some changes that had been suggested in notes of the playwright (such as having Orfeu killed on the top of the Morro by sharp-edged plants), but he eliminates complete aspects of the original play, such as a dialogue between Apolo and Clio (Orpheus's parents) in act I, as well as Clio's terrifying descent into madness in act III, and the sorrowful remembrances by the people in act III.

11. Jared Banks, "Cinematic Adaptation: Orfeu Negro da Conceicao," *Canadian Review of Comparative Literature* 23.3 (September 1996): 799.

12. *Candomblé* is based on the worship of *orixas* (or *orishas*, anthropomorphized nature deities). Afro-Brazilians merged African deities with the Catholic church's saints, with the result being a syncretic tradition similar to the Santería of the Caribbean. The African roots become especially apparent in the dance elements of the ceremonies.

13. Barbara Browning, *Samba: Resistance in Motion* (Bloomington: Indiana University Press, 1995), 47–58.

14. Marty Roth, "Carnival, Creativity, and the Sublimation of Drunkenness," *Mosaic* 30.2 (June 1997): 8.

15. Robert Stam, *Tropical Multiculturalism: A Comparative History of Race in Brazilian Cinema and Culture* (Durham, NC: Duke University Press, 1997), 175.

16. Carlos Diegues (b. 1940), one of the founders of the Cinema Novo movement, is best known outside of Brazil for his films *Bye-bye Brazil* (1979) and *Quilombo* (1984). De Moraes is known for the lyrics he wrote to the song *The Girl from Ipanema.* Carlos Diegues has also explored the setting of Rio in his 1994 film *Rio's Love Song,* inspired by the songs of Jorge Ben Jor, Gilberto Gil, Chico Buarque, and Caetano Veloso. De Moraes passed away just as the cinematic project was beginning, so it took more than a decade to deal with legal rights to the play and resume the cinematic work. Some of the songs from Camus's 1958 version can be heard in *Orfeu,* and new musical selections, ranging from the late thirties to the late nineties, were coordinated by Caetano Veloso.

17. Randal Johnson and Robert Stam, eds., *Brazilian Cinema* (New York: Columbia University Press, 1995), 65. This statement was originally published in *Movimento* 2 (May 1962), the journal of the National Students' Union.

18. The actress who plays Conceiçao, Zezé Motta, compares her character to Jocasta. See New Yorker Films press kit, n.d., 12.

19. Ibid., 5.

20. Ueda's book, published in 1776 but begun in 1768, was originally titled *Kinki kaidan* (New and old tales of wonder). All of the stories were set in the chaotic periods before the Edo period, or at the end of the Heian period. Mizoguchi

adapted two of the nine stories "Jasei no in" (The lust of the white serpent) and "Asaji ga yado" (House among the reeds).

21. Dudley Andrew, "The Passion of Identification in the Late Films of Kenji Mizoguchi," in *Film in the Aura of Art*, Dudley Andrew, ed. (Princeton: Princeton University Press, 1984), 173–75.

22. Arthur Thornhill, "The Spirit World of Noh," in *Noh and Kyogen: An Interpretive Guide* (Honolulu: Center for Japanese Studies, 1989), 17.

23. It is important to remember in this context that the elegant *nō* dance, which developed from more rustic harvest and folk dance forms, is considered to have possible connections to earlier shamanistic traditions. In the *nō* drama, the protagonist (known as the *shite*) often reveals himself or herself to be a spirit from the dead, returned to earth to avenge some wrong or, in some other way, to work through entanglements that took place while the *shite* was alive.

24. Kunio Komparu, *The Noh Theatre: Principles and Perspectives* (New York: Weatherhill/Tankosha, 1983), 42.

25. Kenneth Johnson, "The Point of View of the Wandering Camera," in *Cinema Journal* 32.2 (winter 1993): 51.

26. In the original story on which the film was based, *D'Entre Les Morts* by Thomas Narcejac and Pierre Boileau, the murdering husband had fled from Paris when the police questioned him, and he was killed in a German air raid. Flavieres (the "Scottie" character) sees a newsreel from Marseilles in which a woman who looks like Madeleine appears. He finds her but she (now named Renee Sourange) denies his story. Flavieres persists and she finally admits that she was involved in the plot. In his anger and shock, Flavieres strangles Renee and then surrenders to the police.

27. Robin Wood, *Hitchcock's Films* (New York: Castle Books, 1969), 79.

28. Ibid., 72.

29. Actually the actors were put on a turntable, and the background was filmed with a gentle track backward, then forward again, as the actors were turning.

30. Royal S. Brown, "Vertigo as Orphic Tragedy," *Literature/Film Quarterly* 14.1 (January 1986): 33.

31. Marvin D'Lugo, *The Films of Carlos Saura: The Practice of Seeing* (Princeton: Princeton University Press, 1991), 216–218.

32. S. Brent Plate, "Religion/Literature/Film: Toward a Religious Visuality of Film," *Literature and Theology* 12.1 (March 1998): 29.

33. D'Lugo, *The Films of Carlos Saura*, 214–215.

34. Robert A. Segal, *Theorizing about Myth* (Amherst: University of Massachusetts Press, 1999), 129.

35. The play *Orpheus Descending* opened on March 21, 1957, but was met with mixed reviews and lasted for only 68 performances. Other (more well-known) films by Sidney Lumet include: *12 Angry Men* (1957), *Long Day's Journey into Night* (1962), and *The Pawnbroker* (1965).

36. In his 1988 stage (and 1990 television) version of the play, Peter Hall adds to the ending a Ku Klux Klan parade retreating and a naked and wounded Val in a cruciform position. Val's full name, "Valentine Xavier," contains overtones of a savior. For more information on Hall's interpretation, see Donald Costello,

"Tennessee William's 'Conjure Man' in Script and Screen," *Cineaste* 27.4 (1999): 263–270.

37. Note, for example, the chapter by Inez Hedges in *Breaking the Frame: Film Language and the Experience of Limits* (Inez Hedges, ed. [Bloomington, IN: Indiana University Press, 1991]) entitled "Truffaut and Cocteau: Representations of Orpheus," which includes a discussion of Truffaut's film *La chamber verte (The Green Room,* 1978). Other films that could be included are: Rick Schmidt's independent film *American Orpheus* (1992) and Marcel Hanoun's French film *La nuit Claire* (1978).

38. Quoted in Susan L. Schwartz, "I Dream, Therefore I am: *What Dreams May Come,*" *The Journal of Religion and Film* 4.1 (2000). Available at http://cid.unomaha.edu/~wwwjrf/IDream.htm/.

39. Kim Newman, "Rubber Reality," *Sight and Sound* 9.6 (June 1999): 8.

40. Mircea Eliade, *Images and Symbols: Studies in Religious Symbolism* (Princeton: Princeton University Press), 18.

41. Yves Bonnefoy, *Asian Mythologies* (Chicago: University of Chicago Press, 1991), 4.

42. Barthes, "Mythologies," 118, 158.

43. Maurice Blanchot, *The Gaze of Orpheus and Other Literary Essays* (Barrytown, NY: Station Hill Press, 1981), 99–104.

44. Ibid., 104.

45. Ibid., 100.

46. Paul Monaco, "Film as Myth and National Folklore," in *The Power of Myth in Literature and Film* (Tallahassee: University Press of Florida, 1980), 37.

Chapter Four

Between Time and Eternity:

Theological Notes on *Shadows and Fog*

Paul Nathanson

Even those who have expressed shock and dismay over Woody Allen's private behavior, or what they know of it from the scandal mongers, generally admit his films are worth taking seriously. It is common sense (which might or might not have any standing according to fashionable aesthetic theories) to recognize that a work of art should be evaluated primarily or even solely in terms of its own characteris tics, and not the biographical background of its creator. How else, after all, could anyone value the anonymous works of art that were once most common in our own society and still are in many others? But at this particular time—Mia Farrow's version of her life with Allen is still being reviewed and sexual perversion is still the mainstay of almost every talk show—the point is worth making as a preface to any discussion of Allen's work. Artists, like all human beings, are inconsistent. They are wise in some ways and foolish in others. They are wise at some times and foolish at other times. Richard Wagner was an arrogant snob and anti-Semite, for example, but he was also a musical genius. What he produced transcended, at least in some respects, what he was. Reality is complex and messy. And maybe it is just as well. Otherwise, we would have to banish, for one reason or another, virtually everything of value that has ever been created.

And many of Allen's films are indeed of great value. For some reason, though, one of the best has been neglected. *Shadows and Fog* (1992) is a cinematic commentary on the problem of how to find meaning in a modern and secular world. In that respect, of course, it is by no means unique. Almost every work of "serious" art over the past century has, in one way or another, explored the very same terrain. But at least two things make this one highly unusual. In the first place, it rejects cynicism—the great tempta-tion of our time—*without* succumbing to naiveté; on the contrary, it fosters compassion and even joy *in spite of* pervasive suffering and chaos. Then, too, it represents a specifically and characteristically (but not exclusively) Jewish way of thinking—one that is based on religious tradition, moreover, not merely on ethnic psychology or sociology. Rejecting cynicism constitutes an act of bravado. As such, it is highly reminiscent of an ancient Jewish custom. Not many Jews remember now that opening the front door on the eve of Passover, symbolically inviting Elijah to attend the seder, once implied direct exposure to a very hostile world outside. At the same time, and for that very reason, it implied a deliberate affirmation of hope over despair and joy over fear.

In some ways, *Shadows* is another version of Allen's earlier movies. Like *Manhattan*, its cinemato graphy is black and white, its music originated in the early twentieth century, and its central character is a neurotic urban Jew. In other ways, though, *Shadows* is a new departure for Allen. Unlike his earlier movies, this one is stylistically abstract, even expressionistic. The cinematic world presented here is a closed but intense one. Space is confined to small rooms and narrow alleys. Time is confined to a single night. Every scene was filmed inside a studio; everything that might distract the eye, therefore, could be removed. As a result, the sets have a visual purity and perfection that renders them less realistic but also more evocative and powerful than they would otherwise have been. Nevertheless, they are not totally abstract. They strongly suggest a time and place in the recent past. The result is a world that is, paradoxically, both eternal (far removed from the distracting clutter of everyday life) and historical (overtly reminiscent of Europe in the twenties but also, as I hope to show, covertly redolent of America in the nineties). Before proceeding, a brief review of the story is necessary.

An Overview of the Film

The protagonist is one Max Kleinman (Woody Allen), a mild-mannered, middle-aged man intimidated by life in general but by his domineering landlady (who has marital designs on him) and his punctilious boss (who has little or no use for him) in particular. In the middle of the night, he is woken up by a gang of neighbors. These are vigilantes who have formed a posse to do what the police cannot do: capture a crazed killer at loose in the streets. Kleinman is clearly afraid of the killer, to be sure, but he is even more afraid of public opinion. While the others wait outside, therefore, he reluctantly dresses. Once on the street, though, he finds that they have gone off on their own. He has no idea of where to go, what to do, or how to act if he should actually meet the psychopath. He spends the rest of the movie wandering through the empty and eerie streets looking for, well, someone or something to give him direction. For want of anywhere else to go, he visits the coroner. This man, like Dr. Frankenstein, is preoccupied with corpses and preserves parts of them in neat jars. His ultimate aim is to dissect the monster scientifically and find the physiological origin of evil. After sharing a glass of wine with the coroner, Kleinman is glad to get away. On the nearby circus grounds, meanwhile, a disagreement breaks out between the clown (John Malkovich) and his lover (Mia Farrow), a sword-swallower. Irmy the sword-swallower runs away, disappointed by his unwillingness to have a baby and angered by his interest in another woman. That leaves her alone in the deserted streets. Before long, she is brought home by a kind prostitute (Lily Tomlin). Though merely a "nonprofessional" visitor, Irmy agrees to service one customer, a wealthy student, for a top fee. Strangely enough, she enjoys the encounter. Then the brothel is raided.

At the police station, Irmy is forced to pay a fine. Kleinman turns up there too, looking for information about local plans to trap the murderer. He learns, however, that circumstantial evidence has been found that might incriminate him: After the coroner had been strangled by the psychopath, a wine glass with fingerprints had been found. Clumsily snatching the glass and stuffing it under his coat, Kleinman steps out into the street. There, he meets Irmy. The two become friends as they wander aimlessly through the menacing alleys. Passing a church, Irmy asks Kleinman to go inside and donate the money she earned at the brothel. Then they meet a distraught woman carrying her baby; she is alone and has nowhere to go. Irmy now asks Kleinman to return and ask for half the money back! The priests, who had been suspicious and contemptuous of him from the first, are now even more so. Later on, the two friends come across a voyeur peeping into a window. Assuming that this is the killer, Kleinman tries to attack him. The voyeur turns out to be his self-righteous boss, Mr. Paulsen. Paulsen immediately fires him, sputtering with outrage. Finally, the killer appears. In spite of himself, Kleinman actually stands his ground and defends Irmy. Running for their lives, they reach the circus grounds. Kleinman is overjoyed to meet the magician whom he has always admired, and to whose profession he has always aspired. He and the magician trap the killer with trick mirrors and eventually chain him to a chair. But when the good citizens arrive, the killer has escaped once more. The movie ends as Kleinman accepts the magician's invitation to leave his humdrum job and run away with the circus.

Interpreting the Parables of the Film

Most movies, and this one is no exception, can be interpreted at more than one level. I begin with the most obvious one. Allen evokes the atmosphere of a central European city between the wars. He does so indirectly, though, by evoking the atmosphere of German movies made at that time. Given the title, viewers should not be surprised at what they see and hear. Mist swirls past dimly lit windows, down twisting alleys, or through gothic archways hung with iron lanterns. Shadows loom menacingly against blank walls. Footsteps crack sharply against cobbled pavement. Corresponding to all this is what viewers hear: the music from Kurt Weill's *Threepenny Opera,* a musical play by Bertolt Brecht that was filmed by G. W. Pabst in 1931. Except for its anachronistic references to American "dollars" and English dialogue spoken with American accents, this movie might almost be mistaken for one made in the Weimar period—that is, the period immediately preceding the rise of Hitler and the Nazis. It seems clear from the foreboding mood of their movies—many of them metaphorical references to the degeneracy or even insanity of a crumbling society—that directors such as Fritz Lang, Friedrich Murnau, and Pabst himself must have known how soon the end would come. In retrospect, at any rate, it is now almost impossible not to associate those movies with the Nazi nightmare that lay just ahead. That gives another level of meaning, albeit a slightly less obvious one, to the title chosen by Allen. Not only does most of this movie take place in the fog but all of it takes place at night. At least some viewers will recall what came to be known as the "night and fog laws," under which people were mysteriously scooped up by the Gestapo, spirited away to concentration camps, and never seen again. The movie refers directly to this. Kleinman, a Jew, is told by the vigilantes (which is to say, the storm troopers) that an obviously Jewish family—the name is Mintz—has been arrested on suspicion. When he protests that no one in this family could possibly be involved with anything evil, they tell him that actual guilt or innocence is entirely irrelevant since scapegoats are wanted by a public on the verge of panic and thus required by the state. And when Kleinman complains to a police official, he is told the same thing.

Allen has not produced a documentary on European history. At this level of interpretation, it could be said that he has used European history as a way of saying something about our own society. The Nazis themselves are gone, to be sure, but not the moral, spiritual, and intellectual abyss they represented. Like Kleinman, we would all prefer to stay home in our warm beds at night, dreaming of happier times. But like Kleinman, we are sometimes woken up to find ourselves terrified in a world where evil (personified by the psychopath) runs rampant, and confused in a world where those said to be evil (prostitutes and outsiders) turn out to be good and those said to be good (clergymen, respectable community leaders, police officers, and businessmen) turn out to be evil. Not surprisingly, therefore, a well or fountain outside the police station is boarded up: The life-giving source that once sustained society has either dried up or been contaminated. The implication is that modern America is not so very different from Weimar Germany.

But *Shadows* lends itself to interpretation at much deeper levels. Most critics use art—avant-garde art—as their paradigm. To be avant garde, art must be (1) original, innovative, or just new; (2) intensely personal; (3) shocking, challenging, or subversive; and, for some critics, (4) autonomous, an end in itself rather than a means to some moral or social end. This definition is highly idiosyncratic in both historical and cross-cultural terms. In effect, it excludes almost every form of visual (or other) expression except for what was produced in the West since Expressionism, say, or dadaism, and all movies except for "art films" (accessible only to elite viewers who are conversant with the theoretical discussions of academics). Other movies are dismissed as "bad art," partly because they are considered aesthetically unsophisticated but mainly because they are considered ideologically sinister (intended by a ruling class to dupe the masses). Woody Allen clearly considers himself an artist in the avant-garde sense. And most critics would agree with this auteur. Some of his productions, nevertheless, cannot be examined adequately on this basis *alone*. To understand *Shadows* adequately, we must replace the paradigm of art with that of religion.

Religion itself begins, at both the individual and the collective levels, with an *experience* of the "other," the spirit, the god, the cosmos, the infinite, the eternal, and, in a word, the sacred (or holiness). By definition, this experience is ineffable. But the need to communicate something of its essence, so that other individuals and later generations can share the experience to some degree, is intense. Not surprisingly, ways are always found. Among the universal and primary *expressions* of religion are myth and ritual. These two are very closely related, in fact, because myth is always enacted through ritual, usually in connection with festivals. Another common expression of religion, though, is parable. In many ways, it is the opposite of myth.

My understanding of the word "parable" and its relation to "myth" is based on the work of John Dominic Crossan.[1] He identified a whole range of oral and literary genres that express religion. The two of interest here, though, are myth and parable. The former genre includes *traditional* stories that *establish* or *support* a commonly held worldview. They set the stage, as it were, for the drama of human existence. In symbolic terms, they describe a cosmos to which everyone is connected. They provide the community with its sense of origin and destiny, its sense of meaning and purpose in the larger scheme of things. The latter genre, parable, includes *innovative* stories that *challenge* or *subvert* the commonly held worldview. Crossan had biblical myths and parables in mind when he made this distinction.[2] The parables of Jesus, he wrote, were intended to make people question conventional wisdom, to jolt them into thinking about reality in new ways.

(In this way, clearly, a parable is like a Zen *koan*.) Both myth and parable have theological content. And both are necessary, no matter what form they might take, in every society. Myth is primary, of course, because without an established worldview to question there could be no parables. More important here, though, is the fact that each approaches what Westerners call "theology" from the opposite point of view.

The connection between all this and film is very simple: Some movies come to function in a modern, secular society very much (though not completely) the way either myth or parable function in traditional, religious societies. They are what I call "secular myths" and "secular parables." These movies cannot be understood adequately in terms of art. Although parable can be identified with the avant-garde notion of art, to some extent, the link is not strong enough to be of much use. It is true that both are associated with subversion of the established order. But avant-garde art is seldom associated, as parable always is, with an *alternative* order. Jesus did not want merely to destroy; he wanted to rebuild. Even when avant-garde art is associated with an alternative order, though, it is a different kind of alternative order. Jesus did not want to replace the culture he had inherited with some alien one; he wanted to purify it. Some people would argue that the proper analogy is between film and art understood in terms of *deconstruction*. I disagree. Deconstruction is not what it purports to be: an attempt to destroy the whole idea of cultural order. On the contrary, it is an attempt to clear the public square of a "dominant" cultural order in order to replace it with another. But those who use deconstruction for ideological purposes make it clear that the new order must be *radically different* from the old one; virtually nothing of the bourgeois or patriarchal order is to escape deconstruction (or destruction). My point is this: Parable, no matter how surprising or even shocking any story might seem at first, functions (as myth does) *within a traditional worldview*. There is nothing cynical or opportunistic about traditional parables.

Shadows is highly unusual in that it seems to combine features of both parable *and* myth. Like a parable, it has been created by someone who speaks primarily as an individual (with his own distinctive and innovative style). And one thing he does is challenge conventional wisdom or, at the very least, make people think again about the way things are. Like a myth, on the other hand, it has been created by someone who speaks to and for those nourished by a tradition. And one thing he does is support traditional ways of perceiving reality or, at the very least, think again before discarding them. I suggest, however, that this movie is *primarily* mythic rather than parabolic. Its atmosphere alone evokes the wonder associated with both childhood and myth. And its archetypal characters are associated with those of dreams, both individual and collective. Of greatest importance here are the latter.

The protagonist himself is an archetypal figure in several ways. Kleinman means Little One, or Everyone. Most of us, like him, respond to the humdrum quality of everyday life by protecting ourselves whenever possible from conflict or disturbance. What happens, though, when the routine is suddenly interrupted? Security and complacency are shattered. Confronted directly with danger, hidden anxiety and confusion come to the surface. Why is this happening? What are we to do? What does it all mean? And so it is with Kleinman. Ostensibly referring to his lack of instruction by the vigilantes, he asks: "What's the plan? How do I participate in it? What role has been assigned to me?" But Kleinman is also the archetypal Jew. This is made clear on several occasions. At the police station, for example, an officer tells him that the murders have been linked somehow to the poisoning of wells. Allen alludes here to the fact that mass hysteria brought on by eruptions of the black death often led to accusations that Jews had contaminated the water supply. It was with this in mind, no doubt, that he placed that well or fountain just outside the police station. Having received no acceptable response, Kleinman moves on, roaming the streets. In doing so, he becomes the legendary "wandering Jew." According to the folklore of many European countries, a Jew mocked or struck Jesus on the road to Calvary. For this crime, he was cursed by God. His punishment was to wander from place to place, always the hated outsider, until the end of time—that is, until the Second Coming and the subsequent inauguration of God's kingdom. Only then, as a witness to the truth of Christianity, would he be forgiven. By implication, of course, the entire Jewish people has been cursed to wander throughout Europe living at the mercy or pity of Christians. The Jews themselves have traditionally understood their "dispersion" theologically as a divine punishment (though not for rejecting Jesus). For traditional Jews, nevertheless, this has not meant separation from God; on the contrary, God is believed to share the exile—in the joys of everyday life no less than its sorrows—with his people. But for secular Jews, especially in view of the most recent catastrophe, Jewish history for the past 2,000 years is usually seen as a kind of waking nightmare. Maybe this is one reason why the entire movie takes place at night. But this movie is not intended only for Jews. As the archetypal outsiders, they symbolically represent all outsiders. And given the fragmentation of society in our time, almost everyone is an outsider in one way or another.

To the extent that this movie can be called a myth, it would have to be called a "secular myth," because, as I have pointed out elsewhere,[3] it does for an ostensibly modern and secular society what religious myths do for traditional and religious societies. In this case, it brings viewers face to face with a mystery that lies at the core of human existence at all times and in all places: death. It is in this connection that the killer becomes an archetypal figure. He is not just a run-of-the-mill hood. He has no name. He has no family. He has no accomplices. He is a mystery. The coroner asks him: "How did you get in?" And he answers: "Did you think you could keep me out?" Shackled in heavy iron chains at the end of the movie, he nevertheless escapes. More specifically, he disappears. These are the only clues by which viewers can identify him. Given the cinematic evidence, they must conclude that he is a metaphysical being, a cosmic force—that he is Lord Death. As such, he is found in the religious myths of virtually every traditional society. Unlike traditional myths, though, this movie offers only the faintest hint of a context that would confer meaning on death and thus purpose on life. Remember that death is far more than a medical term. Throughout history, it has been symbolically associated with both evil (living in a malevolent universe dominated by sinister forces) and chaos (living in a meaningless universe at the mercy of random forces). And in both cases, it has distinctly metaphysical connotations. Unlike Ingmar Bergman's personification of death in *The Seventh Seal,* Allen's is a personification of evil; his victims die as a result of violence, after all, not of disease or old age.

Unlike many tales of Satan or the devil, though, this movie does not portray him as a simple externalization of evil. He is that, to be sure, but he is also part of every viewer or, to put it differently, every viewer is part of him. The vigilantes have supposedly united to capture him. Within a few hours, though, they fragment into hostile factions. In fact, they begin killing each other. They thus exemplify the very thing they claim to oppose. Also related to death are the anti-Semitic police officials who condone or even instigate the attack on innocent citizens. But the killer represents far more than the evil in all of us (just as Kleinman represents far more than the innocence in all of us). He functions primarily as a personification of chaos in general rather than of evil in particular. Though evil could be considered a form of order (as in the case of totalitarianism), it is more appropriately classified as a form of chaos because it contradicts the order of justice without which human existence is ultimately impossible.

Now consider the killer more carefully. He is a psychopath, someone who is oblivious to reason and thus to order. The coroner asks: "What makes you kill?" But there is no answer. His behavior is entirely irrational; because he strikes at random, viewers must conclude that his motivation has nothing to do with greed, rebellion, notoriety, drugs, personal animosity, or anything else commonly associated with criminal behavior. For him, killing is an end in itself. He cannot be stopped by appealing to shame, guilt, or even fear. Unlike angelic or holy beings, commonly believed to promote whatever society considers good and true, this demonic being lives beyond not only the natural order but beyond the cultural order as well. In literal or cinematic terms, he stalks individuals; in metaphorical or allegorical terms, though, he stalks the human race itself. Unless it is set within a larger context, death mocks whatever we make of ourselves in this world—no matter how wise, beautiful, or noble. In other words, the threat of personal extinction threatens to negate the meaning and purpose of life. Think of it this way: (1) neither life nor death is intelligible except in terms of the other; (2) to make sense, therefore, life must be seen in relation to death; (3) consequently, some meaning must be ascribed to death. In our time, unfortunately, the meaning of death—and thus of life as well—is often trivialized. If death is understood merely as the termination of life, if there is nothing "more," then how can we ascribe any ultimate meaning or purpose to life? It is not enough to argue that biological continuity through reproduction is enough to mitigate the problem of death. If that were so, after all, why has virtually every human society since our ancestors came down from the trees felt a need to address it? Death has always been the primary symbol of everything that threatens order, whether at the individual, collective, or cosmic level. Although the ways of understanding death vary enormously from one culture to another, one thing never varies: a universal and fundamental human need to "solve" the problem it creates. Nor is it enough to argue that we can metaphorically bypass death by passing on some beneficial legacy to our children. Although this "solution" is morally edifying and might even be emotionally comforting for a while, it is nevertheless intellectually inadequate because all those who inherit what we leave behind must also die. And if everyone and everything disappears eventually into the void—if not in the immediate future then in the remote future of civilizational collapse or planetary destruction—then what is the point of doing anything at all? Why not just enjoy whatever material or sensual pleasure we can and let the devil, as it were, take the hindmost? And if we cannot do that, why not just die quickly and get it over with?

Death (and Life)

This last possibility has not been nearly as uncommon as many people assume. Sometimes, life can seem even more problematic than death. This happened at one particularly troubled period in the history of India. Because life, with both its sorrows and its joys, was often seen as an illusion generated by the play of the gods *(maya)*, and because the ultimate goal was release *(moksha)* from the cycle of rebirth *(samsara)*, many began to think that ending this life quickly was a small price to pay for release from despair. Self-willed death became so prevalent, in fact, that philosophers had to take it seriously as an urgent social problem. India pulled away from the brink of chaos by restoring a sense of meaning and purpose to life.[4] Not every society manages to do so. Emile Durkheim coined the term "anomie" to describe a state of social disintegration that leads to collective suicide. He might well have used it in connection with the collapse of aboriginal societies in North America; under such circumstances, drinking on a massive scale dulls what would be the otherwise unbearable pain of a futile existence in a meaningless world. Durkheim might also have used this term in connection with the collapse of social order among blacks in urban ghettoes. Few are surprised, nowadays, when teenage boys accept the likelihood of not living long enough to make education or even the use of condoms seem worthwhile; under the hopeless and meaningless circumstances they call "normal," gang warfare might be just another form of collective suicide.

Most people experience both joy and suffering. It is the suffering, however, that creates a problem and calls for a solution. Even the rich and powerful, after all, experience too much suffering—they fail to achieve goals, endure shame and guilt, encounter malice and grief, get sick and grow old—for life to be self-legitimating. If it has a meaning or purpose beyond mere physical existence, then no amount of suffering will be too much to bear; but if it does not, then no amount of pleasure will be enough to assuage the pain. That is why death—personal mortality—is always the most difficult and most important problem that every society must address. Traditionally, Jews, Christians, and other religious people have ascribed cosmic importance to death and thus placed it in a context that makes continued human existence dignified and worthwhile. (Even so, when death strikes suddenly and on a massive scale—as it did after the outbreak of plague in the fourteenth century, for example, or after attempts at genocide in our own century—even they are often forced to rethink or even reject what might otherwise have been taken for granted.) Secular people, on the other hand, must always either deny or trivialize death; consequently, they try to hide from it as long as possible. Nothing illustrates this trend more clearly than contemporary funeral rites that turn the dealings with death (and the dead body) over to funerary professionals. But death remains with us.

Still, Allen tells us, we can live reasonably happy lives even in the shadow of death. How? He suggests not one but two answers. In the first place, there is always art. Both the clown and the magician are called "artists." What they have in common with painters, say, or sculptors is creative imagination. Through carefully designed illusions—that is, through artifice—they enable people to leave the chaotic world of everyday life and enter an orderly world of their own. There, they can still live *as if* there were some inherent meaning or purpose. Then, too, the artistic world, like the circus, is a community of like-minded people. It is the required "haven in a heartless world." In the circus, Kleinman discovers other people who have rebelled against the meaninglessness of everyday life. With them, he is free from domestic tyranny (his nagging landlady), peer pressure (the vigilantes), corporate hierarchy (the pompous windbag who gets his job), and hypocritical respectability (his boss). The problem has not really been solved, of course, because Lord Death has not been defeated. Even now, he has triumphed over the city—both those he has killed and those who live in constant fear of him. Moreover, he will eventually triumph even over those who find temporary comfort under the big top.

It is in this connection that the meaning of an important visual motif becomes clear. The movie opens with a crescent moon reflected on a pool of water; it concludes with a crescent moon used by the circus as a prop. Both images of the moon are associated with illusion: the former with a mirror image, the latter with artifice. Together, they provide not only a visual frame of reference but also a temporal one. The entire story takes place during a single night: between the rising and setting of the moon. It is thus linked symbolically to dreams—which are illusions—and, more specifically, to nightmares. By extension, this metaphor indicates that life itself—all we know of this cinematic world, after all, is what occurs onscreen—is a dream, or nightmare, from which we either can or will awaken. But the process of waking up—a term used in many religions, both Eastern and Western, as a metaphor indicating enlightenment or grace—is not as easy as it sounds. Immediately following the moon's appearance, Kleinman is woken up *physically* by pounding on the front door; it is only immediately preceding the moon's final appearance, however, that he is woken up *spiritually*.

Not incidentally, each lunar crescent faces the opposite direction. On a purely formal basis, they form parentheses. By implication, the entire story is parenthetical. This, too, is of theological significance. According to traditional forms of both Judaism and Christianity, life itself is a parenthetical experience. Both the individual and the community (or the human race itself) are understood within a larger, cosmic, context. The individual soul is said to be immortal. At one level, that simply means beyond mortality. At a deeper level, though, it means beyond *time* (change, contingency, finitude, decay, and so forth). The soul exists both before birth and after death. In Judaism, for example, each soul has existed in Eden since creation. At birth, it goes into a kind of "exile" from paradise (eternity). But its destiny is to *return* after a brief pilgrimage "on earth" (in time). Something very similar is characteristic of Christianity. The same is true on a collective level. History—that is, the story of Israel, the Church, or the human race itself—is surrounded, as it were, by eternity. What begins in paradise concludes in paradise. Some traditions describe eschatological destiny in agrarian terms. The once and future paradise is a garden. In fact, it is Eden, the primeval garden. Other traditions describe eschatological destiny in urban terms. It is a supernal city. In fact, it is the heavenly Jerusalem. The Book of Revelation, however, makes it clear that the two are identical: growing within the heavenly city, after all, is the very Tree of Life known to Adam and Eve.

It is worth noting here that the parenthetical or dreamlike nature of human existence does not deny or even diminish its value. On the contrary, it is precisely because of its larger context that human existence takes on value in the first place. Whether for individuals or communities, living is understood in terms of preparation for the return. Only by going through the life cycle can individuals *learn* what it means to be with God. Only by going through history can the community *learn* what it means to serve God. Life is both an end in itself (as a divine creation) and the means to a greater end (as the vehicle by which a divine plan is worked out). The significance of every act can be measured not only in terms of its immediate effect in everyday life, therefore, but also in terms of its ultimate effect on cosmic destiny.

All of this is suggested by two lunar crescents. It is in the nature of sophisticated art to suggest eternity or infinity so economically. But do we know that Allen had any of this in mind? In this case, we can be almost certain. Very few movies in the past five or six decades have been as carefully and totally controlled by their directors. Nothing in the film, after all, appears by chance (as it might have in a movie shot on location); everything viewers see on the screen was produced specifically for this production and filmed inside the studio.

In *Shadows,* unlike many of his other movies, Allen alludes briefly to another type of response, one that is characteristic of religion. Still on the run, Irmy and Kleinman stop and look up into the heavens. Irmy notices the stars through a break in the clouds. She explains that these stars might not even exist now because the light has taken so many millions of years to reach Earth. All the same, she and Kleinman look at them with a sense of wonder. As I have indicated, the cinematic world of *Shadows* is characterized primarily by closure. This particular episode, though, provides a window looking outward at a vast and open cosmos (albeit one that might be welcoming, hostile, or indifferent to mortals). What the two friends experience is not unlike what religious people call "the sacred," a sudden awareness of an underlying but often unsuspected dimension of reality. For a moment, they feel connected to a cosmos of infinite beauty, majesty, and mystery.

Allen would probably describe himself as a secular Jew, though one who is interested in theology no less than philosophy. In this way, he is like most other Jews in America and, indeed, like all those who have either willingly or unwillingly accepted modernity. Secularity, after all, is a characteristic feature of modernity. Not all Americans have accepted modernity. Those who do often place religion in a special mental or emotional compartment, thus isolating it conveniently from other aspects of their lives. The result, though, is always some degree of ambivalence. For a quite different reason, though, this tension is a characteristic feature of American life. Most Americans by far profess at least some religious beliefs and many are members, at least nominally, of some religious community. Nevertheless, most staunchly uphold the constitutional separation of church and state. Unlike other modern societies, which maintain state churches no matter how out of touch the latter might be with the lives of most citizens, the United States is officially secular. Though by no means hostile to the religious traditions on which its way of life is based, the state is officially indifferent to any particular one. (Until recently, this theoretical separation was often overlooked. References to God—which is to say, the God of Christianity in general and Protestantism in particular—were common in public life. At the moment, though, Americans are increasingly divided by problems such as the place of prayer in the public schools or that of creation versus evolution in textbooks.) Ways have been found to bridge the gulf between personal piety and collective secularity. These include the estab- lishment of a civil religion, for example, to celebrate the nation's history and traditions. In addition, as I have suggested, popular movies and television shows sometimes become "secular myths." Although the relation between religion and secularity is inherently problematic, in short, it is most obviously and disturbingly so in a country such as the United States. This is why *Shadows* can be described as quintessentially American despite its nod to European stylistic conventions.

To complicate matters, the ambiguous nature of secularity is matched by the ambiguous nature of Western religion itself! Allen seems to have selected only one of the two quite different (though not incompatible) ways that Jews and Christians have traditionally understood the divine-human encounter.[5] One tradition asserts that God is "out there," beyond the knowable universe, but enters it occasionally for specific purposes: creating the world; founding the holy community; rescuing the faithful collectively during history but finally bringing them out of history as well; rescuing them individually during the life cycle but finally bringing them beyond death as well. At its best, this tradition has generated hope and encouraged people to cooperate actively with God in establishing justice. At its worst, though, this same tradition has generated despair and encouraged people to wait passively for God to rescue them. The other tradition asserts that God is "in here," waiting to be discovered *within* the familiar universe. In other words, holiness is built into the very fabric of everyday life; the sacred is inherent in the very structure of reality itself. Consequently, it is directly accessible at all times to those who know how to look and listen. Usually, it is mediated by ritual: the Eucharist for Christians, say, or the Sabbath for Jews. Sometimes, though, the sacred reveals itself unexpectedly (which is what happens, I suggest, to Irmy and Kleinman). At its worst, this ahistorical tradition discourages people from adapting to changing circumstances. At its best, though, it allows them to experience the joy of being connected to a cosmos of infinite beauty, harmony, and mystery. The essential difference between these two theological traditions—and Western religious traditions have affirmed not one or the other but *both*—might be summed up as follows: The former is based on the notion of divine transcendence and the latter on that of divine immanence.

Given the vicissitudes of history, the former way of thinking has always been problematic. But given the rise of secularism, one aspect of which has been the loss of belief in divine rescue operations, it has now become more problematic than ever. If God enters the finite world of time and space to save the weak and innocent, after all, then how can we explain the continuing horrors that stain the pages of every newspaper? The problem of theodicy—explaining the behavior of an allegedly all-loving *and* all-powerful deity who nevertheless permits evil—is as ancient as the Book of Job. For many people, the old rationalizations no longer suffice. It is easier on intellectual grounds and even preferable on moral grounds to reject God, as Elie Wiesel has observed, than to worship a deity who permits Auschwitz for *any* reason, no matter how inscrutable. Many Americans, at any rate, are now either unwilling or unable to accept the notion of divine intervention in history—even though this tradition was the one that shaped collective identity, the sense of national origin and destiny, from the days of Puritan New England until very recently. Does this mean that, for those who reject the notion of divine providence, "God is dead"? It would if transcendence were the *only* theological resource. In fact, Western religion would have disappeared long ago—long before the modern period. But transcendence is *not* the only theological resource, as I say, and Western religion has not disappeared (although transcendence has virtually disappeared, except for some vestigial forms, in many of the official religious institutions). This is because the question of theodicy becomes irrelevant in the context of immanence.

Where was God, ask "holocaust theologians," when Hitler was automating murder? So far, the question has generated no answer that is emotionally or even intellectually satisfying to most Jews and Christians. But the Hasidim seldom, if ever, ask this question. According to these and some other orthodox Jews—and they suffered as much as or more than any other group of Hitler's victims—the answer is self-evident: God was right *there, with them, in* the death camps. For some Christians, too, the answer is strangely simple. Their tradition is based on the notion of a god who suffered, after all, and died on a cross; Christ asked his followers to take up their own crosses, not to expect lives free of pain. But more important even than this theological framework is the simple fact that the sacred can be personally experienced at any time or place. Whatever happens after death or at the end of history, holiness, the intimacy of God's presence, is to be enjoyed here and now in the familiar context of everyday life: a colorful festival, a family meal, a flash of insight, a glance at the stars. . . . Given the rise of secularism—another aspect of which is rejection of the sacred because it cannot be verified empirically—the immanent tradition has also become problematic in our time. Even so, secular functional equivalents of the sacred are usually easier to find or create than secular functional equivalents of divine eruptions into history.[6] And they are certainly less dangerous when you consider those who use the resources of modern dictators to act out their fantasies of divine power.

Shadows and Fog can thus be considered a characteristically (though not uniquely) Jewish response to anxiety generated by "the death of God." Its power is grounded in the fact that it takes seriously the particular situation of modern, secular men and women for whom, as virtually all philosophers and theologians make perfectly clear, the central problem is precisely meaninglessness. This movie avoids condescension: Death really is a problem that must be brought out of the proverbial closet. At the same time, it rejects cynicism: Death does not render life meaningless and decency futile. The result is a truly compassionate view of the human condition in our time.

Notes

1. John Dominic Crossan, *The Dark Interval: Towards a Theology of Story* (Niles, IL: Argus Communications, 1975).
2. The parabolic perspective is not necessarily expressed in the form of a short, pithy, story designed to illustrate some theoretical point. Much of the moral and historical material assigned to Isaiah and some of the other prophets, for example, is parabolic in content (though not in form).
3. Paul Nathanson, *Over the Rainbow: The Wizard of Oz as a Secular Myth of America* (Albany: State University of New York Press, 1991).
4. The Indian notion of self-willed death—not necessarily suicide, which results from personal despair, although the difference is not always obvious—developed in approximately the sixth century B.C.E. At this point, warriors were allowed to kill themselves in some situations (rather than to be killed by enemies) as were the very old, the very sick, and widows. Jains, meanwhile, maintained the goal of eventually starving themselves to death. In the tenth century C.E., Hindu thinkers mounted a critque of self-willed death. They banned, at least in theory, all forms of it except sati (the widow who kills herself by entering her husband's funeral pyre). In the nineteenth century, the British banned all forms of self-willed death—including suicide and sati (Katherine K. Young, "A Cross-cultural Historical Case against Planned Self-Willed Death and Assisted suicide," *McGill Law Journal* 39.3 [October 1994]: 657–707).

5. Even though most Christians (until recently in some circles) and most Jews have preferred to emphasize the differences between Christianity and Judaism, the fact remains that *not everything* is different. Unless either one or the other is classified as something other than religion, both must have at least some characteristics in common (and not only with each other, of course, but with other religions as well).

6. One obvious exception, of course, is provided by Jewish attitudes toward the state of Israel. The reemergence of a Jewish state provided a quasi-theological and quasi-secular "answer" to the Nazi experience (despite the moral problem, whether understood in either religious or secular terms, of something so good being attained at the cost of so much suffering). Given the drama of modern Jewish history, the temptation to believe that some "force" intervened in history is very great. This might explain, at least partially, why it is so intensely disturbing for Jews—especially diaspora Jews—to consider the possibility of moral ambiguity in Middle Eastern politics. If Israel is the vehicle of some transcendent "force," after all, then no course of action by the Israelis could possibly be questioned. Nevertheless, Jews are beginning to acknowledge moral ambiguity. This does not leave them hostile or indifferent to Israel, but it does leave them without the security of what has amounted to a kind of "secular religion."

Section Two

Re-presenting Religion

Chapter Five

The Art of Presence:
Buddhism and Korean Films

Francisca Cho

Film and Religion

The unique multimedia experience offered by motion pictures has the particular ability to create "real time" experience, or the sense of "being there" in the world conjured. Because film appears to be immediate in its visual, aural, and narrative representations, its illusion of "reality" is extremely powerful. For this reason, the arenas of film and cultural studies have been attentive to the ideological capacity of this medium, particularly to its ability to make normative the structures of power that organize society along divisions of gender, race, and class. Crucial to this agenda is the affirmation that human representations always present a point of view that is distinct from some conceit of "the way things are," or perhaps even from the way things ought to be. Hence representations, particularly the most potent ones, are in need of critique.

This chapter will attend to the powers of cinematic representation by shifting this ideological/critical observation into an ontological/religious one. If the reality and persuasiveness of film is ultimately an illusion, is it any more illusory than our individual experience of the world as mediated by our own sensory and interpretive equipment? Since all symbolic representations are human creations, the difference seems to be more a matter of medium rather than a question of "reality." In fact, the medium of film, as an object of public consumption, is easier to scrutinize and discourse upon than the structures of our individual, subconscious ideologies. Hence, art is presumably easier to penetrate than the labyrinths of our own minds. However, I am interested in the moments when art does not bear scrutiny because we are too overwhelmed by its presence and because that presence succeeds in displacing our normal sense of reality. When this happens, one might say that art subjects *us* to ideological critique because it wills us to become free of ourselves. The power that art exerts in this process is in and of itself religious because it can challenge and reorient our sense of the real.

Our specific interest in film here, of course, has to do with its relationship with religion. This essay will explore how we can understand film— and art, generally—as religious discourse. This means more than the idea that one can be personally and spiritually moved by films. We will operate within a metaphysics that presumes the ontological, though not functional, equivalence of all human representations. In this context, an exploration of reality through art is a particular form of religious practice. While the aim of some religions may be to search for a reality beyond human forms, this religious practice is driven by the reasoning that since the illusion of art is equivalent to the illusion of life itself, filmmaking (and viewing) can be a form of life experience that is more potent and directed than one's putative "real life."

What I describe here is a religious practice that evolved in East Asia with the advent of Buddhism. The Buddhist understanding that worldly existence amounts to nothing but an illusory dream affirmed the equivalence of reality and art and explicitly enabled a theory of why art can be a form of religious practice. This will be demonstrated through the example of premodern storytelling traditions, which I argue are the functional equivalent of film, complete with a theory that can likewise be extended to the cinematic arts.

Chinese picture performances *(zhuanbian)*, Japanese "picture explaining" performances *(etoki)*, and Korean *p'ansori* are forms of oral storytelling in East Asia. In all three, a storyteller narrates, sings, and acts out a tale, accompanied by musical instruments. The Chinese and Japanese traditions have the added element of picture scrolls that are used as visual aids. The addition of painting augments the creation of a total audio-visual experience. The Chinese *zhuanbian* and the Japanese *etoki* are secular and professionalized versions of storytelling by proselytizing Buddhist monks, practiced during the Tang (618–907) and Muromachi (1336–1573) eras, respectively. Although the tradition of Buddhist storytelling in Korea is made evident by the tales preserved in *Samguk sagi* (History of the Three Kingdoms, 1145) and the *Samguk yusa* (Memorabilia of the Three Kingdoms, 1285), *p'ansori* performance, which takes distinct form in the eighteenth century, can also be linked to the tradition of shamanic narrative song performance native to the southwestern region of the Cholla Province.[1]

A key unifying feature of all three traditions is that they are live performance traditions that emphasize the event of performance itself. They are linked to textual traditions in that texts (Buddhist sutras, Indian tales) may supply story content, and also in that they give rise to vernacular fiction as performances and prompt books are novelized. These events, however, are peripheral to the performance tradition, which bears within itself a theory of performance and which supplies a livelihood and a lifelong discipline for the performer. In the case of the *p'ansori* singer, or *kwangdae,* training begins in preadolescence under a master and often entails isolated practice in a Buddhist temple.[2] Another important feature is that these traditions are expressions of popular folk culture that flourished in urban settings where Buddhist monasteries often functioned as cultural centers and where imperial and aristocratic patronage could be had. The success of oral storytelling as an art form lay in its ability to captivate a broad audience that cut across class lines and that led to the creation of a common national literature.

The theory of performance in these oral traditions derives from Buddhist views about the nature of reality, which in turn supplies a general cultural understanding of the value of the literary arts.[3] The impact of Buddhism on East Asian literature can be initially attributed to the highly imaginative, metaphorical, and narrative nature of Buddhist texts, which led to the dissemination of Buddhist personalities and motifs into secular literature. More than this, however, Buddhist metaphysics sanctioned the truth value of the literary arts as a means of expressing the similarly artful quality of life itself. The parallel status of art and life as equal forms of illusory play allowed for a conscious affirmation of literary practice as a religious path. If life and art are both illusions, then the distinction between religious and nonreligious practices is inherently meaningless. If the point of religious knowledge is, in fact, to understand the intrinsic "emptiness" *(úunyatā)* of all things, then the artifice of poetry, fiction, and, by extension, film, is a natural place to explore this reality.

In this system of values, the "truth" of any representation—which are all equally illusory, or "empty" *(úunyā)*—is measured solely by its power to edify. Since all of our perceptions of the world are selective descriptions that have no basis in an objective or absolute reality, one can choose representations at will. The *Heart Sūtra's* declaration that the truth of emptiness can only be found in such illusory conventions has traditionally been read as a "no-holds-barred" approach to religious practice—in other words, anything can be a vehicle of liberation. The Chinese picture performances appear to have been understood in this light. The tradition bears a distinct linguistic marker, *bian,* or transformation, whose deeper connotations are quite suggestive. Picture performances are literally "transformation performances" *(zhuanbian),* and the notion of transformation harks back to the "miraculous transformation (that is, appearance or manifestation) performed by a Buddha or bodhisattva for the edification of sentient beings."[4] A "transformation" signifies the miraculous in the sense of

something conjured, as in the magician's apparition. In addition, it elabo-
rates upon the idea that the teachings of the Buddha, and even the Buddha
himself, are skillful but ultimately empty manifestations created for the sole
purpose of the spiritual edification of others. In the present context, such
manifestations pertain to dramatic performance and the illusion of theater.
The term *bian* signifies that the illusion of theater has no less potency than
the transformations of the Buddha.

This sense of art as magical apparition that can function as religious
truth is one way of expressing the general East Asian concept of aesthetic
truth. The truth of art is an affective truth in the sense that art makes present
an actual experience: "[B]ecause the poetic expression conveys the ideas
and feelings of an actual person, it will also move readers."[5] In contrast to
the Aristotelian focus on mimesis, or representation in art, the Asian
criterion centers on the truth inherent in the performance. Not surprisingly,
Asian poetic theory is consistently focused on the actualization of performance and the presence created by the performer. In *p'ansori* criticism, for
example, of the four major attributes of the master *kwangdae,* a commanding stage presence is ranked above the other elements of narrative technique, vocal accomplishment, and dramatic gesture.[6]

In summary, the aesthetic focus on affective truth appreciates art as a
process that induces, for both performer and audience, significant life
experiences. In simple parlance, *p'ansori* was so popular because it was
hugely entertaining—in the sense that performer and audience entertained
in their minds and in their affective reality the reality that the art brought to
life. Buddhist metaphysics lends explicit metaphysical arsenal to this
aesthetic practice and sees in art a natural arena to explore its own sense of
the real.

Buddhism and Film

I will examine two films with explicit Buddhist themes and subject matter:
Chang Sonu's *Passage to Buddha* (1994) and Chung Jiyong's *Beyond the
Mountain* (1991). Films with specific Buddhist content do not make up a
significant percentage of Korean cinema, and among them not many can be
confirmed as the products of self-conscious Buddhist religious practice.
Rather than relying on the self-understanding of the filmmakers, however, I
read the "Buddhist film" within the historical lineage of a specific cultural
tradition of popular oral performances, as well as its derivative tradition of
popular narratives. Seen in this light, the thin trickle of films joins forces
with a well-established and traditional deployment of art as religious
practice. Hence, rather than isolating the films within their modern tempo-

ral framework, I instead view them as the contemporary evolution of a process that began as far back as the eighth century. This strategy allows us to gain a diverse perspective on Korean cinema as well. Korea's film industry has been, for most of its history, an ideological battleground defined by twentieth-century history. During the era of Japanese colonial rule (1910–45), the film industry was monitored for nationalist sentiment and utilized for pro-Japanese propaganda. After the north-south division of the country, which began with the Soviet–U.S. occupation (1945–48) and which solidified after the civil war (1950–53), the ideological standoff between the two Koreas intensified the political use of film on both sides. While North Korean cinema is a state-controlled affair, from production to distribution, the South Korean industry has been only slightly better off, being constantly subject to ideological control and censorship. The Korean Motion Picture Act (1962), for example, suppressed any portrayals of poverty and economic conflict, promoting instead narratives of prosperity tied to the Park Chung Hee regime (1961–79). Since the 1980s, the easing of political pressures has given rise to the use of film as a medium of social criticism—a freer yet equally political utilization. Concurrently, more films have been produced for the international market in the pursuit of national prestige as well as of cultural identity.

The Buddhist film makes its appearance largely since the 1980s and is well represented in the category of the international export film. Its relative novelty can lead one to interpret it as the outcome of contemporary social needs. Hence, the turn to religious themes is read as a "search for a moral vision of society,"[7] particularly in the midst of rapid modernization. Im Kwontaek's *Mandala* (1981) and *Come, Come, Come Upward* (1989), and Bae Yonggyun's *Why Has Bodhi-Dharma Left for the East?* (1989), in fact, all exhibit a social consciousness that is the hallmark of South Korea's "new wave" filmmakers, and they utilize a Buddhist filter in order to address contemporary concerns about class and poverty.[8] The Buddhist film also reflects the vogue of traditional culture and folkways as a subject of Korean cinema, made most explicit in such films as Im Kwontaek's *Sopyonje* (1993) and *Festival* (1996). This new interest in the past bespeaks the contemporary yearning for identity and cultural pride. In addition, the nostalgia for traditional and folk culture can be read as a politics of aesthetics in which "traditional Korean culture" is marketed to the international film community as a way of gaining currency in the global cultural arena.

Bearing these contemporary dynamics in mind, our view of these films can be significantly broadened if we place them within the lineage of Buddhist religious practices. The first film to be examined here, *Passage to Buddha*, is exemplary of the tendency of Buddhist scriptures to be co-opted into more popular and accessible formats. *Passage to Buddha* is the English translation of the Korean film title, *Hwaomkyong,* which is the Korean name for the *Avatamsaka Sūtra* (Chinese: *Huayanjing).* The film borrows its narrative from the final chapter of the sūtra, which also exists independently in the Sanskritic tradition as the *Gandavyūha* (entry into the realm of reality). In this text, the central character—a young boy named Sudhana—sets off on a pilgrimage to attain enlightenment from 53 successive teachers. These "enlightening beings," who are the subject of the first half of the *Gandavyūha,* have two notable qualities. First, they take a multitude of human forms: mendicants, priests, scholars, scientists, doctors, merchants, ascetics, entertainers, artisans, and craftsmen.[9] This variety embodies the Mahāyāna view that all beings are bodhisattvas who have a role to play in the weal of other beings. It also underscores the concept of "expedient means" *(upāya),* and the idea that different people respond to different kinds of teachers. The enlightening beings take on different forms for that reason. This is also related to their second notable quality, which is that they are "phantom" beings who appear to people according to the latter's need: "Having pervaded the cosmos with their emanations, they enlightened, developed, and guided sentient beings."[10] As phantom manifestations, the enlightening beings demonstrate the Mahāyāna view that illusion can be a form of benevolent magic.

The human diversity and the skillful magic of the enlightening beings lend themselves to narrative depiction. The idea that all kinds of beings can function as spiritual guides sets up the possibility of many kinds of narrative scenarios. It offers a leave, if you will, to enter into any number of human predicaments for their inherent dramatic interest. In *Passage to Buddha,* the pilgrim is an 11-year-old boy named Sonje who wanders through modern-day Korea, particularly its social margins. The film opens in a crematorium where the body of Sonje's father, too poor and inconsequential to be identified, is rendered into ashes. Beginning with the loss of his father, who is never seen or named, Sonje proceeds in the rest of the film to search for his mother, who apparently abandoned him as an infant. The themes of orphanage and homelessness, as we will see, are ubiquitous Buddhist tropes. They pervade the medieval biographies of eminent monks and surface in both our films.

Sonje's search for his mother is overtly conflated with Sudhana's search for Buddhahood, as the former declares that his mother can be found in any "good person." The interchangeability of mother and Buddha as objects of yearning is depicted in one Oedipal dream sequence in which Sonje encounters a beautiful older woman who makes love to him. At the end of the film, Sonje has another vision, this time of his mother, who declares to him that she is the mother of all beings, including the Buddhas and bodhisattvas. The ultimate convertibility of signs, or manifestations, is a pointed declaration here, very much in the spirit of the *Gandavyūha*'s teaching that enlightening beings take any and all forms. The specific conflation of Buddha and mother, who is also depicted as a love object, makes the further point that the traditionally antipodal realms of religion and domesticity are oppositions that must be overcome. Interestingly, Sonje has difficulty accepting this lesson in his own life, when he rejects marriage to the young woman he has impregnated in order to continue his spiritual pilgrimage.

Sonje's succession of teachers include a doctor, a blind beggar woman, a political prisoner, an astronomer, and a lighthouse keeper. In keeping with its namesake text, the film narrates a deliberate process in which each teacher sends Sonje on to the next, indicating that each has a particular teaching to give and that a variety of encounters are necessary to attain the full Dharma. The idea that each human encounter imparts a spiritual boon is denoted by the deep bow that Sonje renders to each character before moving on. The one personage that weaves in and out of Sonje's journey is the apostate Buddhist monk, another abiding trope of East Asian narratives. At the very beginning of his travels, Sonje encounters the monk in a restaurant, eating meat and drinking wine. The monk appears again midpoint in the film to exhort Sonje to marry the little girl—now a young woman—whom Sonje initially met at the crematorium. In the final encounter, Sonje sees the monk working with the village women, gutting fish in order to earn money for wine. The meeting culminates Sonje's sense of hopelessness and confusion, triggering a suicide attempt and the ultimate turn toward understanding, as signified by the aforementioned vision of his mother.

The world-embracing monk, with his decidedly nonmonastic ways, is a familiar figure that reaches back to the popular Buddhist text the *Vimalakîrtinirdeúa Sūtra*. The text is named for its principle character, Vimalakîrti, a noncleric who indulges in worldly activities yet who bests the most renowned Buddhist disciples in Buddha wisdom. This second-century Mahāyāna text was extremely favored in East Asia for its emphasis on the value of lay life. The critique of monastic reclusion that is implicit in the world-embracing monk is a prominent theme in Korean Buddhist films. To be sure, *Passage to Buddha*'s overall focus on the social fringes—each of Sonje's teachers bear the pain of a personal or social lack—manifests a political consciousness that is the imprint of post-1980s Korean cinema. The concordance of religious practice and social service, however, is a theme explicitly emphasized throughout the *Avatamsaka,* which embraces worldly activity and skills "guided not by the personal desires of the practitioners but by the current needs of the society that they are serving, according to what will be beneficial."[11]

In simply co-opting the title of a significant Buddhist text, *Passage to Buddha* declares its lineage. Beyond lifting its plot line from Sudhana's famous pilgrimage, the film plays on the theme of enlightening illusions. One method it employs is a classic use of dreams as a way of advancing the tale—as well as Sonje's spiritual knowledge. Both dream episodes entail encounters with mother figures that are emotionally and religiously loaded. In the first, Sonje's Oedipal encounter with his mother/lover abruptly and rather disturbingly ends when she falls from a cliff during a post-coital excursion. In the second, Sonje finally has a vision of a woman who calls herself his mother, as well as the mother of all beings [fig. 5.1]. The dream sequences mark significant nodes in the plot/journey—at the point of maximum loss and absence and at the point of maximum attainment and presence. The ability of dreams—which, after all, are illusions—to function so meaningfully in the course of Sonje's journey can be paralleled to the medium of film itself. This is pointedly suggested by a curious detail in *Passage to Buddha*: The boy Sonje never ages despite the passage of many years. This detail explicitly invokes the conceit of the Buddhist-derived dream tale, in which the protagonist lives an entire life in the course of a short dream.[12] When such dreams are told as stories or acted out as films, the efficacy of the former is extended to the latter genres as functional equivalents. These "transformations," which offer a distilled and potent experience of life, are better vehicles of instruction than the distracted experiences of waking reality.

The tension between the religious and secular paths is the overt theme of *Beyond the Mountain*, which features a love story between a nineteen-year-old Buddhist novice, Chimhae, and a young Buddhist nun, Myohon. Whereas Sonje's story already conflates his journey of life with a spiritual quest, parallel to Sudhana's journey, the young lovers of *Beyond the Mountain* are torn between their religious vows and their desire for each other. Seminal to their passion is the fact that both Chimhae and Myohon were both orphaned as young children, which led them to the Buddhist monastery as a substitute family. Chimhae, abandoned by the seaside, was discovered and taken in by the monastery's master in infancy. Myohon lost her family to a fire and was taken in by an adoptive father and brother. When her relationship with the brother blossomed into more mature, erotic feelings, she was driven out by the father, particularly upon the untimely death of the son. As Myohon informs Chimhae, her attachment to Chimhae was sparked at first sight, because of his uncanny resemblance to the original brother/lover. Hence Myohon and Chimhae's attachment to each other, and their desire to leave the monastic life and to reenter the world, are attempts to address a lack in both their life stories. For Myohon, this is the need to reanimate in Chimhae her prior object of attachment, who is figured not only as a lover but doubly as a substitute for the prior loss of her family. For Chimhae, it is the desire to simply see the world and to begin the journey so abruptly interrupted in infancy.

Parallel to this tale of Myohon and Chimhae is an equally significant relationship between Chimhae's master and the degenerate monk Mubul—a name that is phonetically identical to the Chinese characters for "no buddha." The master and Mubul instantiate two antipodal figures—the orthodox monk and the apostate monk—that form another classic trope in Buddhist literature. Im Kwontaek's *Mandala* and *Come, Come, Come Upward* are also organized around this polarity, figured as two monks in the former and two nuns in the latter. In Im's films, the apostate monk and the worldly nun bear the lineage of Vimalakîrti and tread the superior religious path. The nun Sunnyo of *Upward*, for example, parallels the trope of the degenerate monk through her worldly—particularly sexual—ministry, which is ultimately affirmed as superior to the orthodox monasticism of the other nun. Her sexual largesse, both in being "metonymic for her general social ministry" and "the source of her own spiritual development,"[13] follows the paradigm of the bodhisattva Guanyin and the medieval tales that recount her use of sex and sexuality as an impetus to

Figure 5.1 "Sonje finally has a vision of a woman who calls herself his mother, as well as the mother of all beings. The dream sequences mark significant nodes in the plot/journey.... The ability of dreams—which, after all, are illusions—to function so meaningfully in the course of Sonje's journey can be paralleled to the medium of film itself."

enlightenment.[14] Im takes advantage of laxer industry standards to explicitly depict Sunnyo's sexual ministrations, using the bait of eroticism to draw the audience to a moral and spiritual lesson, much in the same manner as the tales of Guanyin.

Mandala and *Upward* explore the tension between religious renunciation and the imperative to work within the world—a focus dictated, perhaps, by Im Kwontaek's socially conscious filmmaking.[15] In pronouncing the superiority of the one who engages with the world, Im gives voice to the social consciousness of his art and ultimately favors only one half of a fuller dialectic at the heart of Buddhist practice. This dialectic is fundamentally concerned with resolving the polarity between religious and worldly paths as ultimately indistinguishable. The process often entails a preference for the worldly path as an antidote to the entrenched status of the monastic institution. Ultimately, however, the lesson of both orthodox and popular Buddhist literature is that the either/or option must be transcended. Similar to the longstanding association between prostitutes and bodhisattvas—themselves functional signs of nondiscriminating compassion—the Buddha way requires transcending the ultimately empty distinction between high and low, between spirituality and sexuality. The way of passion can be a skillful means because it too partakes of the principle of baselessness.

Beyond the Mountain gives full play to this dynamic in the way it depicts the relationship between the Master and Mubul, whose lives play out in oppositional yet parallel modes. The Master is near death, after 70 years of life in monastic seclusion, and has yet to attain enlightenment. At the beginning of the film, the monastery is abuzz with the rumor that Mubul has returned to the vicinity, having abandoned the monastic life some years ago. When Mubul finally appears, the Master asks him how he found the worldly scents of meat, women, and wine. Mubul replies that he could not find enlightenment in them and that he has returned because he overlooked something of value at the monastery. The unrelenting Master, however, orders him to leave.

For the vast duration of the film, the antipathy of the two figures is demonstrated in their interactions with Chimhae and the way they address his religious/sexual dilemma. The Master, true to his orthodox calling, tells Chimhae to "throw away" his attachments. While this counsel overtly applies to Chimhae's sexual desires, its double-edged quality also cuts against his monastic bonds. Hence the Master's command is ironic relative to his own decidedly familial relationship with Chimhae, for whom he is a substitute father as well as religious teacher. When Chimhae finally leaves the monastery for the world at the end of the film, it is only after he has fulfilled his obligations as a son to his Master/father. It is only after the Master's death that Chimhae is finally able to "throw away" his attachment to the monastic family and brave, alone, the much more uncertain world outside.

Chimhae's final act segues into an embrace of Mubul's opposing imperative to face, rather than renounce, that which beguiles him. The mobius strip that connects the Master's ideal of standing aloof to Mubul's option of confronting one's demons is constructed by the recoil inherent in both their methods. The Master's counsel to throw away attachments ultimately applies to himself and the religious life he holds in esteem. Throwing away something inevitably entails embracing something else, as evident in the Master's attachment to monastic orthodoxy. Mubul's return to the monastery, on the other hand, impugns the judgment that the worldly life is ultimately the better Buddha way. Mubul, much like the Master, describes himself as only half a Buddha. His worldly ministries as a miner, trash collector, and laborer have taught him that the attainment of Buddha only gives way in time to the grip of another devil. Facing the world, interchangeably with abandoning it, forges a link in a endless chain of substitutions. Cracking a massive icicle in the frozen cave where he has taken refuge, Mubul tells Chimhae that the icicle will surely grow back, but that it will take different form. There is in this evolution both resignation and hope.

In parallel sequence, as the Master makes preparations for his death, Mubul throws himself from a cliff in a final act of resignation, or perhaps acceptance. As for his final act, the Master calls Myohon from the nunnery and asks her to take her clothes off so that he can see a woman's body before he dies. When she is fully nude, the Master jolts into awakening and calls out to Mubul at the moment of his death. This final invocation suggests *satori*, or awakening, in which the antinomy of the Master's monastic attachment is swept away and brought to dialectical completion [fig. 5.2]. He too throws away his attachments—a throwing away that is simultaneously an acceptance. In the final act of the film, we see the cycle continue in the younger generation of Chimhae and Myohon. As noted above, Chimhae's renunciation/embrace takes the form of setting off for the world. On the contrary, Myohon makes an offering of her finger to the Buddha, signifying that she will stay on in her monastic cloister. She throws away the attachments that have been played out as a series of substitutions, and yet, her ultimate devotion to the Buddha way is but another. This is overtly suggested in the figurine she carves from fragrant wood. At the beginning of the film, she carves her brother; by the end, she carves the Buddha. The figurine functions throughout the film as a go-between for Myohon and Chimhae, occasioning and reoccasioning their meetings. The floating nature of its significations—brother, lover, Buddha—also parallels the transitions between Myohon and Chimhae, which ultimately move them to their separate paths. The prevalence of transitions and substitutions suggests that religion can be located in this all-encompassing dynamic that surpasses the distinction between the monastic and the secular.

Conclusion

Passage to Buddha and *Beyond the Mountain* are "secular" tellings of stories derived from Buddhist narratives and tropes. In that sense these films continue the tradition of oral storytelling performances, which are themselves derived from religious storytelling practices—both Buddhist and shamanic. In this lineage of performance, entertainment is a logical aspect of religious practice because the ability to "entertain" a reality made present by art is a necessary step to religious truth. *Passage to Buddha* is overt and didactic about linking religion and art, paralleling the religious journey of Sudhana with the film journey of Sonje, and by using the dream trope to implicitly question the distinctions between dream, reality, and film. *Beyond the Mountain* is less preachy and finer in its artistic realiza-

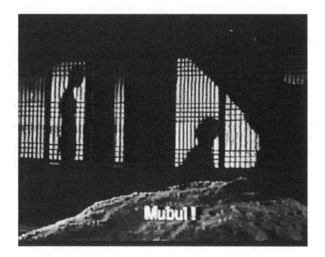

Figure 5.2 "When she is fully nude, the Master jolts into awakening and calls out to Mubul at the moment of his death. This final invocation suggests *satori*, or awakening, in which the antinomy of the Master's monastic attachment is swept away and brought to dialectical completion. He too throws away his attachments—a throwing away that is simultaneously an acceptance."

tion. It takes up the secular/monastic distinction, which is an abiding element of canonical discourse, and renders it into a narrative structure and process. Its subtle and substantive inquiry into the nature of religion entertains our sense of reality, and to that degree, the film itself instantiates, and even resolves, the dilemma of its internal narrative. The qualitative performance of the religious question in the medium of film enables one to transcend the distinctions between the religious, the secular, and the aesthetic as merely functional qualifications of the greater truth of presence.

Notes

1. Marshall Pihl, *The Korean Singer of Tales* (Cambridge: Harvard University Press, 1994), 60–63.
2. Ibid., 104
3. William LaFleur, *The Karma of Words: Buddhism and the Literary Arts in Medieval Japan* (Berkeley: University of California Press, 1983); Francisca Cho Bantley, *Embracing Illusion: Truth and Fiction in the Dream of the Nine Clouds* (Albany: State University of New York Press, 1996).
4. Victor Mair, *T'ang Transformation Texts* (Cambridge: Harvard University Press, 1989), 49.
5. Earl Roy Miner, *Comparative Poetics: An Intercultural Essay on Theories of Literature* (Princeton: Princeton University Press, 1990), 119.
6. Pihl, *The Korean Singer of Tales*, 98.
7. Hyangjin Lee, *Contemporary Korean Cinema: Identity, Culture, Politics* (Manchester: Manchester University Press, 2000), 61.
8. David James, "Im Kwon-Taek: Korean National Cinema and Buddhism," in *Im Kwon-Taek: The Making of a Korean National Cinema*, David E. James and Kyung Hyun Kim, eds. (Detroit: Wayne State University Press, 2002).
9. *The Flower Ornament Scripture: A Translation of the Avatamsaka Sutra*, Thomas Cleary, trans. (Boston: Shambhala Press, 1993), 1169.
10. Ibid., 1168.
11. Ibid., 41.
12. Cho Bantley, *Embracing Illusion*, 85–107.
13. James, "Im Kwon-Taek," 76.
14. Chun-fang Yu, *Kuan-yin: The Chinese Transformation of Avalokitesvara* (New York: Columbia University Press, 2001), 419–38.
15. See James, "Im Kwon-Taek."

Chapter Six

Pentecostalism, Prosperity, and Popular Cinema in Ghana*

Birgit Meyer

Introduction

Heaven, according to a popular painting by an anonymous Ghanaian artist, is a big city up in the sky, with modern skyscrapers and office towers, surrounded by trees and flowers. In the painting *Judgement Day*, Jesus arrives in the blue sky and has his angel select the good from the bad. There is a signpost indicating that heaven is up the stairs, whereas hell and the world are on the ground floor, so to speak. Those dressed in white climb up, whereas those dressed in black—a number of youngsters and a man wearing a Fez—are bound to end up in hellfire guarded by a monster that obviously represents the devil. The picture, of course, refers to passages in the book of Revelation and is reminiscent of the depiction of Jerusalem as the heavenly city in popular Protestant imagination and literature, which was introduced to Africa by Pietist missions in the course of the nineteenth century (e.g., John Bunyan's *Pilgrim's Progress* and the well-known lithograph of the *Broad and the Narrow Path*[1]). What is new, and interesting in this image, however, is heaven's distinctive high modernity, with skyscrapers featured as icons of pride and emblems of prosperity.

This image is not idiosyncratic but part of a genre of similar paintings that are based on a Christian framework. The image pinpoints a particular attitude toward the imagination of salvation in terms of modern urbanity and prosperity in Southern Ghana. The intimate link between Jesus and skyscrapers, and the promise that good Christians will end up in an urbanized heaven, is widely shared in Christian circles.[2] Above all, this view is stressed in the Pentecostal-charismatic churches, which have been able to attract a great number of followers and sympathizers in Ghana in the course of the last two decades. There has been a spectacular rise, still going on, in the number of Pentecostally oriented churches and prayer groups, which often carry an epithet like "global" or "international" in their name, advertise the prosperity gospel, and criticize the theologians of the established mission churches for advocating a stance characterized as "to be poor to be holy."[3] God, in this perspective, wants his children to enjoy life before they die, and Pentecostalists claim to know the access route to a heavenlike life already on earth.

Their emphasis on consumption as a sign of divine blessing occurs in conjunction with the opening up of Ghana to neoliberal capitalism, instigated by the state together with the World Bank in the late 1980s, which resulted in flows of much-desired commodities into the country yet made many people realize their limited access to the sphere of consumption. Significantly different from the ascetic Pietists in Max Weber's analysis of the link between the Protestant ethic and the spirit of capitalism, Ghanaian Pentecostalists emphasize consumerism as part and parcel of a modern life style.[4] Far from wondering about the question as to whether one belongs to the elect, they regard financial success as a sign of divine blessing and, by contrast, poverty as the work of the devil. The prime emblem of success is the Pentecostal pastor, lavishly dressed in the latest style, wearing gold jewelry, living in a high-class mansion, and driving an expensive car, preferably a Mercedes. Openly engaging in conspicuous consumption, a pastor parades the fact that he, and his church, are blessed by the Lord. While the origins of wealth are usually mystified, spending is foregrounded all the more.[5] Believers are de facto constructed as consumers.

All this is not entirely new but links up with and rearticulates the Christian project of modernity from the point of view of consumption. Even if orthodox mission churches, ever since the late nineteenth century, when Christianity was introduced, propounded an antimaterialist attitude, in practice Christians held privileged positions in society and were the first to have access to well-paid jobs in the colonial administration and consumption of Western goods.[6] Conversion to Christianity also was a conversion to modernity, and Christians formed the new elites in colonial society.[7] When Pentecostalism got a mass following in the mid-1980s, a period marked by political disillusionment and serious economic hardships, preachers did not formulate a completely new message but rather revitalized the old, unfilled promises of modernity and claimed to be able to fulfill them through new means, by privileging consumption above production and by emphasizing and reworking the individual self.

Far from remaining confined to a distinct space reserved for religion in Ghanaian society, Pentecostalism has encroached upon the new public sphere that has evolved in Ghana after the return to democracy and the liberalization and commercialization of the hitherto state-owned and state-controlled media in 1992. Pentecostal-charismatic churches have understood the power of media to reach people, thereby creating a Pentecostally inclined Christian public. Realizing that mastery of media technology is a symbol of modernity and thus a power resource, Pentecostals make active use of media such as video, TV, cassettes, and FM stations in presenting and advertising themselves.[8] The FM stations, constituted as secular yet in practice colonized by Pentecostal churches, testify to Pentecostalism's capacity to raise its voice in public and to thus fill secular public space with religion. In the marketplace of religions, which Ghana has become, Pentecostal denominations forcefully compete with each other and offer their religious services as commodities to believers, who are addressed as consumers and clients.[9]

Pentecostalism also has a considerable impact on cultural productions in the field of music, the press, literature, theater, and popular film. In a sense, what has been evolving in Ghana in the aftermath of democratization is what I would like to call a Pentecostally infused or, perhaps better, *Pentecostalite* public culture. By this I mean a whole array of popular expressions, from popular paintings to posters, from theater to video, from music to popular literature, that adopt Pentecostal modes of representation. The emphasis is on style, rather than on content or message as such. It is important to make this distinction, because it would be a mistake to view the proliferation of Pentecostalism in public culture simply in terms of an increase of religiosity. The point I wish to make here is that Pentecostal modes of representation offer a repertoire that is adopted by even formally independent cultural entrepreneurs and artists who consciously make use of Pentecostal styles, without necessarily defining themselves as believers.[10]

While Ghana's public culture hosts more voices than the Pentecostal, the latter is truly remarkable because of its loudness and impact. Products of Pentecostalite public culture run remarkably counter to different visions, which idealize the village as a space of truthfulness, morality, and happiness—a virtual space to be cherished as "African Heritage"—and contrast it with the moral corruptness of the big city emanating from the moral perversion that went along with colonial modernity. These visions are part and parcel of different politics of identity. Whereas the positive association of urbanity, prosperity, and Christianity is emphasized in Pentecostal-charismatic circles, which now form a majority among Christians in Accra, state-promoted cultural policies seek to root national identity and pride in the village, which is conceived as a heritage space.[11] If until 1992 it was possible for the state to control the public sphere and propagate its own politics of culture and identity, this has become increasingly difficult with the liberalization of both the media and the economy. In Ghana's contemporary public culture, these different positions regularly clash with each other. While these positions oppose each other in terms of temporal (past versus future) and spatial (village versus city) schemes, it is important to realize that both are articulated in and with regard to the present, and struggle to make sense of the fact that the present appears to be out of tune with the ideal. Those talking about the village in terms of a heritage to be retrieved (often calling upon the Akan symbol Sankofa)[12] struggle also to appropriate notions such as "development," whereas those imagining salvation in terms of the modern heavenly city seek to come to terms with the fact that the city they inhabit is much more ambivalent and resembles hell more than heaven. This essay focuses on the Pentecostalist view and seeks to unravel the reasons for its appeal.

In so doing, the main emphasis does not lie on the Pentecostal message as it is preached in churches as such, but rather on the ways in which Pentecostalist modes of representation are incorporated into expressions of popular culture. A particularly interesting case in point is the popular video film industry, which has emerged since the mid-1980s and took off in full swing after 1992. In the wake of the liberalization and commercialization of the media, there developed a flourishing video-film scene.[13] As independent video-filmmakers, in order to stay in the business, fully depend on the approval of their urban audiences, "Ghanaian films" zoom in on the desires and horrors of ordinary people. Far from taking up colonial and postcolonial, statist modes of filmmaking, which regarded film as a medium par excellence for the enlightenment and education of the general public, the new video-movies are above all concerned with visualizing what resonates with the structures of feeling of their audiences.

Given the high popularity of Pentecostalism, as indicated above, it will not come as a surprise that there is a striking overlap between the prosperity gospel promoted by these churches and the video-films. It is the main aim of this essay to explore the articulation of a new social imaginary that evolves at the intersection of popular cinema with Pentecostalism, made possible by the opening up of the public sphere. In order to do so, I will investigate the complex ways in which popular video-movies and the Pentecostal-charismatic movement relate to each other, examine the relationship between prosperity and faith as well as the new notions of self and family propelled by these films, reflect on the emerging nexus of religion and entertainment, and discuss the question of imagination in the context of globalization. The main argument I would like to put forward is that video-films, by operating in the sphere of entertainment, popularise Pentecostalism on a mass scale, beyond the confines of churches as such. Its marked presence in the public sphere contributes to the spread of a social imaginary that is geared toward the recuperation of the project of modernity under the new condition of an open public sphere and the retreat of the state.

Pentecostalism and Popular Cinema

The entanglement of Pentecostalism and the cinema can best be evoked by pointing to the fact that in present-day Accra, many cinema houses are, albeit partly, used as churches by Pentecostalist congregations. While many Pentecostalist pastors have a negative attitude toward the cinema—they regard the cinema hall as a potentially immoral, dark, and unholy space in need of being cleansed through their prayers and are suspicious of the overkill of sex and crime in films—it is certainly significant that Pentecostalism and film cohabit in the same space. When the cinema was introduced in the 1920s, it generated new audiences and a new public culture in the evolving urban spaces of the Gold Coast. Appropriated by the British colonial administration, the cinema was used to visualize the message of "civilization" and "modernization"[14]; it became a modern temple of vision, testifying to the superiority of Western knowledge and the legitimacy of colonial rule. As a new social practice, going to the movies constituted "an experience that was always much more than the viewing of the film itself"[15]; it contributed to the emergence of a new urban class. An emblem of colonial modernity, the cinema occupied a new public space, which entailed new disciplines concerning the ordering of space and time,[16] and a new mode of vision in which education and entertainment were presented as flipsides of each other. It attracted urban audiences eager to go out in their leisure time, thereby opening themselves up to new regimes of visual representation characterized by an entanglement of discipline and pleasure.

The Ghana Film Industry Corporation (GFIC), which replaced the Colonial Film Unit after independence, was owned and controlled by the state, and produced newsreels, documentaries, and feature films—in line with Nkrumahist views—all devoted to the enlightenment of the nation, the education of the people, and the genesis of national pride in African culture and heritage. With the rising popularity and accessibility of TV in the course of the 1970s, the state increasingly addressed the people in their own homes and invested little in the upkeep of the state-owned cinema halls and the production of films. Material got spoiled, and many cinemas became ghostlike remnants of a past when the cinema still was the key mediator of the nationalist vision of the independent state. Pentecostal-charismatic churches, which became increasingly popular in the course of the 1980s, a period marked by political and economic instability, brought the buildings back to life. Transforming the space of the cinema into a church,[17] Pentecostalists tied into the symbolism of the cinema hall as a modern temple of vision and started to propagate their distinct vision of Christian modernity—a project, as will be shown below, evoking yet going beyond older colonial and state-driven versions of modernity.

From the early 1990s onward, video producers started to show their video feature films in cinemas with the help of "telejectors" (as video projection units are called in Ghana), thereby blowing up the hybrid medium of video to cinema proportions. At this point in time, the state-run film industry was virtually defunct, and all the cinemas could show were low-budget films from abroad, provided the projectors were still operating. The video-film producers eagerly came to fill the void by producing local films to be screened in the cinema theaters. Being able to draw large audiences, video-film makers generated their main income through these screenings. They would only sell exposition rights to GBC and TV3, Ghana's two TV channels, once they were sure that the market created through the cinema was saturated. Pleased with audiences' demand for locally produced films, cinema owners and operators screened the latest "Ghanaian films," especially in the weekends, and rented the hall to churches on Sunday mornings. In the 1990s, when the "culture of silence" characteristic of the period between 1987 and 1991 was over,[18] and entertainment started to flourish, video-films and Pentecostalism shared the space of the cinema [fig. 6.1]. Recently, however, cinema attendance has dropped again because many people started to watch films at home, both on TV (where many Ghanaian and Nigerian films are screened nowadays at prime time) and VCR. There are now many video shops and also mobile vendors selling the latest films. Many filmmakers now market their films as home videos on a massive scale, sometimes even without showing them on public screens at all, thereby contributing to the further erosion of cinema and the full conversion of cinema halls into Pentecostalist churches. Despite the apparent disentanglement of church and cinema, it is important to realize that there are new spaces in Ghana's flourishing mediascape shared by video producers and Pentecostalists. A case in point is the well-equipped editing studios that are owned by Pentecostal-charismatic churches and rented out to video producers.

Video-filmmakers themselves have realized that they resemble pastors. This is not simply a question of individual belief. While some producers call themselves Christians and seek to convey a Christian message, others don't—and yet their products very much resemble each other. It is important to realize that these products are not "auteur" films, conveying the particular perspective of its producer or director, as would be the case in artistic genres. Many directors told me that they did not necessarily believe in the narrative structure and message of their films and complained that one could only make a profitable film if one echoed concerns from the street and, above all, as one filmmaker put it: "all this Pentecostal crap," thereby foregoing the chance of being celebrated at prestigious African film festivals such as the Pan-African Film and Television Festival (FESPACO). Because of this closeness to audience expectations, filmmakers can safely be regarded as mediators of popular views. Fixing and visualizing rumors, video-films refashion stories circulating in society by adopting a particular narrative form and representational style, the form and style propagated by Pentecostalism.

One important characteristic is the dualism on which most of the plots thrive. There usually is a struggle going on between "the powers of darkness" and the way they have a firm grip on irresponsible husbands, loose girls, selfish businessmen, greedy mothers-in-law, bad friends, or even ritual murderers, killers, and members of secret cults, on the one hand, and divine power, which always supports the pious housewife, the innocent child, and, of course, the Pentecostal pastor, on the other.[19] Some films, interestingly, also bring in the personage of the pastor going astray; this, however, does not challenge the general appreciation of pastors, for those going astray are always dismantled as "fakes." Needless to say, much in line with Pentecostal sermons, in the end, good overcomes evil in the same way that God is stronger than the devil. Moreover, often films are framed as confessions, thereby echoing a distinct genre of Pentecostalist ways of speaking. By introducing a film as a "true story," based on a person's own

Figure 6.1   "Pleased with audiences' demand for locally produced films, cinema owners and operators screened the latest 'Ghanaian films,' especially in the weekends, and rented the hall to churches on Sunday mornings. In the 1990s . . . video-films and Pentecostalism shared the space of the cinema." Photograph by Birgit Meyer.

experiences with greed, selfishness, and occult powers prior to his or her conversion, filmmakers claim to offer eyewitness revelations about the machinations of evil spirits. Important here is that, much like Pentecostal discourse, a good deal of time is devoted to a voyeuristic encounter with the powers of darkness, where ample use is made of special effects. Diverting markedly from the agenda of both colonial and post-independence state-driven cinema to do away with so-called superstitions and educate the masses, popular films confirm—and to some spectators even prove—the existence of all those invisible forces that stand central in Pentecostal discourse, as well as in popular experiences. Thus films are populated by witches, Mami Water, elementary spirits, shrines in the bush, and different types of magic.

Both popular films and Pentecostalism trade in a particular mode of vision: claiming the power to reveal what remains invisible to the eye yet determines the course of life and addressing spectators as voyeurs. Far from exposing the nonexistence of invisible forces, in popular film the camera zooms in on their operations, thereby creating the illusion of offering firsthand views deep into hell. In this way, the work of representation that constitutes film is mystified—mise-en-scène appears as a revelation of the invisible real. Thus both filmmakers and pastors engage in certain forms of make believe by constructing the powers of darkness through speech, image, and special effects.[20] In so doing both excessively dramatize transgression into evil, thereby adopting one of the most striking figures of Pentecostalist representation, the spectacularization of the spectral.[21] While it would be too simple to reduce filmmakers to pastors because both operate in different, yet increasingly intersecting, arenas—the sphere of entertainment and the sphere of religion—there certainly is an elective affinity between both spheres that will be further discussed below.

In addition, as far as the story is concerned, most video-movies are very much in line with the message of the Pentecostal-charismatic churches: In teaching Christian morals, and, above all, depicting the awful consequences of their violation, these films offer a perfect visual supplement to Sunday's sermons.[22] Indeed, many churches show video-films to their congregations, in particular the youth, in order to alert them to dangers of modern life and teach them morals while at the same time propagating a Christian version of modernity. Both video-films and Pentecostalism actively struggle with modernity. On the one hand all sorts of aspects of modern life—enjoying a prosperous life, with a posh car, a beautiful villa, fine clothes, etc.—are represented as ultimately desirable and harbingers of happiness. On the other hand both films and sermons address the temptations of modernity and the destructive impact these may have on people's lives. Modernity, it should be noted, is not represented as an option to reject or adopt but as a context of life in the big city. The problem rather is how to handle modernity's promises and temptations, and the answer that both sermons and films offer is clear: In order to make the best out of everything, one has to have faith in God and be filled with his Holy Spirit; then one will certainly prosper.

Video-Films as Mediators of Christian Modernity

In video-films, usually much emphasis has been placed on the visualization of the local setting as part and parcel of urban modernity. Films are usually replete with long scenes—in fact, too long for spectators from outside Ghana—in which cars take the audiences on a ride through the wide alleys of Accra (and sometimes Takoradi or Cape Coast, but virtually never places further north), passing buildings of national and touristic importance, multistory buildings, fly-overs, expensive hotels, Labadi beach, chic boutiques, air-conditioned supermarkets, exquisite restaurants, and other places to enjoy life—and, interestingly, these scenes are usually accompanied by Western-style music. The magic of the cinema that stems from the transfiguration of Accra as a cinematic space—and thus as a simulacrum of the modern city—has a remarkable impact on the audiences.[23] Again and again I heard from spectators that it was wonderful to see the beauty and "development of Ghana" (actually, the capital, which is taken for granted as the symbol of the nation) on the screen. People were thrilled to see cinematic representations of familiar sites, which would always appear much nicer than from the usual pedestrian perspective. Life appears more enjoyable from the perspective of a flashy limousine that takes audiences on a mimetic ride through town during daytime and, even more excitingly, in the night. Watching films in the cinemas, I often overheard audiences make remarks about the beauty of the cityscape; they were keenly interested in seeing the latest hotels, office buildings, and fly-overs on screen and emphasized their beauty.[24] For sure, the mediation of the local through a global medium such as video does not merely mirror the local cityscape but transforms it into a series of icons of pride comparable to the Western settings that people know through TV and cinema[25] and represents the limousine as the prime vehicle toward modernity.[26] As being put on the screen means being made part of the wider world, watching locally produced video-films should not be understood as a retreat into local worlds but rather as a practice through which people may assure themselves that they, too, have access to global forms and are able to reconfigure the local in the light of the global. In short, these video-films are not just products of the global accessibility of modern media but are above all mediators of modernity and globalization, offering a mimetic spatial mobility,[27] which echoes the Pentecostalist promise of prosperity and upward social mobility.[28]

The most prominent location featured in Ghanaian films is the upper-middle-class mansion. Fenced by a huge wall guarded by an—often funny—watchman, this type of house has a number of rooms, and the camera often offers the audiences a sightseeing tour through the house: There is the well-furnished kitchen, the living room with beautiful sofas and a room-divider containing a TV, VCR, and stereo installation, and, of course, the fine bedroom of the married couple. While most of the viewers live in much more simple circumstances, they enjoy seeing this type of house on screen and tend to make a lot of comments about the interior. In films, the main protagonists often visit air-conditioned supermarkets and restaurants, and the camera zooms in on the exquisite articles for sale and on the food served. These scenes are usually quite long and give the audiences ample time to discuss the food displayed. In the same way, the hairstyles and costumes—always a bit more fashionable than what people, even the rich, would wear in real life—are subject to discussion and sometimes even generate a new style, adopted especially by young, female viewers.

Interesting in this context is the fact that films, similar to Pentecostal discourse, focus on consumption and keep silent about production. The only site of work that appears in films is the modern office, but it is always presented as an icon of pride, stuffed with computers and phones and populated with beautiful secretaries and their elegantly dressed bosses, not as a place where people struggle hard in order to earn the money they spend. No hard work, no sweat; and in case films reveal the origins of a person's riches, they refer to occult practices, entailing the exchange of life for money.[29] This is in line with Arjun Appadurai's suggestion[30] that consumption is crucial in processes of binding people together, because it enables them to become a class *for* themselves, even if, from a perspective of production, they belong to different classes. It seems to me that the strong emphasis on consumption and the neglect of production reflects the fact that in Ghana, modern identity is being achieved and affirmed through such a shared life style. Consumption certainly features as an imaginary equalizer.

Another significant feature of the films, again fully in conjunction with Pentecostal discourse, is the emphasis on the nuclear family, often living in a very nice, secluded, middle- or upper-class home. The absolute highlight of many films is the marriage celebration, with the groom, meticulously dressed in a dark suit, taking the bride, in her white gown, to the altar, to the sound of the usual marriage march. In many ways, films speak to and reiterate the Pentecostalist stance toward morals, marriage, and, of course, the role of demons in destroying happiness. Interestingly, the films are virtually always in favor of the Christian housewife and highly critical about her morally weak husband, his mother, and his young lover. Often, there is a more-or-less open struggle going on between the powers of good and evil, and in the end the former will overcome the latter and the ill-treated mother and wife will triumph. Take for instance *Mariska* (Akwetey-Kanyi Films 2001), in which a devoted wife (Mariska, who refused to marry the elderly rich man—who later turns out to be a drug dealer—whom her mother chose for her) struggles to support her husband Mawusi, who needs expensive hospital treatment. Mariska has a very jealous friend who snatches Mawusi by making use of love magic derived from a shrine in the forest (there are spectacular scenes, in which his double is kept in a calabash, signifying the fact that he lost his will and is under a spell). In the end, after much suffering and having to bring up Mawusi's child all alone, Mariska marries a rich, nice man, who is a Christian like her; Mawusi ends up in jail.

Remarkable in this film, as well as in many others, is the emphasis placed on personhood and agency. In a sense, it is not entirely Mawusi's fault that he leaves Mariska, because he is—unconsciously—in the power of higher spiritual forces. This danger of not being in control over one's life features in many films, and the implicit or explicit solution to this problem is the warning to keep on praying, in order to be sure to be filled with the spirit of God, so that no evil spirit can intrude and eventually destroy one's happiness. This echoes the Pentecostal practice of deliverance, which seeks to drive out all sorts of evil forces that may control a person, even if he/she is completely unaware of the fact.[31] Yet it would be too simple to see personhood only as a question of remote control by outside forces, either satanic or divine. For a good Christian will make the appropriate choices also on the basis of his/her conscience. In *Mariska*, there are a number of scenes depicting an inner dialogue between good and evil, showing a person in between two doubles who both make suggestions. The bad voice—on the left—is dressed in a Western style, the good one—on the right—in a respectable African dress [fig. 6.2].[32] It is the silent person in the middle, listening to both voices, who will decide to whom to listen and what to do. This image of the inner dialogue runs counter to the image of the person captured under a calabash, put under the spell of higher forces. The former image testifies to a notion of moral personhood, emphasizing individual responsibility, agency, and the possibility of choice, which is now increasingly foregrounded and promoted in Pentecostalist circles.

Looking back at my research on local appropriations of Christianity and the popularity of Pentecostalism in Ghana (started in 1988), I see that the emphasis on what Max Weber called *Lebensführung* (conduct), characterized by permanent, methodological self-control, gradually is more emphasized than the previous notion of the person as an empty room, to be filled

and governed by either the spirit of God or evil spirits.[33] While the
leadership and intellectuals in the orthodox mission churches have always
affirmed the importance of conduct and personal responsibility, for many
believers this notion, as well as the notion of sin, has been difficult to adopt.
Indeed, Pentecostalism initially became so popular because it claimed that
possession was a hidden source of trouble and suffering to be taken
seriously by Christians. Practicing deliverance as a countermeasure, they
proposed an image of the person as being subject to higher powers rather
than being personally responsible for his/her deeds in general, and mishap
in particular.[34] Now, as the film *Mariska* also indicates, the notion of
personal choice and responsibility is increasingly popularized, without,
however, neutralizing the notion of possession. What is emphasized here is
the ideal of a closed self that is not vulnerable to any intruding, evil forces
from outside (from witchcraft to local village- or family-based gods, from
Mami Water to Indian spirits, from ancestors to black magic) and able to
act in a morally sound way on the basis of inner reflection. Of course, this

Figure 6.2 "In *Mariska*, there are a number of scenes depicting an inner dialogue
between good and evil, showing a person in between two doubles who both make
suggestions. The bad voice—on the left—is dressed in a Western style, the good one—on
the right—in a respectable African dress."

notion of the self is difficult to attain and maintain. Hence the continued obsession with the threat of parasitic forces that would subvert the Christian ideal of self-control. In a way, films such as *Mariska* offer a space to imagine an ideal Christian personality, as well as to address the difficulty of attaining it in everyday life. They emphasize personal responsibility for one's actions and warn people to not easily follow the attraction of women and money. Films may be viewed as a laboratory for the investigation of Pentecostalist regimes of subjectivity and technologies of the self, which are being celebrated as the most suitable guarantee for individual success.

While a "morally-controlled materialism"[35] is idealized, films usually pinpoint that there are also immoral, selfish ways to achieve wealth; they emphasize how modernity is full of temptations and seductions, which mainly operate through the desire for sex and money. A prosperous way of life is depicted as beautiful and desirable, yet dangerous because of the seductions that come with power and success. While the wife and the pastor usually feature as positive heroes, husbands are shown to easily fall prone to modernity's temptations, for once they have a bit of success, they indulge in hedonistic pleasures without taking any responsibility, thereby becoming subject to manipulation by occult forces. At the height of their power and success, they appear too weak to exert self-control and lose everything. A number of films, especially Nigerian ones,[36] also tell stories about a person's deliberate pact with occult forces, which make him indulge in ritual murder and crime. These films reflect increasing concerns about personal safety in the big city, with its numerous dark, immoral spaces. There are also films addressing the much-heard criticism that certain pastors run churches in order to make money—a criticism that is, interestingly, also fuelled by many exponents of prosperity gospel, who assert that they are not "fake" pastors but genuine. Certainly all this opens up a space to express second thoughts about Pentecostalism's actual success to guide people toward heaven on earth and the actual efficiency of prosperity gospel.[37] Still, most currently produced Ghanaian video-films affirm the need to adopt Pentecostal religion in order to engage with modernity in a safe and disciplined way.

Films especially appeal to young women, many of whom told me in interviews that they loved to see such films in order to learn about possible problems in marriage life, and to see how to avoid them from the outset. Filmmakers usually get a lot of mail from the audiences, and often people tell them that they have been in similar situations and learned something from the film. In a marriage conflict, one spouse may even remind the other of all the Ghanaian films on the subject in order to bring him/her back to reason. The gift of video-films to female audiences is the celebration of their point of view. Indeed, wives and girlfriends are eager to make their partners watch Ghanaian films because they illustrate dramatically how the failure of the husband to choose for the benefit of his wife and children inevitably leads into unbearable troubles, and how Christianity, especially its Pentecostal-charismatic variant, may bring moral superiority and enduring success in modern, urban life. To them, this appears as an attractive project within reach, geared toward reshaping everyday life by adopting Pentecostalist styles and forms of conduct.

As mentioned above, films are watched both as home videos and in the cinema. Even if viewing takes place at home, it is an intensely social affair with many people present in the room (and possibly uninvited guests peeping in through the window). Usually, audiences discuss buildings, food, dress styles, and moral behavior. This ongoing stream of comments is incidentally interrupted when something spectacular is happening on the screen. Then viewers may shout at the character in question, call Jesus for him or her, or just applaud. In a sense, watching films is a truly interactive affair. A good film lasts longer than the screening as such: It may generate discussion after it is finished, cause viewers to write letters to the producers in which they relate their own life to the film, and be called upon in marital struggles ("Didn't you see that Ghanaian film? It shows where your behavior will lead to!!!!")

Religion, Entertainment, and the Work of Imagination

The marked presence of Pentecostal styles in public culture, so typical for the process of democratization setting in after 1992, was facilitated by three developments. One concerns the end of the symbiosis between the media and the state, which entailed a considerable control of the state over civil society and the virtual exclusion of popular culture from the mass media.[38] The second, related to the first, has to do with the turn to neoliberalism and the opening up of Ghana to the global market. Commercialization and privatization have become the buzzwords of a new mode of production, not only in the sphere of the economy in a narrow sense but also in shaping the dynamics of the public sphere. The third concerns the changing place and role of Pentecostalism in society. Thriving in a niche and keeping silent in public well into the 1990s, Pentecostal-charismatic movements quickly and eagerly appropriated the mass media once they became accessible through liberalization and commercialization. Far from confining themselves to addressing their own followers through media such as radio and TV, Pentecostalists assumed a loud voice in the new public sphere. In various contexts, they publicly condemned African culture and tradition, so much cherished by the state, as "devilish" and "backward" and propagated their alternative views on Christian modernity. With much success—for as we have seen, individual cultural entrepreneurs, such as the video-filmmakers discussed above, adopted Pentecostal styles and representations in order to appeal to the audiences. A film running counter to Pentecostalism simply does not sell.

Interestingly, the forces of commercialization, vital in the opening up of the public sphere, reshaped both popular culture and religion as such and facilitated a liaison between popular film and Pentecostalism. This liaison is not incidental but stems from the fact that Pentecostalism, compared to Catholicism, orthodox Protestantism, and Islam, has been much more inclined to adopt and effectively use electronic media. The fact that Pentecostalism appears to be everywhere, however, should not be interpreted simply in terms of an increase of Pentecostal believers and religiosity. The fact that in Pentecostal circles there are concerns about the danger of corrupting religious content as a result of its mediatization and commercialization—often, but not always, raised with regard to other denominations and not one's own—indicates the extent to which these developments actually have already transformed the place and role of Pentecostalism.

These developments are quite similar to the intersection of religion and popular culture occurring in the course of the nineteenth and twentieth century in the United States, especially as a result of the rise of cinema. At that time, the successful public presence of religion, rather than being confined to a particular niche and thus culturally bounded, depended on its ability to locate itself in the marketplace of culture.[39] In this view, commodification makes possible the public presence of religion in modern society, a presence that is realized in the sphere and mode of entertainment. Indeed, this is not a matter of sheer coincidence, but—at least in part—a result of actual contacts between American televangelists and Ghanaian Pentecostals. While both in the United States as well as in Ghana, the intersection of entertainment and religion evokes criticisms on the part of some believers, who lament the watering down of religion, it is equally clear that Christian entertainment is able to bind large numbers of people and instigates the rise of new communities of sentiment that go far beyond congregational particularities.

Liberalization and commercialization of the media not only blurred the spheres of religion and entertainment and curtailed the power of the state to control public culture but also entailed new possibilities for the imagination. The video-film industry is an excellent example of how, as a result of the easy, global accessibility of mass media and the declining power of the nation-state to retain the privilege to monitor the imagination of community, "ordinary people have begun to deploy their imaginations in the practice of their everyday lives."[40] The video-filmmakers are people with little capital and no formal training in the state-run film school, the National Film and Television Institute (NAFTI). Excluded from and looked down upon by the class of professional filmmakers,[41] their greatest asset is the fact that they share the life worlds of their audiences and are able to successfully visualize popular views with relatively cheap means. Video technology enables them to become the mediators of a new social imaginary,[42] which develops more or less independently from the state yet is all the more indebted to Pentecostalism. Their films strike a chord with viewers' life worlds, or at least with their envisioned future and the morality they would like to endorse. Resonating with prevailing structures of feeling, popular films contribute to the spread of this Pentecostalite social imaginary, which is geared toward Christian modernity and a morally controlled access to prosperity. Quite similar to the ways in which print media facilitated the imagination of community in terms of the nation,[43] video-films contribute to connecting as a public great numbers of hitherto unconnected people in the big city who would previously define themselves primarily as members of particular churches and/or as members of different ethnic groups (and only in certain, limited contexts as "Ghanaian"). While ethnic and congregational identities certainly remain important,[44] films address a more general audience and offer public screens for the imagination of Christian modernity from a Ghanaian perspective. At stake here is the dissemination and affirmation of a distinctly Christian conception of the moral order of society[45] and life style among large strata in society, in particular in the urban zones.

Epilogue: Christian Modernity and the Global in the Local

Video technology and Pentecostalism certainly both have a global dimension, yet the question is how this dimension is being worked out on screen. A clue to a possible answer could perhaps be found by returning to Walter Benjamin's famous, much-quoted analysis of cinema as blowing apart the prison of metropolitan space by "the dynamite of the tenth of a second" and offering adventurous traveling among the ruins.[46] We have seen that in Ghana, too, video-films propound a cinematic mode of vision. Yet, in contrast to the background against which Benjamin formulated his view, in Ghana the cinematic mode of vision is not backed by an experience of being "locked up hopelessly" in "our taverns and our metropolitan streets, our offices and our furnished rooms, our railroad stations and our factories."[47] For there has not been a successful transformation of metropolitan space in modern terms, and, worse still, people experience urban space as increasingly deteriorating. Likewise they experience their own personal and domestic circumstances as defective and in need of betterment. Cinema has always operated as a messenger of the superiority of the West and represented the local as inferior, yet did not grant it a space on the screen. Popular video-films, by contrast, set out to beautify the mess and the dirt that characterizes life in Accra, thereby cinematically recreating Accra as a modern city—on screen. By keeping the audiences in the seats, yet enabling them to mimetically travel in modern space, popular video-films engage in a practice of *symbolic transfiguration,* in which the local is recreated in the light of the global, as being part and parcel of the wider world, yet still accessible in the here and now.

It would be a mistake to view this simply as a matter of escapism, as a mere outward orientation toward participation in global arenas at the expense of engagement on the level of the nation. It would be equally wrong to dismiss the dream of high modernity and prosperity simply as old-fashioned, a point also made forcefully by James Ferguson.[48] Rather, popular cinema symbolically recreates the local life world on screen in the light of the global, thereby making up for actual shortcomings and disappointments and claiming access. This, as it were, can be viewed as a local theory of globalization, not geared toward an imaginary escape from problematic conditions of life but rather toward the transfiguration of the local and personal mobility. In many ways, the project of Christian modernity to which this vision is tied even links up with the discourses of development propounded by the state, which makes use of the same iconography when it depicts development (fly-overs, high buildings, cars; fig. 6.3). It is not the project of development as such that is looked upon critically but the failure of the state to achieve it. This has been brought forward by a number of Pentecostal preachers in the wake of the recent elections in 2000, when they criticized the government for mismanagement, corruption, and the failure to create a safe urban environment. Disappointed by the incapacity of the state to lead them out of the mess and make them progress, people call upon Christianity, and especially Pentecostalism, in order to reconstitute their lives—on a personal level first, yet with a vision for society at large—and thereby desperately try to overcome Africa's actual disconnection from global flows and fulfill the old promises of modernity.

While media and Pentecostalism, both in their own ways, certainly have reconfigured many people's sense of time and place by offering a transnational orientation,[49] it is important to emphasize that, at least in the case analyzed here, both are geared toward, and operate in, the Ghanaian public sphere. Here a globalizing orientation is made to speak to longstanding local concerns. Both popular films and Pentecostalism are engaged to develop

Figure 6.3 "In many ways, the project of Christian modernity to which this vision is tied even links up with the discourses of development propounded by the state, which makes use of the same iconography when it depicts development." Photograph by Birgit Meyer.

new forms of visual representation, addressing and constituting a new public, which cannot easily be recuperated by the state and represents Pentecostalism as the most suitable harbinger of prosperity and most reliable guide in handling globalization.

Notes

*This article was originally published in *Culture and Religion* 3 (2002): 67–87. Permissions to reprint granted by Taylor & Francis, Ltd. Available at http://www. tandf.co.uk/journals.

The data on which this essay is based have been collected during a research project conducted in the framework of the research program "Globalization and the Construction of Communal Identities" sponsored by the Netherlands Foundation for the Advancement of Tropical Research (WOTRO) between 1995 and 2000, and my PIONIER research program "Modern Mass Media, Religion and the Imagination of Communities" sponsored by the Netherlands Organization for Scientific

Research (NWO). I would like to thank Gerd Baumann, Brian Larkin, Peter van Rooden, Rafael Sanchez, Jojada Verrips, and Marleen de Witte for their comments on earlier versions of this paper.

1. Birgit Meyer, *Translating the Devil: Religion and Modernity Among the Ewe in Ghana* (Edinburgh: Edinburgh University Press, 1999), 31ff.

2. But compare this picture with a work painted by Charles Anderson in 1974 (in Simon Coleman, "Moving Towards the Millennium? Ritualized Mobility and the Cultivation of Agency among Charismatic Protestants," *Journal of Ritual Studies* 14.2 [1999]: 16–17), which describes the city as a hell, with traffic jams, and, because the work appears after September 11, 2001, a plane sticking out of a skyscraper. Interestingly, in Ghanaian Pentecostal circles the landscape of the big city is cherished as highly desirable, a space people wish to access, whereas the countryside is regarded as backward ("bush") and a place for the poor and uncivilized.

3. Paul Gifford, *African Christianity: Its Public Role* (Bloomington, IN: Indiana University Press, 1998); Rijk Van Dijk, "From Camp to Encompassment: Discourses of Transsubjectivity in the Ghanaian Pentecostal Diaspora," *Journal of Religion in Africa* 27.2 (1997): 135–60; for Nigeria see Ruth Fratani-Marshall, "Mediating the Global and the Local in Nigerian Pentecostalism," *Journal of Religion in Africa* 28.3 (1998): 278–315. While the strong popularity of Pentecostalist churches in Southern Ghana is matched by their presence in public space—with Christian stickers and mottos on cars, canoes, and shops; posters advertising prayer meetings on virtually any free wall; radio and TV programs advertising these types of churches; loudspeakers broadcasting what happens within churches far into the neighborhood—it is difficult to come up with statistical information. To my knowledge, the latest survey was conducted by the Ghana Evangelism Committee (1993), which showed that between 1987 and 1993 the number of Pentecostal churches increased 43 percent and church attendance was up 38 percent. Orthodox mission churches remained more or less stable, whereas so-called African Independent or Spiritual Churches declined. See also Gifford, *African Christianity*, 61ff. It seems that this trend has been further enhanced in the last decade.

4. Colin Campbell, *The Romantic Ethic and the Spirit of Modern Consumerism* (Oxford: Basil Blackwell, 1987).

5. See also Ruth Fratani-Marshall, "Prospérité miraculeuse: Les pasteurs pentecôtistes et l'argent de Dieu au Nigeria," *Politique Africaine* 82 (2001): 24–44.

6. Birgit Meyer, "Christian Mind and Worldly Matters: Religion and Materiality in Nineteenth-Century Gold Coast," *Journal of Material Culture* 2.3 (1997): 311–37.

7. Peter Van der Veer, *Conversion to Modernities: The Globalization of Christianity* (New York: Routledge, 1996); Meyer, *Translating the Devil*, 1–14.

8. Rosalind I. J. Hackett, "Charismatic/Pentecostal Appropriation of Media Technologies in Nigeria and Ghana," *Journal of Religion in Africa* 28.3 (1998): 1–19.

9. Franklin-Kennedy Asonzeh Ukah, "Media Publicity and Pentecostal Proselytization in Ibadan," paper presented for the workshop "Religion and Media in Nigeria," School of Oriental and African Studies, London, February 25–26, 1999.

10. Birgit Meyer, "Pentecostalite Culture on Screen: Magic and Modernity in Ghana's New Mediascape," paper presented to the symposium "Magical Modernities in Africa," University of Wisconsin, Madison, April 7, 2001.

11. Cati Coe, "'Not Just Drumming and Dancing,' The Production of National Culture in Ghana's School" (Ph.D. diss. University of Pennsylvania, 2000).

12. This symbol depicts a bird looking back and embodies the message "Go back and pick it." It is often called upon in discourses on the importance of the national heritage.

13. Birgit Meyer, "Popular Ghanaian Cinema," and "African Heritage," *Africa Today* 46.2 (1999): 93–114; Birgit Meyer, "Money, Power, and Morality: Popular Ghanaian Cinema in the Fourth Republic," *Ghana Studies* 4 (2001): 65–84; see also Brian Larkin, "Hausa Dramas and the Rise of Video Culture in Nigeria," in *Nigerian Video Films,* Jonathan Haynes, ed. (Athens, OH: Ohio University Center for International Studies, 2000).

14. See also P. Morton-Williams, *Cinema in Rural Nigeria: A Field Study of the Impact of Fundamental-Education Films on Rural Audiences in Nigeria* (West African Institute of Social and Economic Research, University College, Ibadan, 1959); Birgit Meyer, "Ghanaian Popular Cinema and the Magic in and of Film," in *Magic and Modernity: Dialectics of Revelation and Concealment,* Birgit Meyer and Peter Pels, eds. (Stanford: Stanford University Press, 2003).

15. Brian Larkin, "Theaters of the Profane: Cinema and Colonial Urbanism," *Visual Antropology Review* 14.2 (1998/99): 55.

16. Karin Barber, "Preliminary Notes on Audiences in Africa," *Africa* 67.3 (1997): 347–362.

17. It seems that this use of theaters by Protestant churches is not confined to Ghana. In the United States, for instance, in the nineteenth-century revivalists gathered in former theaters.

18. Paul Nugent, *Big Men, Small Boys and Politics in Ghana: Power Ideology and the Burden of History* (Accra: Asempa Publishers, 1996), 163ff.

19. For examples of particular films see Meyer, *Translating the Devil*; Meyer, "Money"; Meyer, "Ghanaian."

20. This became very clear to me in an interview with the filmmaker Socrate Safo (Amsterdam, September 9, 2001), who told me about a phone-in radio program in which callers defended the claim of a Pentecostal pastor that witchcraft was real by making references to film. Safo stated that most viewers would regard film as a representation of reality. Special effects, although deliberately created by computer programs, would often be seen as "real magic." He felt a dilemma between the responsibility to represent "truth" and the fact that he had to give the audiences what they wanted to see in order to be successful.

21. See also Jean Comaroff and John Comaroff, "Occult Economies and the Violence of Abstraction: Notes From the South African Postcolony," *American Ethnologist* 26.2 (1999): 21.

22. See Jojada Verrips and Birgit Meyer, "Kwaku's Car: The Struggles and Stories of a Ghanaian Long-Distance Taxi Driver," in *Car Cultures*, Daniel Miller, ed. (Oxford: Berg, 2001).

23. See Thomas Looser, "Post-cities: Transfigurations in the Architecture of Globality," paper presented at the third ASFRP symposium, "Globalization and the Urban Community," Rikkyo University, June 29–July 1, 2001.

24. I sometimes remarked to filmmakers that I was surprised that they would invariably put this type of car ride into their productions and refuse to show scenes from the market or bring in a pedestrian's perspective working himself or herself through the crowded, messy streets of Accra. The reply I usually got was that audiences knew the pedestrian perspective all too well from daily experience and that they rather longed to see "beautiful things." My own liking for market scenes and similar stuff was dismissed as a typically Western interest in things that they deemed not nice enough to put on the screen. "Why do you people always want to depict the mess over here?" was a question I often got.

25. Several times, I have been able to meet Ghanaian filmmakers and actors in the Netherlands. I found it striking to notice a certain disappointment with the city of Amsterdam. All these old, narrow houses alongside the canals, which Western tourists craved to see, did not match my Ghanaian friends' imagination of the West.

26. See Achille Mbembe and Janet Roitman, "Figures of the Subject in Times of Crisis," in *The Geography of Identity*, P. Yaeger, ed. (Ann Arbor: University of Michigan Press, 1996); Verrips and Meyer, "Kwaku's Car."

27. See Larkin, "Theaters of the Profane," 46; Rafael Sanchez, "Media, Mediumship and State Authority in the Maria Lionza Cult (Venezuela)," in *Religion and Media*, Hent de Vries and Samuel Weber, eds. (Stanford: Stanford University Press, 2001).

28. A fine example for the appeal of modernity is the film *Future Remembrance* by Tobias Wendl and Nancy du Plessis (1998), in which they insightfully document how people in Ghana actively create desirable images of themselves by having their picture taken in photo studios. These studios offer fascinating backdrops depicting icons of modernity such as a cupboard containing a TV, VCR, CD player, and well-stuffed fridge, a beautiful mansion, or the stairway of an aeroplane. See also the exposition and catalogue *Snap Me One* (Tobias Wendl and Heike Behrend, *Snap Me One. Studiefotografen in Afrika* [München, London, New York: Prestel, 1998]); and Wendl, "Visions of Modernity, in Ghana: Mami Wata Shrines, Photo Studios and Horror Films," *Visual Anthropology* 14 (2001): 269–292.

29. Birgit Meyer, "'Delivered from the Powers of Darkness': Confessions about Satanic Riches in Christian Ghana," *Africa* 65.2 (1995); Meyer, "Prières, fusils et meurtre ritual: Le cinéma populaire et ses nouvelles figures du pouvoir et du success au Ghana," *Politique Africaine* 82 (2001); see also Comaroff and Comaroff, "Occult Economies."

30. Arjun Appadurai, "Keynote Address," presented at the third ASFRP symposium, "Globalization and the Urban Community," Rikkyo University, June 29–July 1, 2001.

31. See Birgit Meyer, "'Make a complete break with the past': Memory and Post-colonial Modernity in Ghanaian Pentecostalist Discourse," *Journal of Religion in Africa* 28.3 (1998).

32. This is certainly not simply a question of opposing Western and African styles in terms of pro- and antimodern. The African dress also is distinctly modern and fashionable and, in my view, stands for a Ghanaian version of Christian modernity. Dress codes in films to a large extent mirror everyday life (although film characters usually are a bit overdressed). Actors usually wear both Western and African style clothes, and it depends somewhat on the age and occasion what is being put on. For celebrations, characters would usually wear African designer clothes, whereas on the beach they would wear shorts. During work businessmen always wear Western suits. While young women mainly wear Western-style dresses, in a later stage of life they shift to African styles.

33. Meyer, *Translating the Devil,* 145–146.

34. Meyer, "Make a complete"; Meyer, *Translating the Devil,* 204ff.

35. Fratani-Marshall, "Mediating the Global," 282.

36. Nigerian films have become increasingly popular in Ghana in the course of the last three years. Much more than is the case with Ghanaian films, Nigerian films depict transgression into the realm of the occult and are replete with brutality and excess. In order to deal with the threat of Nigerian films to the business, recently Ghanaian filmmakers have started to refashion their stories by bringing in elaborate special effects and more sex, violence, and occult matters. See Jonathan Haynes, ed., *Nigerian Video Films* (Athens, OH: Ohio University Center for International Studies, 2000); Meyer, "Prières."

37. Meyer, "Prières."

38. See Emmanuel Akyeampong, *Drink, Power, and Cultural Change: A Social History of Alcohol in Ghana, c. 1800 to Recent Times* (Oxford: James Currey, 1996).

39. See Lawrence R. Moore, *Selling God: American Religion in the Marketplace of Culture* (Oxford: Oxford University Press, 1994).

40. Arjun Appadurai, *Modernity at Large: Cultural Dimensions of Globalization* (Minneapolis: University of Minnesota Press, 1996), 5.

41. Most of them were employed as civil servants at the state-owned media. As a result of the privatization of the film industry, many of them lost their jobs and were forced to try their luck by producing films for the market.

42. In studies of mass communication, there has been much more attention to the use of video technology in the context of projects described as emancipation, alternative communication, mass participation, or alternative, locally grounded notions of development, than to the use of video in the context of popular culture and religion.

43. Benedict Anderson, *Imagined Communities: Reflections on the Origins and Spread of Nationalism,* rev. ed. (London: Verso, 1991).

44. Carola Lentz and Paul Nugent, eds., *Ethnicity in Ghana: The Limits of Invention.* (London: Macmillan, 2000).

45. Charles Taylor, "Social Imaginary," paper presented to the Global Imaginaries Group, Chicago, March 24–25, 2001.

46. Walter Benjamin, "The Work of Art in the Age of Mechanical Reproduction," in *Illustrations* (New York: Schocken Books, 1978), 236.
47. Ibid.
48. James Ferguson, *Expectations of Modernity: Myths and Meanings of Urban Life on the Zambian Copperbelt* (Berkeley: University of California Press, 1999).
49. David Morley and Kevin Robins, *Spaces of Identity: Global Media, Electronic Landscapes, and Cultural Boundaries* (London & New York: Routledge, 1995); Karla Poewe, ed., *Charismatic Christianity as a Global Culture* (Columbia, SC: University of South Carolina Press, 1994).

Chapter Seven

The Islamic Apocalypse:

Mohsen Makhmalbaf's Moment of Innocence

Lloyd Ridgeon

In 1994 the Iranian film director Mohsen Makhmalbaf placed an advertisement in a Tehran newspaper announcing that he would be holding auditions for the casting of his next film in a local park. Makhmalbaf was visibly shocked to see about 5,000 young Iranians turn up, the significance of which extended beyond the number of hopefuls, for as he himself stated, it was the one-hundredth anniversary of cinema in Iran.[1] Iranian cinema has a long pedigree, but the early modern era (1960s-78) was largely dominated by the Filmfarsi genre, which has been described as "inane" and "commercial" and which included popular music and dance, comedies, and tough-guy movies.[2] During this period Egyptian and Indian melodramas and song and dance films were screened regularly, and their success encouraged the production of similar indigenous productions, casting singing stars (such as Googoosh, the Iranian "pop diva") in leading roles.

It was only in the 1960s that "socially engaged" films began to increase in number, the most famous being Dariush Mehrjui's *Gav* (The cow) (1969), which reflected the "reality" of Iranian village life. Another acclaimed director of the time was Masoud Kimiai, whose tough-guy movies such as *Qaisar* (1969) and *Dash Akol* (1971) utilized the good-bad dichotomy. Such films have been understood by some as an attempt to uphold traditional Iranian values as opposed to the importation of the more gross and unsophisticated aspects of Western culture.

This "new wave" of socially engaged Iranian films was interrupted by the Islamic Revolution in 1978, which demanded the "Islamization" of culture. Naturally this affected filmmaking, and the new Islamic standards meant that Islam could not be criticized in film, the promotion of immorality (drugs, prostitution, corruption, etc.) was prohibited, and women were to be portrayed modestly.[3] Some directors of the first new wave continued to make films in Iran (such as Kimiai, Abbas Kiarostami, Ali Hatami, and Bahram Bayzai), and one of the notable aspects of post-revolutionary films was the attention paid to children. Focusing on children allowed film directors to avoid the barriers created by Islamic censorship yet still deal with important social issues such as race discrimination[4] and oppression.[5] As Kiarostami has stated: "Children know how to carry on living in the midst of . . . cumbersome traditions and social contracts."[6] Yet by the time Makhmalbaf held his famous auditions in 1994, commentators were speaking of a second new wave of Iranian film directors who were socially engaged yet worked within Islamic parameters without necessarily following any official line and without resorting to focusing on children in their films.

Makhmalbaf's film of 1995, *A Moment of Innocence,* the casting of which attracted those 5,000 Iranians, is an example of the kind of second new wave films that focus on themes relevant to modern Iranians. Perhaps the most important of these themes is modernity and its relationship to Islam, the interpretation of which is now the subject of intense debate both within Iran and among its expatriates. This chapter reflects on the Islam/modernity relationship and, in particular, on the role of the individual in the community by focusing upon Makhmalbaf's *A Moment of Innocence.* In order to appreciate the intricate nature of this relationship it is necessary to delineate the specific characteristics of Iranian Islam, which enjoys the heritage of two spiritual currents, namely mystical Islam (Sufism) and Shi'ism. Following this there is a brief survey of Makhmalbaf's career and a discussion of *A Moment of Innocence,* which he says is his favorite film.[7] It is only after all of this that one can fully appreciate the Islam/modernity debate that is embedded in the film.

The Iranian-Islamic Apocalyptic Tradition

The basis of Islam is the Qur'an, the book that Muslims believe was given to Muhammad by the angel Gabriel over the course of 23 years until Muhammad's death in 632 C.E. If one element predominates in the Qur'an, it is its apocalyptic nature, its stress on the need for moral renewal because the Hour, the Resurrection, and Judgement are at hand. References to and passages about the Hour are scattered throughout almost all of the Qur'an's chapters, so that Norman O. Brown has commented: "There is an apocalyptic style or eschatological style: every sura [chapter] is an epiphany and a portent; a warning, 'plain tokens that haply we may take heed' (24:1)."[8] The time of the Hour is not given in the Qur'an. Only God has knowledge of this (43:85), however, it will occur soon (54:1, 33:63, 42:17) and suddenly (47:18). The good believers are promised paradise and the delights therein, whereas punishments are vouchsafed for the sinners, whose own hands, feet (41:19–23), and skins (36:65) will confess their actions. As a result, the believer is required to repent of any sin and turn constantly to God. The only sin that God will not forgive is *shirk* (4:48), the association of other gods with God.

The Hour is closely connected to a figure known as the Mahdi (the rightly guided one) in Shi'ite Islam. Shi'ites are those Muslims who believe that the rightful successor to Muhammad was his cousin 'Ali, who became the fourth caliph (or successor). Moreover, mainstream Shi'ites claim that 'Ali's descendants should have been subsequent political/spiritual rulers or "Imam," but they were deprived of their rights by two dynasties, the Umayyads (661–750 C.E.) and the Abbasids (750–1258). Perhaps as a result of the persecution of Shi'ites, the twelfth Imam went into a period of occultation, in other words, he is still alive and exists in the world but is absent from human eyes. He will return as Mahdi just before the Hour to establish a period of justice that rights all the wrongs committed against Shi'ites. According to Shi'ite sources, the Mahdi will return to the Shi'ite community when injustice prevails throughout the world and when the "normal" order has been stood on its head. One tradition states that he will become manifest when men are satisfied with men, women cohabit and rule society, and forbidden things are made legal.[9]

Throughout Iranian history there have been manifestations of millenarian expectation. This has lasted from the eighth century, when the Islamic armies defeated the Sassanian empire, until the establishment of the Safavid dynasty in Iran at the beginning of the sixteenth century (when Iran became officially a Shi'ite land), and even in the nineteenth century there was much millenarian expectation. Space does not allow a detailed discussion of this topic,[10] however, and so we will limit ourselves to an example of how the apocalypse was understood in the Persian Sufi tradition. 'Aziz Nasafi was a thirteenth-century Persian mystic who testified that in his own lifetime there were many pretenders to Mahdihood,[11] and, more importantly, his writings provide an interiorized depiction of the apocalypse. Nasafi spiritualizes the events related to death and the Resurrection and locates them within the immediacy of the individual's own lifetime.[12] He claims there are four resurrections: the lesser, the intermediate, the great, and the greatest. The lesser resurrection is when a child is born from the mother's "tomb," which is why it is called "the day of resurrection" (a term that appears 70 times in the Qur'an). The intermediate resurrection occurs when the child gathers life, intelligence, and the comprehension of religious laws within him, and so this is the "day of gathering," another Qur'anic term (42:7) that is usually associated with the gathering together of all people for judgement. The great resurrection takes place once the individual comprehends the nature of things and can distinguish good from evil, and so this is the "day of distinguishing," a Qur'anic term (37:21) that is more commonly taken to refer to God's separation of good people from sinners on Judgement Day. And finally, the greatest resurrection occurs when the individual appreciates the nature and similarity of his own and God's existence. This is linked with the apocalypse by Nasafi since it is the "day of judgement" (another Qur'anic name for the Resurrection [1:3]) because the individual becomes content, is forgiven by God, and attains paradise, and all this is his recompense for his own hard effort. It is important to bear in mind that while Islam is a communal religion (see below), the Sufi interiorization of Islamic doctrine permitted the self to develop. This is significant because it suggests that modernity, with its dominant focus on the individual as opposed to the community, is not necessarily alien to Islam.

Whereas the Sufis were able to internalize ideas concerning the apocalypse, the Shi'ite clerics were faced with an awkward dilemma because of their attachment to the Imam who had disappeared with the occultation. There was a clerical reluctance to assume the Imam's function of guiding the community for three reasons. First, even though the Imam was in occultation, he was still alive and it was his prerogative to rule. Second, the Imam was infallible, as he alone possessed esoteric knowledge of the Qur'an, which meant he knew the correct action or guidance in any given circumstance. Third, he had been designated for the task of leadership by the previous Imam, making a chain of links back to Muhammad. For these reasons the Shi'ite clergy has generally held that it is only the Mahdi who should be considered the legitimate political leader in society.

Yet for practical reasons, the Shi'ite clerics realized that society's religious affairs required some kind of direction in the absence of the Imam, and so on occasions they have entered into the "secular" realm to ensure that the spiritual welfare of the community was not endangered. Such clerics realized that the logical consequences behind the Imam's occultation and the lack of spiritual guidance would have been a society characterized by decay and corruption. (Paradoxically, from a Shi'ite perspective this might have precipitated the Mahdi's appearance, given the signs of his manifestation mentioned above.) Moreover, had the clerics adopted a quiescent attitude they would not have been able to follow the Islamic moral and ethical commitment. Indeed, each of Islam's so-called "five pillars" recognize and are based upon communal obligations of religion. In addition to the five pillars, there are two imperatives to build and strengthen the community. The first is *jihad*, which seems originally to have been a concept designed to defend the Islamic community against its opponents. The second is contained in the expression "commanding the good and forbidding evil" (a phrase derived from the Qur'an[13]), which encourages all Muslims to promote Islamic morality within the community. This is reinforced by the codification of Islamic laws that regulate many acts of daily life, the performance of which is always encouraged by the more religiously inclined neighbor.

The conflict between political quietism and activism became the central issue for Iranian Shi'ite clerics from the 1960s onward, especially in light of the secularizing, westernizing, and corrupt policies of the second Pahlavi Shah, Muhammad Reza. The response given by Ayatollah Khomeini, one of the leading Iranian clerics, was a call for activism, claiming that a cleric (or clerics) could rule as guardian(s) until the Mahdi appeared,[14] and the community was obliged to follow him/them.[15] At the same time that Khomeini called for reform, there emerged a similar message from the lay ranks, namely that advocated by 'Ali Shari'ati. Shari'ati's message drew on the Sufi tradition of interiorizing the end, for he argued that the apocalypse is here and now: The yearning expectation for the Mahdi will result in the victory of the oppressed, and the destruction of the masses will occur on this very earth and before death, not in the Resurrection after death.[16] Such language also indicates Shari'ati's attraction to the liberation theology emanating from the third world (for example, in the writings of Franz Fanon). Recently, Shari'ati has been criticized by Iranian scholars because of the tensions within his worldview. On the one hand, he viewed the people as a whole, the community, as tied to a deterministic socialist framework,[17] yet on the other hand as individuals people had free choice, and this was further complicated by Shari'ati's religious idealism.[18]

The worldviews of both Khomeini and Shari'ati offered limited space for the individual, yet in the desperate circumstances of Iran in the 1970s, it was the community as a whole that was the focus of attention. Moreover, both Khomeini and Shari'ati were astute enough to lace their language with apocalyptic themes that, as we have seen, have wound their way throughout Iranian history, leaving an imprint on the Iranian religious *imaginaire*. The return of the Mahdi is never deferred for religious Muslims in Iran; indeed, there are benedictions for the Imams and prayers said on regular occasions in hope of the Mahdi's quick return.[19]

Mohsen Makhmalbaf: From Revolutionary to Poet

The message of revolution and the clerical guarding of the community struck a chord with Makhmalbaf, who in 1974, at the age of 17, hatched a plan with his friends to steal a gun from a policeman so that they could then rob a bank to finance their revolutionary aims. The plan backfired as the revolutionaries could not disarm the policeman, who, despite being stabbed, put up stiff resistance and shot Makhmalbaf in the side. Makhmalbaf was arrested and thrown into prison, and he served about four years before his release in the wake of the Islamic revolution. He then began work as a newsman and writer in the radio while composing his own film scripts. By his own taxonomy, it is possible to classify Makhmalbaf's films into more than four periods. The first includes the films made between 1982 and 1985,[20] which are moralistic and influenced by his religious beliefs. There are three films within the second period, between 1986 and 1988, reflecting social issues that show Makhmalbaf's disappointment at the revolution's inability to solve many of Iran's problems.[21] Between 1990 and 1992, he made films that each illustrated problems of relativity.[22] In the fourth period Makhmalbaf claims that his films show a multiplicity of perspectives and human sorrow,[23] and these films have become more personal: He states that as a child he wanted to save humanity, and after growing a little he wanted to save Iran, and now his desire is to save himself. He has forsaken the ideal of changing the world for the better and comments that "any person who has tried to take the responsibility of the world upon himself has done nothing but corrupt it in the end."[24]

Mohsen Makhmalbaf is now a veteran of the second new wave of Iranian films, having produced 16 feature films and 6 short-length films. The characteristics of the second new wave of Iranian films have been discussed by Makhmalbaf himself, identifying two main components: realism and its praise for life and hope. The realistic element of the second new wave has many manifestations, ranging from the use of nonprofessional actors to the documentary style of filming. Such realism is perhaps a conscious effort by Iranian directors to move away from the Filmfarsi genre and Hollywood-style films. Another consideration is that the style of such second new wave films makes them comparatively cheap. As Makhmalbaf states, he made his acclaimed film *Gabbeh* (1996) with a crew of eight, including the driver and cook![25] To a certain degree, this democratizes the process of filmmaking and widens the horizon of the public sphere that much more. Such a process was also discussed by Samira Makhmalbaf (Mohsen Makhmalbaf's daughter) at the Cannes Film Festival of 2000. She spoke of the digital revolution and "camera-pen," which will eventually make filmmaking as cheap as writing, as the centrality of capital in the creative process will be radically diminished.[26] The second characteristic of the second new wave, the celebration of life and hope, is certainly evident in Mohsen Makhmalbaf's films as recurrent themes include the battle against repression and censorship (see *Nasir al-Din Shah, Aktor-e Sinema* [1991] and *Gabbeh* [1996]), and the attempt to improve the self against all odds (see *Salaam Sinema* [1994] and *Sokoot* [1997]).

Aside from his own films, articles, and books, Mohsen Makhmalbaf's presence is also felt in his scripting of films made by members of his family, including *The Apple* (1997) and *The Blackboard* (1999), which were both directed by Samira Makhmalbaf, and *The Day I Became a Woman* (2000), which was directed by his second wife, Marzieh Meshkini. The artistic and commercial recognition and the financial success Makhmalbaf has enjoyed has allowed him a certain degree of independence from the Iranian central authorities and their censorship, and this limited freedom is perhaps one reason why the Makhmalbafs have been able to engage in explicit criticism of certain individuals within the Iranian government and to produce films that censure aspects of Iranian culture. It is interesting to note how artistic space has been created within the confines of an Islamic state that by and large has attempted to restrict the individual in favor of the Islamic community.

There are several ways that the Makhmalbafs have manoeuvred within the public sphere despite the restrictions of the Iranian Ministry of Culture. Makhmalbaf's financial success has allowed him to rely on his own sources to produce films. For example, when it became clear that the Ministry of Culture wanted to cut some of the scenes in *A Moment of Innocence*, Makhmalbaf decided to proceed with producing the uncut version, even though it would result in a ban (which was to last from 1995 to 1997) and thus financial failure. He was able to secure enough capital to finish *A Moment of Innocence* by mortgaging his own house. Moreover, Makhmalbaf was financially secure to the extent that beginning in 1996, within a four-year period, he was able to retire temporarily from directing films and establish a school to train film directors. He had intended to accept 100 students in this new school, but when the Ministry of Culture denied him permission, he founded his own independent school, located in his own house, on a much smaller scale. It was composed of eight members (his family and friends) and has been remarkably successful, evidenced by the acclaim given to the films produced by the Makhmalbaf family, such as Mohsen's *Sokoot* (1997), *Qandahar* (2001), *The Afghan Alphabet* (2001), and the films by Samira and Marzieh Meshkini mentioned above.

Another way in which Makhmalbaf has slipped through the snares of the Ministry of Culture has been to use the information technology revolution to his own advantage.[27] He has been able to promote his family's films on the world wide web, on the site "Makhmalbaf Film House," which is colorful, glossy, and informative; contains reviews, articles, photographs, music, and video clips; and mentions the films that have been subject to the Iranian censors.

In addition, there are always devious ways to bypass censorship. For example, Samira's film *The Blackboard* was made and edited in Iran, yet it was smuggled out of Iran (without having been submitted to the censors) and shown at the Cannes Film Festival in 2000. Paradoxically, following the praise received by the film (it won the "Jury Prize" in Cannes), *The Blackboard* was screened in Iran as an example of great Iranian filmmaking.

A Moment of Innocence

Makhmalbaf's disillusionment with politics and religion is revealed most graphically in his 1995 film *Noon va Goldoon*. (The title is a colloquial form of Persian, meaning "the bread and the vase" but the English title is *A Moment of Innocence* because MK2, the French distributor of the film, desired to preserve a rhyme in the title [*un instance d'innocence.*]) The film is a re-creation of young Makhmalbaf stabbing the policeman, but it is much more than a regurgitation of events. A literal reenactment would probably have been quite uninteresting for the Iranian viewers given that most Iranians are aware of the events of Makhmalbaf's radical youth. *A Moment of Innocence* is a tapestry that weaves real events with pure fiction and permits the director to relive the stabbing episode with the benefit of hindsight. The oscillation between reality and fiction has resulted in the film being termed a work of "factasy," as the viewer is never really sure where the boundaries lie in Makhmalbaf's collage.

The film starts with the character of the policeman that Makhmalbaf stabbed in those revolutionary times seeking the director's house and expressing his desire to act in his next film. We learn that Makhmalbaf is to make a film based on the stabbing, but the two protagonists (Makhmalbaf and the policeman) will each select an actor to play their young self. Makhmalbaf chooses a youth who, during the auditions, states that he wants to save mankind, reflecting the idealism that fired Makhmalbaf as an adolescent [fig. 7.1]. A clue is given to the "older" Makhmalbaf's present perspective on life in the same scene when another young hopeful declares that it is enough to solve one's own problems rather than those of the whole of mankind.

The policeman will be recognized by those in the know as one of those who auditioned for parts in the Tehran park in 1994 and appeared in the film *Salaam Sinema*. In *Salaam Sinema* this character expresses his desire to be cast in "positive roles" rather than as the criminal, and in *A Moment of Innocence* he also says he wants to be portrayed positively. However, the "old" policeman turns out to be something of a ridiculous figure: Notable for his large stature and nonphotogenic appearance, the "old" policeman selects a handsome youth to play his young self, a choice that the "old" Makhmalbaf rejects and replaces with another youth. In the course of the film, we learn that while on duty all those years ago, the policeman had fallen in love with a young girl who regularly passed him by in the street and asked him for the time or for directions. He had just decided to present the young girl with a flower and declare his love for her when he was stabbed by Makhmalbaf. The policeman never saw the young girl again, although he later met a girl who resembled her and who seemed to be interested in him since she thought he was an actor. When he confessed that this was not the case the girl lost interest, and it was at that moment that he decided to turn to the acting profession in an attempt to win her love.

The "old" and the "young" Makhmalbaf then go in search of an accomplice for the "reenactment" of the stabbing. The "old" Makhmalbaf wants to cast his female cousin's daughter in the role because it was his female cousin who was his accomplice all those years ago. However, she refuses to let her daughter act in the part, and so the "young" Makhmalbaf suggests his own female cousin. The "young" idealistic Makhmalbaf acts out his role with his cousin and asks her if she is willing to be the "mother of mankind," saying that together they will plant trees in Africa and feed the starving. This term, the "mother of mankind," has a certain resonance with the Qur'anic description of Muhammad's wives as "mothers of the believers" (33:6). Interestingly, this female accomplice is not prepared to accept the title, as she does not desire the burden of responsibility for the community's welfare. But it becomes clear that her role in the plot is to distract the policeman's attention while Makhmalbaf stabs him with a knife.

Figure 7.1 "Makhmalbaf chooses a youth who, during the auditions, states that he wants to save mankind, reflecting the idealism that fired Makhmalbaf as an adolescent. A clue is given to the 'older' Makhmalbaf's present perspective on life in the same scene when another young hopeful declares that it is enough to solve one's own problems rather than those of the whole of mankind."

As the "young" Makhmalbaf practices his part, he becomes somewhat reticent about having to stab the policeman, especially when the "old" Makhmalbaf hands him a knife (albeit, one with a false blade). He asks the "old" Makhmalbaf if there is another way to save mankind, and the latter approvingly pats his "younger" self on the cheek. Moreover, the "young" Makhmalbaf breaks down in tears once he reaches the site of the incident and states that he no longer wants to stab the policeman.

The contrast between the "young" Makhmalbaf and the "old" Makhmalbaf is revealing. Initially there is a dramatic difference between the idealism of the 17-year-old youth and the maturity of the 38-year-old film director. As the film progresses, the differences between the two become less obvious as the reformed ideas of the seventeen year old mirror those that the "old" Makhmalbaf wishes he could have had at that age.[28] Meanwhile the "old" policeman is busy training his "younger" self by showing him how impossible it was to hand his beloved the flower when she approached him with her questions. On the one hand he wants to train his younger self to be a policeman on guard, but on the other hand he wants to convey how difficult it was for him to give the flower to his beloved.

As the film draws to its climax, the "young" Makhmalbaf and his female accomplice approach the "young" policeman standing on duty in an empty alley in the bazaar. When the filming commences the "old" policeman is shown directing his "younger" self, but when he sees the "young" Makhmalbaf approach with a young female who asks the "young" policeman the time, he realizes that the girl he had been in love with for all those years had been in collusion with Makhmalbaf. He storms off and says he does not want to be associated with the film. Added to the injury of his heart is the insult that he has not been given a positive part. Nevertheless, the "old" policeman is seen rehearsing with the "young" policeman and instructs him to shoot at anyone who disturbs his sentry duty, even if is the young girl.

The final scene of *A Moment of Innocence* recreates the incident of the stabbing/shooting. As the young female accomplice asks the "young" policeman the time, the "young" Makhmalbaf stands before them, with the knife in his hand hidden by some flat bread. The young girl asks the policeman for the time, once, twice, three times, and the policeman dithers, his eyes shifting from the girl to the "young" Makhmalbaf, while fingering his holster. Suddenly, the "young" policeman picks up his potted flower and presents it to the girl at the same time that the "young" Makhmalbaf offers bread instead of thrusting his knife into the policeman [fig. 7.2]. In exchange for a bullet and a knife the new generation of Iranians offer bread and a flower. The old generation is redeemed: The expectation of the Mahdi is to be undertaken in a more poetic fashion; the hungry should be fed and trees should be planted in Africa. The young generation becomes the Mahdi to restore justice and order in a peaceful way to the world.

Makhmalbaf's redemption raises fundamental questions. His resolution of the conflict between the "old" Makhmalbaf and the "old" policeman stands in contrast to the Islamic revolution (the overthrow of the Shah and his corrupt administration) and the subsequent cultural revolution with its violence and bloodshed. It would seem that Makhmalbaf regards the means of such a revolution as untenable, and it comes as no surprise therefore, that the Iranian authorities banned the film.

The film does not include explicit references to the Mahdi or to the Apocalypse, yet there are subtle signs that lead the viewer to the conclusion that the film indeed is a spiritual, Islamic perspective of the apocalypse. One of these signs concerns time, a theme that reoccurs in several contexts. The most obvious is the young girl's attempt to find out the time; not only does she ask the "young" policeman on more than one occasion, but she also asks the "young" Makhmalbaf and goes into a clock-repair shop in the bazaar, only to be informed that all the clocks have stopped and are to be repaired. Time is running out, and maybe it has stopped, so there is an urgency, a need to seize the moment and make things right before the return of the Mahdi. Iranians must act now before it is too late. This is reflected in the scene in which the "young" policeman is searching for his potted flower. Having left it in the bazaar, in a shaft of sunlight, he asks one passer-by, "Have you seen a ray of sunlight?" and receives the reply, "The sun doesn't stay in one place."

Makhmalbaf expresses the immediacy of the moment through the reversible temporal structure of his cinematic narrative. For example, there

Figure 7.2   "In exchange for a bullet and a knife the new generation of Iranians offer bread and a flower. The old generation is redeemed: The expectation of the Mahdi is to be undertaken in a more poetic fashion; the hungry should be fed and trees should be planted in Africa. The young generation becomes the Mahdi to restore justice and order in a peaceful way to the world."

is a scene in which the young girl rushes off down a bazaar alley and innocently asks the "young" policeman the time. In a later scene, the "young" and "old" policemen are busy rehearsing the part, and the "old" policeman describes how the young girl would approach him each day with a question. Just at that moment, the young girl hurries up to the "young" policeman and asks him the time, which is a replay of the previous scene, but now within a larger context. This technique encourages a sense of self-reflexivity, a recognition that small, "unrelated" incidents really do matter, that we are accountable. Time is of the essence, as the apocalypse is here and now. Therefore, the believer must prepare himself in the most suitable of ways by atoning for his misdemeanors. The return of the Mahdi (one of whose titles is the "Owner of Time" *(Sahib-e Zaman)* that is, the Lord of the Age) is imminent. Makhmalbaf wants to save himself, and perhaps he may also change others in the process. This is a modern form of Shi'ism, an individualist Shi'ism that accords more with many of the forms of modern-ism and individualism found in the West. The apocalypse is not postponed, but it is anticipated and interiorized by the individual, leaving him with the responsibility to act. It is similar to the way that the medieval Persian Sufis understood the apocalypse, for there is the external variety that is located in time future, and there is the imminent, interiorized apocalypse that occurs in time present. The interiorized apocalypse almost lends itself to a postmodern interpretation of *A Moment of Innocence.* The breakdown of the linear structure in the film, the confusion between fact and fiction, and the collapse of a communal ethic, which is replaced with individualism, situates Mohsen Makhmalbaf as a film director who can sit comfortably within Western postmodernism while at the same term preserving a distinct Iranian and Islamic heritage. This is not so say that Makhmalbaf is no longer concerned with his perceived duty to the community; however, the community no longer takes precedence. Makhmalbaf wants to save himself first: "I criticize myself everyday, I try to break myself everyday. I am a filmmaker, and I hope that nothing I say will ever lead to an assassination or to someone being killed in defending what I have said."[29]

Notes

1. These events were captured in Makhmalbaf's film *Salaam Sinema.* See also Amir Khusrawi's introduction in *Salaam Sinema: Chand Goftagu* (Tehran: Nashrani, 1376/1997), 9–11.
2. See Massood Mehrabi, *Film International* 3.3. Available at http://www.neda/film/vol3–3/yearsidl.html (downloaded June 13, 2002).

3. See Hamid Naficy, "Islamizing Film Culture in Iran," in *Iran: Political Culture in the Islamic Republic,* Samih Farsoun and Mehred Mashayekhi, eds. (London: Routledge, 1992), 190–91.

4. The problem of race discrimination and children is shown in Bahram *Bayzai's Bashu, Gharibeh Kuchek* (Bashu, the little stranger) (1986).

5. Issues relating to oppression and children are shown in Abbas Kiarostami's *Khaheh-ye Dust Kojast?* (Where is [my] Friend's House?) (1987).

6. Kiarostami's comments appear in "Art Matters: The Films of Abbas Kiarostami," in *Life and Art: The New Iranian Cinema,* by Rose Issa and Sheila Whitaker (London: National Film Theatre, 1999), 91.

7. See the article "Makhmalbaf Film House," available on the Makhmalbaf website, http://www.makhmalbaf.com/articles.asp?a=a04.

   This film has also stimulated much attention from academics, evidenced in Hamid Dabashi's article "Mohsen Makhmalbaf's *A Moment of Innocence,*" in Rose and Whitaker, *Life and Art: The New Iranian Cinema,* 115–128, and Nasrin Rahimieh's article "Capturing Cultural Transformation on Film: Makhmalbaf's *A Moment of Innocence," Edebiyat* 12 (2001): 195–214.

8. Norman O. Brown, *Apocalypse and/or Metamorphosis* (Berkeley: University of California Press, 1991), 88.

9. See Moojan Momen, *An Introduction to Shi'i Islam* (New Haven: Yale University Press, 1985), 167.

10. On this topic see Said Amir Arjomand, "Islamic Apocalypticism in the Classic Period," in *The Encyclopedia of Apocalypticism,* vol. 2, Bernard McGinn, ed., (New York: Continuum, 1998), 238–283.

11. See Lloyd Ridgeon, *Persian Metaphysics and Mysticism* (Richmond: Curzon Press, 2002), 83.

12. Nasafi, *Kashf al-haqa'iq,* Ahmad M. Damghani, ed. (Tehran: Bongah-e tarjuma va nashr al-ketab, 1344/1965), 210–13.

13. See for example the Qur'an, 7:157.

14. See his comments in *Islam and Revolution,* trans. and annotated by Hamid Algar (London: KPI, 1985), 61–2,

15. Ibid., 94.

16. See Abbas Ammanat, "The Resurgence of Apocalyptic in Modern Islam," in *The Encyclopedia of Apocalypticism,* vol. 3, Stephen J. Stein, ed. (New York : Continuum, 1998), 253–4.

17. On Shari'ati and the deterministic framework see Ali Rahnema, "Ali Shariati," in *Pioneers of Islamic Revival,* Ali Rahnema, ed. (London: Zed Books, 1994), 208–50. Criticisms of Shari'ati's thought in relation to modernity were discussed at the Society for Iranian Studies Conference, held in Washington, DC, in May 2002.

18. Ibid., 230–31.

19. For example, there is a special lamentation prayer (called the *nudba*) that is usually recited on Friday, the day for congregational prayers. The *nudba* prayer expresses the desire for the imminent return of the Mahdi.

20. See *Tawbeh-ye Nasuh* (Nasuh's repentence) (1982) and *Du cheshm bi su* (Two blind eyes) (1983) and, to a certain extent, *Boycot* (The boycott) (1985) which also bear some similarities with the second group of films.

21. See *Dastforush* (The peddler) (1986), *Baysikalran* (The cyclist) (1987), and *'Arus-e Khuban* (The marriage of the blessed) (1988).
22. See *Nawbat-e 'asheqi* (A time for love) (1990), *Shabha-ye Zayandeh Rud* (Nights on the Zayandeh River) (1990), *Naser al-Din Shah, Aktor-e Sinema* (Once upon a time cinema) (1991), and *Honarpisheh* (The actor) (1992).
23. See *Salaam Sinema* (Salaam Cinema) (1994), *Noon va Goldoon* (A moment of innocence) (1995), and *Gabbeh* (1996). Since then Makhmalbaf has directed two feature-length films, namely *Sokoot* (The silence) (1997) and *Qandahar* (2001).
24. See Hamid Dabashi, *Close Up* (London: Verso, 2001), 211.
25. See World Socialist website: "An Interview with Mohsen Makhmalbaf." Available at www.wsws.org/arts/1996/sep1996/iran-s96.shtml (downloaded June 18, 2002).
26. Samira Makhmalbaf's speech of May 9, 2000 is reproduced on the world wide web at, www.makhmalbaf.com/articles.asp?a=a06 (downloaded June 18, 2002).
27. The Internet is not censored in Iran. There were 400,000 people on the Internet in Iran during 2001, but government figures expect this to rise to 15 million over the next three to four years. See Alfred Hermida, BBC News Online, Monday June 17, 2002. Available at http://news.bbc.co.uk/hi/english/sci/tech/newsid_2044000/2044802.stm.
28. That Makhmalbaf desires change not through the "sword" but through the "camera" is illustrated in his comment that " We filmmakers are here only to illuminate, to bring joy to life. All I seek is that, after seeing a film of mine, a person feels a little happier, and acts with a little more kindness towards the world. I don't think that cinema can hope to do much more" (cited in Dabashi, *Close Up*, 211).
29. Ibid.

Chapter Eight

Performative Pilgrims and the Shifting Grounds of Anthropological Documentary*

Luis A. Vivanco

Introduction: Debating the Maya Calendar during "una Gran Romería"

On the day of the spring equinox every March, one of the pyramids at the renowned Maya archaeological site of Chichén Itzá in Pisté, Yucatán, Mexico, experiences a phenomenon in which the sun casts a serpentlike shadow on one of its balustrades. In any given year, this phenomenon attracts thousands of Mexican, North American, and European tourists, professional and amateur archaeologists and archaeo-astronomers, practitioners of New Age religions, ambulant vendors, and state authorities. Most of these people come, at least ostensively, to acknowledge and celebrate the genius of the ancient Maya, although, importantly, many also come to maintain control over the tourist masses or to make money selling souvenirs and food. In 1995, the equinox event drew more attention than usual, attracting record numbers of visitors, among them conspicuously large numbers of New Age religious practitioners, who came because of the apparent calendrical significance of that particular year. For New Agers, this equinox was to usher in the "Age of Aquarius," and they had converged on Chichén Itzá because of their belief in the propitious coincidence of this event with a cyclical renewal on the Maya calendar, itself apparently marking the arrival of the "Age of Itzá."

Among the visitors for this particular occasion was a pair of cultural anthropologists, Jeff Himpele and Quetzil Castañeda, gathering video footage for a documentary film about the tourism spectacle surrounding the equinox phenomenon. In the video they produced, *Incidents of Travel*

in Chichén Itzá, the ethnographers explain in a brief voiceover narration
that this event has been described by a Yucatecan intellectual as *una gran
romería,* or "a great pilgrimage," which in Spanish carries with it connotations of bacchanalia and carnival.[1] The concept of pilgrimage frames the
video's approach to its subject matter, which is an inquiry into the various
representations and meanings that visitors and workers project onto each
other and onto the archaeological site, its ancient inhabitants, contemporary Maya, the equinox phenomenon, and the religious activities taking
place because of it. The video shows that a preoccupation with imagery of
tragedy, death, the sacred, and saintly figures are central elements in the
development and experience of Chichén Itzá, as they are at other popular
pilgrimage sites.[2] The video also shows that, whether they are there to
engage in specific ritual activities or out of general curiosity, people come to
this place on a quest, seeking something that lies outside the normal
patterns of their everyday lives, possibly some form of affirmation or
completeness. In these senses, the video has certain goals and techniques
one would expect of the ethnographic documentary genre, namely a
commitment to representing actually existing peoples, struggles, and events
in service of persuasive arguments about the world. But these goals and
norms alone do not define how this video was produced or its narrative
structure, for in important respects, the film also demonstrates a profound
skepticism toward certain basic assumptions about documentary filmmaking, especially filmmaker omniscience and an unproblematic ability to
"capture" an unfolding social reality on film. Differing from traditional
approaches in this genre, it engages in a deliberate blurring of boundaries
between documentary and fiction, participant-observation and performance, and social analysis and the recognition that knowledge is always
partial and incomplete.[3] Seen in this light, the filmmakers themselves seem
to be performing a pilgrimage of their own, balancing a search for the
ancient Maya (through the eyes of others) with an intention to participate
in a raging debate about the future of anthropological documentary film.

In an effort to explore the contours of this debate and the shifting
grounds of ethnographic documentary emerging from it, this chapter
examines how *Incidents of Travel in Chichén Itzá* internalizes critiques of,
and offers a provocative alternative to, certain realist conventions of filmic
representation. This exploration is not inspired by a taxonomic impulse to
classify emerging techniques of documentary film production but by a
desire to evaluate how this work reflects ongoing debates about the
dilemmas of visually representing religious experience and cultural processes more broadly. The videomakers take seriously the now well-known
assertion of a crisis in ethnographic representation and filmmaking, where
the defining qualities of nonfiction documentary—realist narratives, rhetoric, and meanings in which the emphasis is on making expository argu-

ments through the use of visual ("factual") evidence—are not acceptable given the aesthetic, interpretative, and political manipulations and asymmetries at the heart of representational processes. Because the status of film and video as document is not persuasive[4]—films and videos are themselves cultural representations, each with specific qualities, techniques, and dilemmas—the choices about how to represent other cultures and cultural processes on film are less clear-cut than ever.

Paradigms of polyvocality, reflexivity, transparency, and dialogism alert us to new representational possibilities and increasingly normative frameworks in which a central goal includes the revision of unquestioned hierarchical relationships inherent in cross-cultural research and visual representation. Performativity is another complementary possibility, in which disembodied observational techniques give way to interactivity and the challenges of rendering visible the filmmaker's embodied experience and subjective position. Within this framework, ethnographic authority and authenticity, which have been based on the separation of subject and object (the greater the rhetorical distance, the more authoritative), can no longer solely render the object visible while both ethnographer and ethnographic processes remain invisible. Its highly suggestive potential, according to Bill Nichols, who has written extensively on ethnographic documentary and its alternatives, is that "Performative documentary suspends realist representation. Performative documentary puts the referential aspect of the message in brackets, under suspension. . . . These films make the proposition that it is possible to know difference differently."[5]

This commitment to self-reflexive performative action becomes apparent during an early scene in the film. It is a scene in which we view one of the ethnographers, Quetzil, in front of the camera (which Himpele is operating), self-consciously entering a pyramid, where he encounters a middle-aged man explaining to a couple of young women in English that a basic aspect of the Mayan calendar is the 52-day cyclical period. After eavesdropping for a short time, Quetzil turns to the camera with a questioning look, inquiring if it is on, to be sure that the following interaction will be filmed. He greets the man in Yucatec Maya, and asks in English, "How do you know so much?" We learn that the man is a Catholic priest from the U.S. Midwest, working in a Yucatec Maya community not far from Chichén Itzá. The priest explains that the contemporary Maya themselves do not appear to appreciate the calendrical details of which he speaks and adds that they do not understand that this particular day—the equinox—had long been acknowledged in their culture as a celebration of new life; today it is seen as a Christian celebration. He concludes, "They've lost all their knowledge of their own culture. . . . The more they learn about themselves, the better." A woman standing nearby dressed in white (common dress among New Agers) interjects, in a low voice, that the last equinox was 520 years ago. Quetzil challenges her, pointing out that it happens every year. The woman continues to explain that "This is really big, I mean in the Maya calendar, which is two hundred and sixty years, this is five hundred and twenty years." She adds that because it is the end of the millennium and a time of such significance ("The Maya believe that we must change from the age of belief to the age of knowledge. . . . They call it the Age of Itzá, and we call it the Age of Aquarius") that she came to play her didgeridoo "and to do a healing." Quetzil begins to ask how she came up with the numbers she used, but the priest announces in a tone of voice implying a bemused dismissal of the New Ager, "me voy amigo!" ("I'm leaving, friend!"). Quetzil coos to the man, "I would very much like for you to participate!" And so the priest stays.

What ensues is an inspired interaction, in which the anthropologist, New Ager, and priest debate about the various cycles in the Maya calendar, their meanings, and how they articulate with changes in the universe. Assuming the tone of an expert, Quetzil makes technical assertions about Maya time periods and cycles (explaining the various meanings of *May, katuns,* and *tuns*), and asks the woman to explain from whom she got her own calculations. The priest says to the New Ager, perhaps more because Quetzil asked him to stay than out of his own desire to educate, that "the Mayans here are not aware of what you're talking about." The woman protests that her assertions "are very common knowledge right now" and eventually concludes, "It's not an issue I have any desire to question. . . . I respect the culture of the Maya." The camera pans to eavesdropping tourists listening in on the discussion. After a back and forth of several minutes, there is neither a resolution of the debate nor a formal closure of the conversation, and the three each self-consciously go their own ways.

It is necessary to ask what is the point of this segment, for there are others like it in the video, in which the eavesdropping ethnographer participates on camera in unresolved discussions about the meanings of Chichén Itzá, ancient and contemporary Maya cultures, and why all these people have come to this place on this day. This scene demonstrates, in several important respects, that this documentary diverges from epistephelic expectations of the genre that emphasize objectivism, omniscience, and a "closer indexical relation to the real world."[6] Foremost, it puts the purported expert front and center, willingly (and not so willingly) being drawn into debate with the presumed subjects of investigation. This can have the effect of rendering authorship open to new scrutiny, including all the vulnerabilities this can project, as we see when Quetzil verbally stumbles, repeating his own explanation of the Maya calendar as if to convince himself that he got it right. In this sense, the video manages imagery of anthropology in the making without assuming its social authority or editing out (at least some of) its uncertainties, in the process evocatively showing us an uncomfortable space where the dictates of conceptual relativism and seeing the world "from the native's point of view" butt up against the positivistic legacy of anthropology's commitments to "get the facts straight" through description. Significantly, the videomakers are very careful to not resolve the debates or correct their contradictions, and there is no voiceover narration through most of the video to reinforce the claims made by the anthropologist or to override what people say on camera (a most facile solution during editing to ensure anthropological authority). Committed to representing multiple and competing perspectives on the equinox and its meanings, the scene tries to avoid imposing any singular or privileged authoritative interpretation of events. Anthropology, it is projected, is but one voice among many clamoring for attention and authority in ongoing struggles to impose normative interpretations on Chichén Itzá.

Does *Incidents of Travel in Chichén Itzá*, which self-consciously employs techniques of self-reflexivity and embodied performance to achieve its goal of decentering anthropological authority, help us know difference differently?[7] What is the difference that is known? These questions get to the heart of performative documentary's potential to reconfigure the relationship between filmmaker and Other, documentary and fiction, description and evocation. This is an especially compelling question in light of this volume's concern with representations of religious belief and practice on film, in that it forces us to ask if and how these techniques (re)constitute representations of the sacred, which happens to be a central concern for many of the visitors to Chichén Itzá. Not everyone is as sanguine about the possibilities of reflexivity and transparency to resolve the representational asymmetries and epistemological dilemmas of ethnographic documentary making.[8] A crucial reason for this is that reductionistic attention to images and their creation does not alone necessarily stimulate ameliorative action. What happens outside the imagery on film and filmmaking processes—political, economic, and other structural inequalities; deeply held orientalisms; the fact that viewers are not "cultural blank slates"—is just as relevant in determining the outcomes of documentary film, so that techniques of transparency, self-photography, performance, and so on, do not necessarily lead to an alteration in the status of the people being filmed (if indeed that is a goal). Similarly, even audiences attuned to the politics of cross-cultural representation do not necessarily focus on the specific construction of imagery itself in ways that filmmakers intend, much less know how to distinguish and analyze the subtleties of the embodied action of anthropologists. As we reach the limits of such technical filmic practices to radically transform the anthropologist's and the viewer's relationships between self and Other, West and non-West, the point is not to reinstate a positivistic vision of ethnographic documentary but to acknowledge the possibilities these newer practices and norms raise for ongoing cross-cultural dialogues both within and outside the vision of the camera's lens.

Beyond "The Sacred Journey"

By adapting the name of John L. Stephens's "classic" nineteenth-century explorer's travelogue *Incidents of Travel in Central America, Chiapas, and Yucatán,* Himpele and Castañeda imply a connection between Stephens's adventures and their own quest to make sense of Chichén Itzá.[9] But the goal of the anthropologists is not an explorer's quest to reveal an unknown and primitive Other, much less a region outside of world history, but an appreciation for what Beatriz Sarlo has in another context called "the exacerbation of the heterogeneous."[10] It is simply not possible to view the area in terms of its isolation from the world; just as the Yucatán has become a key site of first-world leisure tourism, the Maya have become major icons of indigeneity in global cultural flows. Many contemporary visitors to Chichén Itzá have assumed Stephens's legacy, though, and underlying their visit to the Yucatán is a quest for a particular exotic Other, the lost Maya. These are a people of genius and sophistication who built great cities and astronomical observatories but had a fatally flawed social order that led to their ultimate collapse and disappearance. One of the major assertions of this video is that there is no unity to this search, and in fact everybody seems to be in search of and doing something different. New Age religious practitioners of various nationalities and forms of worship and dress (Tibetan lama imitators, Korean monks, people dressed in white flowing robes, etc.), middle-class North American beach tourists and college "spring breakers" visiting from nearby Cancún, nonindigenous Mexican youths, Mexican National Institute of Anthropology and History (INAH), personnel who police the site, tourism guides, souvenir vendors from Pisté (the Maya village nearest the archaeological zone) and the surrounding region, regional Maya tourists and political leaders—each at some point enters the frame of the camera, willfully and in some cases unwittingly expressing opinions, confusions, critiques about the archaeological zone, the equinox, and why they are there.

Early in the video, we overhear the voice of an American tourist who says "Everyone's doing their own thing." The video adopts this point of view, and a major goal is to document the jostling, confrontations, denials, dismissals, and convivialities that take place between visitors (including the videomaker anthropologists), between visitors and vendors, between state officials and various visitors, and between state officials and vendors, among others. There is a proliferation of voices and perspectives, with the result that there is no one group or individual who can fix the meanings of Chichén Itzá and what is taking place there. Representations flow in many directions, and these incongruities are reflected in the nonlinear narrative structure of the video. Although organized very loosely around the flow of a single day in the life of the archaeological zone (that is, from morning to the afternoon, when the "big event" of the shadow-casting occurs), and interspersed with atemporal visits to surrounding tourist sites and communities, it does not seek to taxonomize the various visitors or their perspectives, and it jumps from scene to scene in a fragmented fashion. The fact that it was filmed using a video camera, which provides an aesthetic of immediacy and informality, reinforces the visual sensation that the videomakers were inclined to "take things as they come."

This (fragmented) narrative of fragmentation is reflected in, and reflects, the number of highly differentiated activities that take place in and around Chichén Itzá. Tourists take pictures of the archaeological zone, carefully seeking images of the ancient city without any other tourists in the photograph. They eavesdrop on each other and make fun of other tourists. They especially spy on and make fun of the New Agers, as when a group of young Mexicans sarcastically chant like the New Agers they are watching, ending their chants in a storm of laughter. Maya visitors explain why they came ("to see the shadow"), and suggest that New Age chants referring to Hunab Ku ("the one true god of the Mayas") mean nothing to them ("We are Catholics," says one Maya woman). Between their efforts to prevent New Agers from practicing their rituals, INAH officials criticize New Agers for their naïve reliance on the Gregorian calendar to calculate the arrival of the "Age of Itzá" (which will actually come in 2012). They also point out that "real Mayas do their rituals elsewhere," not here in the archaeological zone. In a scene far from the archaeological zone, an elder Maya man considers the casting of the serpent shadow ("is it true?" he asks), and explains the phenomenon by demonstrating how a rope casts a shadow if you put it in front of the light. Asked what he thinks is the meaning of the serpent shadow, he impatiently sputters, "Meaning?! The meaning . . . how it . . . how it . . . the sun . . . the . . . the . . . the change of the sun. That's what it means." And so on.

As the brief voice-over narration at the beginning of the video explains, there is an important theoretical point in this heterogeneity and lack of neat closure.[11] Many people come to Chichén Itzá seeking to clear a space for themselves in order to create an unobstructed vision of the ancient Maya city. This process began with the very invention of Chichén Itzá as an archaeological site in the early twentieth century, as Anglo-American archaeologists "peeled back" the jungle to reveal this place. This process marks the Maya as a mystery, a "lost civilization," based on a vision of

Chichén Itzá as an abandoned city, which is inscribed on this space through its (re)construction as an empty ceremonial center. Today, visitors, vendors, and tour guides ceaselessly reinscribe the vision of the archaeologists in their movements through the space and the meanings they project onto the reconstructed pyramids. It is a vision that highlights the mystery of the ancient Maya while largely rendering contemporary Maya invisible. This is reflected in photographic practices of visitors; as one woman explains, she wants to take a picture with nobody in it, to show what things were "really like." Nonetheless, anthropology's authority is never complete, because its vision and inscription on the space of the archaeological zone compete with other intentions and uses—New Agers seeking to practice eclectic rites that affirm a dramatic shift in universal spirituality, the Mexican state's construction of Chichén Itzá as a museum of national patrimony and identity, INAH personnel trying to control the physical movements of visitors and maintain a secular zone free of religious activities, Maya vendors who see the space not as a place of "lost Maya," but as a space to sell goods, etc. That is what the narrative says, but there are other elements here, for we have to add to this dynamic a couple of American cultural anthropologists, Himpele and Castañeda themselves, whose goal seems to be a critique of anthropology itself, and any closure about archaeology's hegemony here is in question. This, of course, is a long way from *National Geographic*–type documentaries about Chichén Itzá, whose singular focus on the mysteries and genius of the ancient Maya is so dedicated that they ignore the contemporary realities of archaeological invention of the site itself and that Chichén Itzá itself is a form of tourism infrastructure built to host thousands of people a day all year long.

In several respects, the nonlinear formal structure of the video and its theoretical argument suggest a critical departure from certain structural-functionalist frameworks and dichotomies that have held sway over tourism and pilgrimage studies. For example, one of tourism studies' basic presuppositions, that the activity of tourism can be divided into "hosts" and "guests" in which the boundaries, expectations, and relationships between the two sides is defined in terms of their cultural differences, economic inequalities, and so on, is blurred in favor of a more complex vision of tourism.[12] Such a binary orients one of anthropology's most influential films on tourism, *Cannibal Tours* (1998), in which filmmaker Dennis O'Rourke seeks to capture tourists ("guests") in their quest for the exotic and in their acts of constructing the Other, while Papuan Iatmul ("hosts") themselves develop and express their own alienated and suspicious representations of Western tourists.[13] The film is "a representation about making representations,"[14] whose goal is to show the vast cultural divide between tourist and the Other and whose effect in the end is an Othering and exoticization of tourists themselves. O'Rourke's point is that powerful representations and orientalisms frame the touristic quest for native peoples, blurring the lines between the ugliness and primitivity often imputed to native cultures and the presumed modernity imputed to tourists. Although inspired by O'Rourke's film (in the sense that they are also interested in the fact that tourists arrive with and seek to confirm certain specific visions of the Other), Himpele and Castañeda reject the possibilities for unitary "hosts" and "guests" at Chichén Itzá. The most destabilizing presence to a simple host-guest binary is the presence of local Mayas touring the archaeological zone, themselves engaging in a complex process of curiosity seeking and identity destabilization. Vendors describe the ongoing conflicts resulting from the infusion of new vendors coming from other villages because of regional economic downturns. Late in the video, we see the deep dissatisfaction among locals—and their threats of political action—at the state government's displacement of vendors from the main tourist avenue and the archaeological zone. There is also a scene in which several leaders in Pisté describe struggles between their community and the state government, which led to their kidnapping of a state-owned bulldozer and establishment of a road blockade to achieve recognition of their political claims.

The destabilization of this simple binary has several important effects. For one, the notion that there might be "resistance" to tourism and tourists among local peoples does not play out in a straightforward way. Indeed, as the film shows, when locals engage in resistance movements or actions related to tourism at all (as in the kidnapping of the bulldozer and conflicts between vendors about who can sell souvenirs and where they can sell them), they are engaged in resisting other Mexicans or the Mexican state, not necessarily the tourists themselves. Perhaps even more important, this approach does not reduce the film to an analysis of the "impact" of tourism upon local populations, a near-sacred lens within tourism studies.[15] This orientation is so powerful that much of the anthropological study of tourism seems to exist as an exercise in "impactology."[16] Within this framework, tourism is understood in rather simplistic terms as a core-periphery phenomenon, reducing tourist activity to market penetration, often with overtones of economic domination. "Hosts" are both passive and "traditional," with something to lose (their culture), while "guests" represent the agency and forces of modernity. In contrast, Himpele and Castañeda suggest that what is taking place at Chichén Itzá are disjunctive and multicentered practices of tourism and pilgrimage, opening an intellectual space to consider how a highly dynamic and contingent phenomenon becomes a resource for defining and articulating religious practices and new cultural identities and for interacting with others.

This vision of Chichén Itzá automatically complicates the construction of tourist activity as a "sacred journey." According to this influential formulation, which draws heavily on Victor Turner's ritual process theory, travel is understood as "structurally-necessary, ritualized breaks in routine that define and relieve the ordinary."[17] What gives the act of tourism special meaning, like other rituals of sacralization, is the passage from the ordinary and "profane" world of work to the symbolically and morally "sacred" world of travel. Furthermore, it is supposed that between tourists a form of *communitas* emerges, in which people are bound together in a common experience of liminality and equality. This theoretical framework arguably makes a strong linkage between tourism and pilgrimage, for it endows tourism with the qualities of explicit religiosity emphasized in notions of pilgrimage, without the experience of religiosity being defined in terms of any single religious tradition. Indeed, as Edith and Victor Turner have asserted, "A tourist is half a pilgrim, if a pilgrim is half a tourist," emphasizing that the experience of pilgrimage need not be defined solely in terms of its explicit religiosity or that tourism be understood as a purely secular endeavor.[18] Undoubtedly, *Incidents of Travel in Chichén Itzá* contributes to this deconstruction of any rigid lines between the implicit religiosity of tourism and the explicit religiosity of pilgrimage, if we accept that the common denominator between them is a "journey out of the normal parameters of life, the entry into a different, other, world, the search for something new, the multiple motives of participants, ranging from homage and veneration to the simple impulses of curiosity."[19] But by emphasizing divergent practices, conflict, and competition over *communitas* and integration, and by expressing a multiplicity of meanings about why people are there and what they are doing, it is apparent that the experience of *communitas* is neither universal nor expected. If anything, instead of creating an alternative and inclusive functionalist order, the experience of touring Chichén Itzá serves to define and reaffirm differences among people.

For example, there is a scene that takes place in the ball court area, in which Quetzil approaches a group of several Americans to ask them what their opinions are about an activity taking place nearby that looks like a New Age ritual. A man answers, "I was just eavesdropping," to which Quetzil responds with a self-conscious laugh, "So are we!" The man suggests that he will find out, and seemingly emboldened by being on camera, asks a participant about it and finds out that it is a ceremony of solar initiation for the Age of Itzá. Invited to join in, he and one of his companions join a circle of people holding hands and stand there for a while seeming to meditate. They seem uncomfortable and awkward. After the ceremony, as he and his companion return to their titillated friends, the man asserts, "None of us really knew what we were doing, you could get whatever you chose from it." His companion differs, suggesting that she felt a vibration that "was kind of weird. It was calming, it felt different." Perhaps what this woman felt is what Victor Turner referred to as a sensation of "spontaneous communitas," an unexpected feeling of unity and integration.[20] However, what is significant is that there is a clear lack of resolution here. Whether it is the continued skepticism of the man or the dismissive, even mocking attitude of his companions, it is reaffirmed that the New Agers are still Other, and indeed, part of the spectacle of visiting Chichén Itzá on this day.

Situations of *communitas* compete with forces of disjuncture not only because of the different motivations and practices that bring people to Chichén Itzá but also because different visitors occupy asymmetrical positions within the highly policed realm of the archaeological zone. This is apparent in the ways INAH officials regard and treat New Agers, for they are a potentially destabilizing presence given the fact that they are openly practicing religious rituals. There are several scenes in which INAH officials interrupt New Age ceremonies, asserting that it is illegal to practice religious activity on the grounds of the archaeological zone. But, interestingly enough, INAH officials seem to target small groups of New Age worshippers and not a large tour group of New Age practitioners who have come with their Mexican tour guide/spiritual leader. This group's activities consist of walking in circles around one of the main pyramids, which elicits confusion among the participants of the "what-are-we-doing-now?" variety one might expect to see in any large tour group. As one woman explains, they have "Lunch at Mayaland hotel, do a ritual, and then I'm not sure, we get instructions one step at a time." They also have a brief ceremonial encounter with members of the Maya Council, composed of regional political authorities, in which their tour guide/spiritual leader admonishes the Mayas of their need to reclaim the spiritual legacy of their ancestors. Yet the INAH officials seem to let these activities happen without interruption. Perhaps it would be too difficult to control so many, or perhaps it is related to the fact that they are not burning incense and chanting (an example of an explicit ritual in one scene), which means that they can "pass" as not engaging openly in religious activity. Perhaps the efforts to control them were simply not caught on film. But in their filming, editing, and brief and sporadic voice-over narrations, the videomakers leave many such loose ends and uncertainties.

Such narrative uncertainties persist largely because Himpele and Castañeda are resistant to impose a totalizing account about what they see going on around them. This does not mean, however, that there is a corresponding collapse in their search for the diverse meanings of visiting the site as tourists and pilgrims. This is apparent in the way that the video manages questions of origins. The first frames of the video are presented as questions about the ancient Maya—Who were they? How did they build these pyramids? What is the meaning of the serpent shadow? And so on. The suggestion is that these are the kinds of mysteries and questions that orient a pilgrimage to Chichén Itzá and are the basic categories with which pilgrims (and archaeologists) regard the Maya. The final question is "What is the origin of these questions?" The video does not attempt to answer this last question literally, which establishes this project's difference from other anthropological pursuits that deliberately, through objectivist means and rhetoric, seek to account for origins. It is these very questions, and even more importantly the fact that they are unanswerable—that origins are ultimately unfixable—that underlies the creation of meaning. The fact that Quetzil is regularly asked on camera "where are you from?" by other tourists and New Agers, but seems to have a different answer every time (New Jersey, the U.S. Midwest, Houston) confirms his own skepticism toward fixing origins. The point is that the specific meanings people make of the world around them are not, for example, simply the product of movement through structural positions in a ritual process or their existence in states of perpetual *communitas* but are the products of partial knowledge, fragmented understandings, and unstable perspectives.

Reforming Visual Anthropology

Certainly, such an argument derives from and speaks to a secular discourse on pilgrimage that seeks to examine and understand it in sociological terms—asking questions about its social dimensions, interpreting its cultural forms—as opposed to a theological appreciation in which the experience of the sacred exists as the central concern. This is not to say that the possibility for an experience of the sacred disappears completely, or that the pilgrim's quest for completeness and wholeness consistently fail in the face of the forces of cultural disjuncture. But in vital ways, religious experience exceeds the visual medium,[21] and Himpele and Castañeda, while wholly committed to an experientially based methodology and narrative, seem more committed to exploring the methodological implications of the embodied actions and performances of visitors and visiting anthropologists than in finding ways to account for the presence of the sacred.

The video manages performativity on two levels, in one sense offering a conceptual model for social action, in another, an approach to decentering and renewing ethnographic methodology. In the first sense, Chichén Itzá itself represents a large-scale stage upon which various social actors enact their differentiated meanings of the archaeological zone, as we see in the performances of diverse New Age ceremonies, in tourists and tour guides using scripts initially laid out by archaeologists to know how to see the space of the archaeological zone, and in visitors making fun of New Agers by mock-performing their ceremonies. The metaphor of performance offers a novel alternative to the supposition that Chichén Itzá and the things taking place there are "socially constructed." The metaphor of "construction" implies that people or groups of people are building something according to an engineered plan, or providing a skilled realization of an underlying structural blueprint.[22] By moving to the concept of performance (which is still an actor-centered theory of human action), there is an acknowledgement that certain scripts and discourses underlie social action and the creation of meaning from raw experience, but that there is more possibility for fluidity, improvisation, and the practices and interactions of actual bodies. As people enact a specific set of scripts or visions of Chichén Itzá, they come into both social and physical contact with others engaged in a similar process, creating suggestive possibilities for dialogic encounters and improvisations, as in the case where the woman above realizes the possibility of "something weird . . . and different" because of her participation in the New Age ritual.

In the second sense, which is more relevant for our purposes here, performativity as embodied action offers a self-reflexive approach to and critique of the processes of fieldwork, visual documentation, and the construction of cultural knowledge more generally. The narrative approaches this theme most directly through the character of Quetzil, who is never distant from, and usually at the center of, the events and conversations taking place on camera. More specifically, it is through Quetzil's concrete experiences of interacting with people in and around the archaeological zone that we gain access to a diversity of perspectives and meanings on the experience of pilgrimage. Our reliance on his willingness (hubris?) to eavesdrop and his ability to enter into and carry on conversations are made explicit in a short section of the film in which Himpele's voiceover explains that in doing this collaborative project with Quetzil, he was himself engaging in an ethnography of the latter's ethnographic style. Expanding on the theme of Quetzil the fieldworker, they interview a resident of Pisté. As Quetzil looks on, the man describes him as "folkloric," explaining (more to Quetzil than the camera), "You can't not be a gringo in Pisté—you are one! But you are also now more than that. You are a friend of many people, a friend because you understand their difficulties. People appreciate it, and when the people appreciate something, that means it is true, it is authentic." In this view, Quetzil exists in a space of cultural fluidity; he can assure access to many people (especially Pisteños) because he is seen as a sympathetic person who listens, marking him as something more than other visitors to Pisté ("gringos"), but, of course, as not quite a Pisteño either.

This sense of contingency and improvisation is precisely the effect the videomakers want to generate, for it forces us to realize that what we are seeing on video is the visual manifestation of fluid social relations and embodied identities of the videomakers themselves. Their identities and markings are both conspicuous and distinct. This is partly related to the fact that, unlike other visitors, they are "making a documentary." By doing so, they attract the attention of other visitors, marking themselves as key participants in helping create and confirm the spectacle that is Chichén Itzá on the day of the equinox. Quetzil is also especially marked by his body, which verges on the erotic with his skimpy shorts and suggestive tank-top shirts. But their status as ethnographers is not unproblematic either, as the techniques, attitudes, and performances of ethnography proliferate among visitors to Chichén Itzá. Ethnography is unleashed as tourists listen in on each other, ask questions, and try to analyze what is taking place around them. Some people on camera take to this more than others, often in response to the videomakers themselves explaining what they are up to. The point is that neither Himpele nor Castañeda have a monopoly on doing anthropology, rendering their own professional identities as anthropologists open to negotiability, even competition, with others.

In placing self-reflexivity through performance as a central visual and narrative theme running throughout the video, Himpele and Castañeda are asking us to look at anthropology "behind the scenes," a strategy that represents a challenge to norms of documentary film production, in which filmmaker authority is disembodied and omniscient. Placing the ethnographer in front of the camera marks a difference from a visual discourse that "moves from mind to mind,"[23] rendering visible the affective and embodied aspects of fieldwork, accepting that the creation of cultural knowledge is mediated by these "subjective" processes and is therefore partial and situated. No longer can ethnographic authority rely on its distance from the subject, or on an "us versus them" dichotomy where there is a basic asymmetry in which "we" stage "them." The point is not simply that "they" also stage "us" but that any division of "us" and "them" is in the first place a product of unquestioned norms of ethnographic and documentary film representations. This reformative methodology is based on a phenomenological principle that embodied action is the basis for both knowledge of self and other. The intention is to force viewers to see the film itself as a representation, instead of unproblematically seeing through the film to the data beyond. At its most suggestive, this can suspend realism, creating a distinctive tension and blurring between performance and document, the personal and the typical, description and evocation. We can go even further to suggest that in place of any commitment to a singular notion of truth, there are multiple truths that can only be approached (but not arrived at) through dialectical combinations of strategy and serendipity. Such blurrings, according to Nichols, do not represent "logical confusions" but arenas of ideological contestation in which new interpretive strategies can be explored and can gain acceptance.[24]

Performances that Keep on Performing

The question, of course, is how to evaluate such claims. The position of performative documentary is that by representing the decentering and embodied actions of the anthropological subject, there is a corresponding decentering of the subject of visual anthropology and ethnographic documentary film itself. More to the point, it allows for the possibility to "know difference differently," that is, outside of the Othering tendencies inherent in "we-stage-them" asymmetries, without defining in precise terms what that difference is or even should be. Motivating this is also a distinctive take on the "use-value" of documentary, projecting a concern that the value of documentary to both the subjects of the film and the audiences that will view it requires a shift from documentary as a way to know Otherness to documentary as a way to reflect critically on and modify anthropological processes of representation. These reforms confirm that cultural knowledge does not rise out of the social vacuum of omniscience but is the product of historical and embodied individuals in specific times and places.

In spite of its explicit disobedience to the traditions of documentary film, though, there is something technically reductionistic and atemporal about the way performative documentary is regarded by advocates like Nichols, a basic assumption being that it can accomplish the radical things it sets out to do largely by force of technique. On several levels, this is based on problematic assumptions. One crucial and persistent conundrum is that as much as anthropology may wish to decenter ethnographic relationships and the creation of cultural knowledge by doing away with the aura of omniscience, the editing room remains the ultimate trump card. On film, anthropologists may allow themselves to be staged, negotiated, challenged, and even rejected. It is also possible to replace the explicit authority of a voice-over narration with the submerged authority of multivocality. But what happens to the collaborations, interactivity, and dialogism in the technical and creative process of editing film clips and sound? Is it possible to truly decenter authorship when recording on film, which is where performativity and bodies are highlighted, or is filming itself but an early step in a much larger production process that ranges from prefilming plans and preparations to various stages of post-production? Is this focus on the actual footage of performative ethnographers not just perpetuating another form of structural inequality, since these other processes involve a key shaping of representations from raw footage to finished product? To be fair, the suggestiveness of self-reflexivity through performance in the documentary film genre is not that it means to extend the net of authorship to all participants, because it is radical enough to identify multiple authors and subjectivities where they have not been admitted before. The goal is to induce viewers to acknowledge that what we see on film is the product of specificity—of lens, intellectual framework, physical body, social relationship, etc.—emphasizing the processes of making representations over the objectivity of facts. But it is worth noting that documentary film's historic commitment to using the world "out there" for purposes of argumentation persists in performative documentary: Instead of assuming the transparency of facts on film, there is invisibility in the framing of the project and the editing process, in which film clips and sounds are organized by the author to pursue a particular argument.

Notwithstanding issues of production control, questions arise on another level about the receptivity of audiences to such techniques. In important respects, performative documentary assumes a paradoxical audience, which is to say, both passive and cosmopolitan in its way of viewing film. That is, audiences have to be both open and responsive to the force of certain techniques of filming, but sophisticated enough in the history and subtleties of ethnographic documentary aesthetics and practices that they can comprehend where the lines between ethnographic self and Other, performance and documentary, are being blurred. In terms of this latter argument, there is a sense that even though the genre seeks to overcome an unmediated, "mind to mind" communication, the viewer's mind has to stay intact in order to appreciate that fact. Of course, this is an unrealistic position, given that viewers do not come to any films as "cultural blanks."[25] They come as persons who have seen movies that confirm the savagery of the Other, television documentaries with condescending and simplistic visions of traditional cultures as sophisticated yet mysterious, and newspapers and magazine photographs that emphasize the visually exotic in contrast to modern ways of being.

As a result, audiences do not necessarily experience and comprehend films in terms of the intentions laid out by filmmakers or critics like Nichols. For example, after showing *Incidents of Travel in Chichén Itzá* to undergraduate and graduate student audiences in American universities at least a dozen times—students who were prepared in advance to be attentive to the self-conscious innovations in the video and its critique of visual anthropology—many still come away with a renewed concept of a savage Other. It is not the ancient Maya, the typical savage Other, around which Chichén Itzá is organized, though. Rather it is the New Agers who are incommensurably Other and exotic, and even mocked by students who watch the video, similar to tourists in the video itself who marginalize the New Agers by reducing their practices to irrelevance or joking. When asked why they laughed at New Agers in the video, some students appear to already have a dismissive attitude toward New Age religions, seeing them as marginal and spurious religious practices. Other students, more inclined to view New Age religions sympathetically, feel betrayed that the video does not defend their practices even if they do not share the same values. In either circumstance, the students have been easily drawn into accustomed ways of viewing documentary that see through the process of representation to the ethnographic "facts" on screen. The video deliberately engages New Agers in a collaborative performance in which the goal is to try to overcome the distance between anthropological objectification and peoples' objectifications of themselves. As such it ends up being interpreted by large numbers of viewers as a send-up of New Age religions and suggests that audiences are neither as cosmopolitan nor passive as presumed.

In one significant respect, Himpele and Castañeda appreciate this fact, because they regularly interview audiences about their reactions to the video and its subject matter. This is consistent with one of their arguments, that any totalizing conclusions about Chichén Itzá are impossible given the unfinished and incomplete negotiation of meanings and experiences that take places there. Viewing the video itself engages new participants in the set of negotiations and cultural dialogues over the happenings during the equinox in Chichén Itzá. In this sense, it is possible to think of what takes place in the video as performances that keep on performing, both in terms of the performances happening on screen and the performative ways audiences engage the video during and after viewing it. But this generates a curiously paradoxical effect in which, even while the video highlights the specificity and temporality of the equinox event, the video itself projects a now atemporal, even timeless, set of performances, events, and interactions that have already taken place. This paradox persists largely because performative documentary cannot escape its own genre completely, which is rooted in procedures of objectification. Even while it aims to represent the decentering of cultural knowledge production, it is still committed to representing the struggles of actual groups of people in service to persuasive arguments about the world. The video's argument may be that we cannot objectively and omnisciently know the heterogeneous cultural realities of particular groups of people or events, but that in itself is an argument that at least partially draws its authority from an atemporal, even universalizing, logic.

Reductionistic attention to images and imagery-making does not necessarily resolve this tension. Perhaps one of the more promising aspects of this genre is that film itself generally requires a normative commitment on the part of viewers, filmmakers, and the subjects of film to view filmmaking not as a neutral recording practice but as a site of active dialogue, contestation, and intercultural engagement. But even while inviting dialogue and the staking of positions, Himpele and Castañeda remain agnostic about the sacred and the nature of the pilgrim's engagement with it. It is not a very curious absence, given the unquestioned secularity of the videomaker's own pilgrimage, but it does require us to ask: What would a performative documentary look like if it took seriously the experiential quest for the sacred and its polyvocalities, instead of the polyvocal sociocultural dynamics surrounding it?

Notes

*An underdeveloped version of this essay was presented at the Society for Applied Anthropology Annual Meeting in Mérida, Yucatán, March 2001, on a panel exploring the various Yucatecan responses to *Incidents of Travel in Chichén Itzá*. My friends Quetzil Castañeda and Jeff Himpele have encouraged my participation in dialogues around this video since our shared time at the Princeton University Department of Anthropology. It was Quetzil's invitation and camaraderie that brought me to the Yucatán and inspires our continuing collaborations. I am especially grateful to Jeff Himpele, both for cultivating my latecomer interests in film and visual anthropology and for taking time recently to reflect on why and how they made this video. I should note that my trip to participate in the Yucatán meeting was made possible by the financial assistance of the University of Vermont College of Arts and Sciences Dean's Fund and the Area and International Studies Program. Developing this essay further would not have been possible without the friendship, support, and collegiality of Brent Plate and Edna Melisa Rodríguez-Mangual, whose transdisciplinary promiscuity and acuity have inspired my own increasingly eclectic intellectual travels.

1. Jeff Himpele and Quetzil Castañeda, *Incidents of Travel in Chichén Itzá* (Watertown, MA: Documentary Educational Resources, 1997).
2. Ian Reader and Tony Walter, *Pilgrimage in Popular Culture* (London: Macmillan Press, 1993).
3. Bill Nichols, *Blurred Boundaries: Questions of Meaning in Contemporary Culture* (Bloomington: Indiana University Press, 1994).
4. John Faris, "Anthropological Transparency: Film, Representation and Politics," in *Film as Ethnography*, P. I. Crawford and D. Turton, eds. (Manchester: Manchester University Press, 1992), 171–82.
5. Nichols, *Blurred Boundaries*, 96–7.
6. Barry Keith Grant and Jeannette Sloniowski, "Introduction," *Documenting the Documentary: Close Readings of Documentary Film and Video*, Barry Keith Grant and Jeannette Sloniowski, eds. (Detroit: Wayne State University Press, 1998), 20.
7. Personal communication with Jeff Himpele, July 20, 2002.
8. On this, see Faris, "Anthropological Transparency."
9. John L. Stephens, *Incidents of Travel in Central America, Chiapas, and Yucatán* (New York: Harpers & Brothers, 1841).
10. Beatriz Sarlo, quoted in Nestor García Canclini, *Hybrid Cultures: Strategies for Entering and Leaving Modernity* (Minneapolis: University of Minnesota Press, 1995), 242.

11. It is important to note that this theoretical argument is one that Castañeda also develops in his ethnographic study of Chichén Itzá: Queztil Castañeda, *In the Museum of Maya Culture: Touring Chichén Itzá* (Minneapolis: University of Minnesota Press, 1996).

12. Valene Smith, ed., *Hosts and Guests: The Anthropology of Tourism*, 2d. ed. (Philadelphia: University of Pennsylvania Press, 1989).

13. Dennis O'Rourke, *Cannibal Tours* (Direct Line Cinema, 1988). See also Katharine Young, "Visuality and the Category of the Other," *Visual Anthropology Review* 8.1 (1992): 92–6.

14. Young, "Visuality," 92.

15. See Smith, *Hosts and Guests*.

16. Luis Vivanco, "Categories of Otherness and Tourism in *Incidents of Travel in Chichén Itzá,*" presentation at the Society for Applied Anthropology Annual Meeting, Mérida, Yucatán, March 2001.

17. Nelson Graburn, "Tourism: The Sacred Journey," in Smith, *Hosts and Guests*, 23.

18. Turner and Turner, quoted in Reader and Walter, *Pilgrimage*, 5.

19. Ibid., 8.

20. Turner quoted in Paula A. Ebron, "Tourists as Pilgrims: Commercial Fashioning of Transatlantic Politics," *American Ethnologist* 26.4 (1999): 910–932.

21. Joel Martin and Conrad Ostwalt, eds., *Screening the Sacred: Religion, Myth and Ideology in Popular American Film* (Boulder: Westview Press, 1995).

22. Paul Richards, "Against the Motion (2): Human Worlds are Culturally Constructed," in *Key Debates in Anthropology*, Tim Ingold, ed. (London: Routledge, 1996), 123.

23. Nichols, *Blurred Boundaries*, 76.

24. Nichols, *Blurred Boundaries*.

25. Arjun Appadurai and Carol Breckinridge, "Museums Are Good to Think: Heritage on View in India," *Museums and Communities: The Politics of Public Culture*, Ivan Karp, Christine Mullen Kreamer, and Steven D. Lavine, eds. (Washington, DC: Smithsonian Institution), 34–55.

Section Three

Making Films, Making Nations

Chapter Nine

Perfumed Nightmare:

Religion and the Philippine Postcolonial Struggle in Third Cinema

Antonio D. Sison

"Se esta ultimando la instalacion del cinematografico para der sessiones dentro de pocos dias." With this announcement of the inauguration of the first Lumiere *cinematographe* in a salon in Escolta, Manila (the installation of the cinema is almost finished, and sessions will start in a few days), the Philippines had its first acquaintance with the silver screen, in January 1897, just two years following the invention of the motion picture in Europe.[1] Curiously, it was also the final year of three centuries of Spanish colonization before the fraudulent cession of the islands to the United States for U.S. $20 million in the 1898 Treaty of Paris. The colonial conspiracy would have disastrous consequences in the shaping of Filipino culture:

> Filipino identity and consciousness now faced a concerted threat from the new colonizer. The colonial traits inculcated by the Spaniards—the legacy of ignorance, superstition, hierarchical values—all these still existing beneath the surface of the dynamic new revolutionary consciousness provided the new conquerors with a convenient basis for imposing their own norms. The counter-consciousness that animated the struggle for independence had hardly developed into a new consciousness before the consciousness was again being modified to suit the needs of a new colonial system.[2]

The popular byword that Philippine culture is "a product of three hundred years in a Spanish convent and forty years of Hollywood"[3] then makes sense. Three centuries of Spanish rule left the indelible seal of Roman Catholicism in the Philippines, making it the solitary Catholic nation in Asia, afloat in a sea of Islam, Hinduism, and Buddhism. Nearly half a decade of American rule ushered in a form of "civil religion," the positivist utopia of technology and progress with its promise of a Hollywood ending.

The centuries of colonial baggage had been compounded even further by the Philippine neocolonial class, whose constituents became willing custodians of colonial ideals and values. That said, it is not surprising that Philippine cinema has always coded the colonial/postcolonial milieu from which it emanates:

> The most important cinema in Southeast Asia is that of the Philippines, which offers a full reflection of that country's troubled past and serves as a striking example of the difficulties of establishing a national cinema under colonialism or neocolonial dominance.[4]

From the perspective of this unique, albeit complicated postcolonial scenario, I set out to explore how religion—expressed in the colonially infused Filipino folk Catholicism, and later, as reconfigured in the American Dream—had been worked out in a Filipino film entitled *Perfumed Nightmare (Mababangong Bangungot)*. The thoroughly original, satirical comedy was lensed by Filipino independent filmmaker Kidlat Tahimik (a.k.a. Eric de Guia) in 1976, at the apex of the U.S.-sponsored Marcos dictatorship. Completed on a shoestring budget of U.S. $10,000, *Perfumed Nightmare* became a cult phenomenon as it went on to win the coveted Prix de la Critique Internationale and both the Catholic and Ecumenical Jury prizes at the 1977 Berlin Film Festival and, soon after, found U.S. distribution through Francis Ford Coppola's Zoetrope company.

I choose *Perfumed Nightmare* as my case study for two reasons. First, because the film captures the trajectory of the Philippine postcolonial struggle and its contradictions from a distinctly Filipino perspective. Second, because it is widely acknowledged by scholars as an example of the research category known as Third Cinema, an aesthetic movement and critical theory that provides me with the theoretical framework and optic to posit an ideological analysis of the film. I discuss *Perfumed Nightmare* as Third Cinema in some detail later in the essay. At this juncture, a summary is instructive.

Plot Summary of *Perfumed Nightmare*

Perfumed Nightmare convoys the liberative journey of its principal character, Kidlat (a semi-autobiographical protagonist played by the filmmaker himself), who embodies the postcolonial contradictions of the Filipino. While observing the Catholic piety of his quaint village, Kidlat is bewitched by the American Dream. Images of American pop culture—the 1969 moon landing, the short-wave broadcast of "Voice of America," the Statue of Liberty, bubble-gum machines, and the Miss Universe beauty pageant—fill his imagination with the promise of a better life, a life awash in rapid technological advancement and economic progress. But well-meaning friends and relatives, among them the village guru Kaya, remind Kidlat of his genuine identity and potential as a Filipino. Kaya enthuses Kidlat to draw strength from the subversive memory of his father, a local war hero who lost his life in the years following the 1898 Treaty of Paris. He describes how Kidlat's father superhumanly blew away 15 American soldiers before he was finally killed. He then issues a pithy reminder: " . . . the sleeping typhoon must learn to blow again." Kidlat's ticket to wish fulfillment finally comes when an American businessman hires him to work for a chewing-gum business in Paris. The French capital would be for Kidlat a launchpad to his dream destination—Cape Canaveral in the United States. What transpires instead is a crisis of belief; Kidlat awakens to the inhumanity and injustice of first-world style hypercapitalism. In a startling series of sequences rendered in magic realism, Kidlat literally blows away symbolic images of Western sociocultural domination during a mock farewell party organized by his American boss. He then makes a personal declaration of independence: " . . . I declare myself independent from those who build bridges to the stars."

Perfumed Nightmare as Third Cinema

The quest for identity and justice, indeed, for human liberation, is cinematically problematized in the rich, symbolic images of *Perfumed Nightmare*. Alongside the works of other third-world directors such as Tomas Gutiérrez Alea, Mrinal Sen, and Ousmane Sembene, Kidlat Tahimik's *Perfumed Nightmare* is included in the research category known as Third Cinema.[5] The classification alludes not so much to the geographical origins of a given film as it does to the film's dedication to an authentic representation of third-world peoples who struggle to become agents of their own history in the aftermath of colonialism:

> What determines Third Cinema is the conception of the world, and not the genre or an explicit political approach. Any story, any subject can be taken up by Third Cinema. In the developing countries, Third Cinema is a cinema of decolonization, which expresses the will to national liberation, anti-mythic, anti-racist, anti-bourgeois, and popular.[6]

Founded by Latin American filmmakers Fernando Solanas and Octavio Getino in 1968, Third Cinema began as a social and artistic movement with a combative Marxist agenda, that of launching a "guerrilla cinema" hostile toward the dominance of Hollywood. Thus the Argentinean filmmakers distinguished between Third Cinema and other forms of cinema, necessarily classified as First Cinema (industrial/commercial cinema epitomized by the Hollywood model) and Second Cinema (mainly represented by European auteur cinema).

Reflecting the paradigm of decolonization proposed by Afro-Caribbean thinker Frantz Fanon in his 1961 work *The Wretched of the Earth*[7] and fueled further by their involvement in the production of the radical documentary *La Hora de los Hornos* (The hour of the furnaces, Argentina, 1968), Solanas and Getino saw Third Cinema as a virtual revolutionary weapon in the struggle for liberation and a strident challenge to the unequal symbolic exchange between Western filmmaking and the marginalized cinematic input of the third world. As such, "The camera is the inexhaustible expropriator of image-weapons; the projector, a gun that can shoot 24 frames per second."[8]

Later developments in Third Cinema, particularly the critical, comparative method of Teshome Gabriel, have become less stridulent and more methodical. Gabriel, an Ethiopian film scholar, is credited for his groundbreaking work on the development of a critical theory of Third Cinema in a third-world context.[9] Gabriel eloquently summarizes the Third Cinema experience as "moved by the requirements of its social action and contexted and marked by the strategy of that action."[10] He launches into a critical inquiry of Third Cinema by elaborating on the link between style and ideology, contending that a "study of style alone will not engender meaning. . . . Style is only meaningful in the context of its use—in how it acts on culture and helps illuminate the ideology within it."[11] Gabriel also underscores the role of Third Cinema as the custodian of subversive popular memory, a resource for third-world peoples in the face of colonially infused "official versions" of history. Thus Teshome Gabriel elevated the strident polemics of his Latin American predecessors into the level of critical theory. In its present evolutionary turn, Third Cinema critical theory is not so much a demolition order against the input of the American and European film industries as it is a requisite dialectical initiative that seeks to give voice and visibility to socially resonant films that spotlight the third-world experience and perspective, which have thus far been accorded only token attention in world cinema and in academic debates.

With Third Cinema providing heuristic touchstones, my task at this point is to examine how religion finds filmic representation in *Perfumed Nightmare*.

"You Shall Be With Me in Paradise"

In *Perfumed Nightmare*, the conjoined thematic and stylistic elements are worked out within the general rubric of postcolonial struggle, here taken to mean the ongoing quest for national identity on all fronts—social, cultural, political, economic—by third-world countries in the aftermath of colonialism and all its ongoing ramifications. This is, in fact, the sense of "postcolonial" mirrored in *Perfumed Nightmare*.

In the Philippine context, the experience of multiple colonizations contributed greatly to the misshaping of national culture and the atrophy of national pride. In classic colonial cultural conditioning, the colonizer/colonized dualism had been translated in terms of superiority/inferiority: The foreign culture is presented as the authentic, normative culture from which the indigenous culture, falsely identified in negative categories as inferior, must be patterned. Thus, "the civilizing process itself was predicated on the very notion that something was lacking in the colonial subjects (maturity, education, technology, salvation, and more) that only colonizers could provide, because of their superiority."[12]

That the Philippines is predominantly Roman Catholic is a Janus-faced statement. It can be an assertion of pride, the distinction that the Philippines is, in fact, preciously unique, the only Catholic nation in Asia. On the flipside, it is also a statement that recalls the national trauma of three centuries of oppressive Spanish rule, during which religion became a tool conveniently used by the colonizers to buttress and legitimize the wholesale "ownership" of a country and culture not their own. The systematic racial exploitation committed by Spanish *frailes* (monks) against Filipino nationals, justified under the mantle of the Catholic Church, is immortalized in two nineteenth-century novels, *Noli Me Tangere* (Touch me not) and *El Filibusterismo* (The subversive), the major literary works of Philippine national hero Jose P. Rizal. Rizal experienced untold suffering and, eventually, execution at the hands of the colonial church authorities who had mastered the art of deceit and religious-political intrigue.[13]

In *Perfumed Nightmare*, the representation of religion is first seen in the modification of colonial Roman Catholicism into folk Catholicism, a fusion of official Catholic practices and popular piety. As a former Spanish colony, the Philippines had preserved and perpetuated much of its erstwhile colonizer's religious traditions, at times, marrying them with indigenous religious forms rooted in animism and superstitious beliefs. Filipino theologian Benigno P. Beltran notes, "As the popular religious form of expression of the inarticulate, the unlettered and the disenfranchised, Folk Catholicism is a complex, amorphous phenomenon which does not admit to easy explanations."[14] Nonetheless, the phenomenon is worth examining for its indexical value for a Third Cinema ideological analysis. "Folk Catholicism has implications for the way reality is perceived, constructed and maintained by the masses."[15]

Perfumed Nightmare provides glimpses of Filipino folk Catholicism in the Lenten practice of self-flagellation. The corporal mortification rendered in semidocumentary reality makes for dramatic mise-en-scène. We see the backs of penitents being incised with blades. Masks and veils hide their faces, shrouding the ritual further in mystical enigma. The flagellants then begin to flog themselves with chains before the statue of the Blessed Virgin Mary in a ceremony of sadomasochistic violence. In a series of flashbacks, we see Kidlat among the penitents at varying periods of his life. In one disturbing cut, he is shown flagellating himself at five years old [fig. 9.1].

The practice of penitential self-mortification was unknown to ancient Filipinos. When first introduced by Spanish *frailes,* the reception for the ritual was, at best, lukewarm. Upon the infusion of popular beliefs, however, particularly the precolonial value known as *damay* (solidarity), the ritual began to make sense and take root in the culture. Self-flagellation came to be viewed as empathy for and participation in the passion of Jesus Christ.[16]

In *Perfumed Nightmare,* ritual self-flagellation is the specter of religion's role in the imposition and legitimation of Spanish domination over the Filipino subjects and the consequent perpetuation of a colonial culture of

Figure 9.1   "*Perfumed Nightmare* provides glimpses of Filipino folk Catholicism in the Lenten practice of self-flagellation. . . . In one disturbing cut, [Kidlat] is shown flagellating himself at five years old."

passivity and subservience. The depiction of the flagellants defaced by masks and veils emphasizes the dehumanizing ethos surrounding this phenomenon. Moreover, the portrayal of Kidlat flagellating himself at a very young age dramatizes how the roots of colonial inferiority run deep into the culture so that liberative currents are neither simple nor easy. This is ratified in the portrayal of Kidlat's Marian devotion. Prior to his departure for Paris, the film's protagonist prays to an image of the Virgin Mary, a life-size statue paraded by the townsfolk as part of the annual Lenten procession common everywhere in the Philippines. Kidlat beseeches the forgiveness of the Blessed Virgin for reneging on his yearly vow of self-flagellation: "O Holy Mary, thank you for granting my prayers. Forgive me for not beating myself as in previous years. We leave on Sunday, my wounds would not heal on time."

For Kidlat, self-flagellation takes on the religious imperative of a divine commandment so that being remiss in this duty is tantamount to sin, which, in typical Catholic sensibility, needs to be confessed and forgiven. Again, what is clearly represented here is the pacifying function of religion in the colonial hegemonic project; if submission to colonial domination is God's will, then to transgress this edict is a sin. *Perfumed Nightmare*'s creative layering of meaning clarifies the problematic further when we take a closer look at the very image of the Virgin Mary in the film's mise-en-scène. The statue, like most of the religious images introduced to the Philippines by the Spaniards, looks decidedly Iberian. The equation is not subtle: If the colonizers are spitting images of the gods, then the gods are the colonizers.[17] The portrayal of the divinization of the colonial/neocolonial classes is not unknown in Third Cinema. An equivalent representation can be seen in the Colombian film *One Day I Asked* (Julia Alvarez, 1970), in which a woman devotee praying in the church pronounces, "one thing is sure, he (God) eats at the boss' table."[18] In both the Colombian film and *Perfumed Nightmare*, God is kindred with the colonial/neocolonial powerholders, who are his exclusive image bearers and confidants, while the colonial subalterns are barred from such a privilege.

Syntagmatically, Kidlat and the other flagellating villagers are emblems of the human offerings sacrificed before the colonial altar. Effortlessly, the imagery has eerie resonances of the 1898 Treaty of Paris where the colonizers, in fact, played gods at the expense of the Filipino people, who became the unwitting pawns on the colonial chessboard.[19] It is therefore significant that in the latter portion of *Perfumed Nightmare*, Kidlat would find his own voice and personally "remap" his country's repressed history in the city of Paris.

As the scene of Kidlat's Marian devotion unfolds, we are confronted by a surprise turn, a deviation from realism that compounds the issue of religion in the postcolonial milieu. The statue of the Virgin Mary begins to speak.

Through the film's clever employment of voiceover, we hear the statue hilariously "talking back" to Kidlat. This connotes the perceived active and direct involvement of the divine in the real, day-to-day lives of Filipinos. What is telling for a Third Cinema interpretation of *Perfumed Nightmare,* however, is that the statue's pronouncements are pure comic gibberish spoken in American Hollywood slang:

> Kidlat, stop apologizing. You know my job here is a bore. . . . And you dear Kidlat, remember the first year you wanted to fly. I could not forget that at five years, you started using the chains, praying for a toy jet plane. And last year, that red mask, how sexy! That year you fell from the Mango tree and broke your back, you locked yourself in the ice factory. When they pulled you out, you were as hard as Judas' prick. Kidlat, you're okay in my book. See you in Lourdes, huh?

When interpreting the scene from the thematic framework of *Perfumed Nightmare,* an oppositional reading becomes appropriate. Comical and irreverent, the schizophrenic Spanish-American Virgin Mary trivializes the sacrifices of Kidlat and the other devotees as though all these were done for her enjoyment, because, as she puts it, "my job here is a bore." If it can be accepted that the flagellants emblematize the human cost laid at the altar of the colonial enterprise, then what becomes apparent here is that the altar has become American.

The representation of religion in the film thus segues to the symbolization of American colonial hegemony, which introduced a new civil religion based on the American Dream, with its positivist utopic liturgy of high technology and rapid progress. The concept of religion here is no longer confined to the organized ritual expressions undergirded by official doctrine; it extends to the shared views and values held by groups of people in society on the basis of faith. Robert N. Bellah coined the phrase "American Civil Religion"[20] to describe "certain common elements of religious orientation the great majority of Americans share" that have played a key role in the building of American institutions and have had a profound influence on the American way of life:

> What we have, then, from the earliest years of the republic is a collection of beliefs, symbols, and rituals with respect to sacred things and institutionalized in collectivity. This religion—there seems no other word for it—while not antithetical to and indeed sharing much in common with Christianity, was neither sectarian nor in any specific sense Christian.[21]

While the American civil religion embodies the most cherished principles of American nationhood, Bellah rightly points out that "like all religions, it has various deformations and demonic distortions."[22] The idea of "manifest destiny," a core concept of the American civil religion posited on the moral conviction that America was a nation set apart to spread across the globe as the godsent vanguard of democratic principles,[23] was used as a signet of divine approval for the U.S. expansionist incursion in the Philippines. In the years shortly after the colonial turnover sanctioned by the 1898 Treaty of Paris, between 200,000 to 500,000 Filipinos, many of them innocent civilians including women and children, were summarily killed by the Americans to quell a popular independence movement in what was described as "an orgy of racist slaughter."[24]

The impact of the colonial trauma on the indigenous culture was no less devastating, with its aftershocks still felt by generations of Filipinos until the present. Centuries of living as an oppressed, colonized people in their own homeland ingrained a "colonial mentality" among Filipinos in which things western are almost always taken to connote superiority. Renato Constantino maps the cultural malaise that plagues his own people:

> As a people, we always depreciate what is ours. Local products are discriminated against in our own country. Local talent is largely unappreciated, and whatever is recognized as local talent is merely the best imitation of American artistry, proudly labeled as such. There are brave attempts to rediscover our cultural heritage and to reestablish our ties with the past, but our cultural corruption is so pervasive that the job of rediscovering ourselves is a difficult one. Meanwhile, the majority avidly imitate each new fad of the West.[25]

In *Perfumed Nightmare* this theme is rendered in sharp relief by the American Dream—the ghost of American colonial superiority relentlessly haunting the Filipino psyche. Colonial mentality is enfleshed in the character of Kidlat, who is portrayed as a Filipino bewitched and captivated by American popular culture. There is Kidlat's constant absorption of American news through the short-wave broadcast of "The Voice of America," his idolization of Miss Universe contestants, and his fascination with first-world technological advancement, seen in his obsession with space travel and the American moon landing. When an American businessman asks Kidlat why he loves America so much, the Filipino's naive answer has a painful ring of truth to it, "In America I can be an astronaut. Here [in the Philippines] I am only a *jeepney* driver." Like many Filipinos still driven by colonial mentality, Kidlat derives aspiration and certitude from the civil religion of the American Dream. This is symbolically validated early on in the film when Kidlat cuts out the photograph of Miss U.S.A. from a 1974 Miss Universe poster and frames it alongside an icon of the Virgin Mary. The 1974 Miss Universe beauty pageant is significant because it represents the perpetuation of the American Dream by the Philippine neocolonial class during the U.S.-sponsored dictatorial regime of Ferdinand Marcos.[26] This, in fact, was the circumstantial background reflected in *Perfumed Nightmare*. If Marcos's gameplan with the United States rested on political, economic, and military power, his wife Imelda waltzed to the tune of American popular culture. The 1974 edition of the pageant, which was hosted in Manila, was one of the former first lady's ostentatious pet projects and a mirror of her fascination for Uncle Sam's "soft power." Marcos himself is alluded to in the film in the religious statue of San Marcos (St. Mark) whom, Kidlat believes, will save the Philippines in the eventuality of an atomic war.[27]

As earlier mentioned, *Perfumed Nightmare* represents religion as it is sublimated in the utopian promise of American-style rapid modernization and technological advancement. Before bringing this dimension to sharper focus, it is useful to consider William C. McLoughlin's clarification of the link between the utopian vision of the American civil religion and the normative Biblical conceptions of utopia:

> . . . our dreams of success, our continual evaluation of the pursuit of happiness in terms of higher standards of living and the mass distribution of "creature comforts" can be described better as a variant upon the search for the new Eden or the coming Kingdom of God on earth as we think it is in heaven.[28]

The American reappropriation of the biblical utopic visions unfolds in *Perfumed Nightmare* with the American businessman's decision to relocate his business to the United States. This would be for Kidlat the anticipated fulfillment of his American Dream. The American reminds Kidlat in honeyed words that he would be the first Filipino to fly at supersonic speed via the Concorde jet. In the scene that follows, we see a surrealist rendering of the face of the American on a stained glass window. The backlit window gives the image an ethereal, divinized radiance. Kidlat's face, more softly lit, is seen in the foreground, frame left [fig. 9.2]. In a sinister sequestration of some of the last few words of Jesus Christ in the New Testament crucifixion account, the American addresses Kidlat: "Tomorrow, Kidlat, tomorrow . . . you shall be with me in Paradise."

The equation has bizarre representational implications that dovetail with the earlier portrayal of the Spanish colonizers as exclusive image bearers of the divine. If the American businessman is cast in the role of the messiah, then it follows that Kidlat is the condemned thief in need of salvation. Again, the colonial project surfaces—the inferior colonial subjects are a problem to be solved. However, Kidlat would spot the proverbial "tail of the serpent" as he begins to articulate his simmering doubt: "Is this the Paradise I prayed for? Is this the Paradise I dreamed of?"

The Sleeping Typhoon

The Third Cinema dialectical presupposition is that religion can be used to oppress as well as to empower. It does not criticize religion per se but the powerholders who use it for their own national profit and collective egoism. In *Perfumed Nightmare,* religion that continues to be haunted by the phantoms of colonial superiority and domination is judged as false; it is presumed not to be a reflection of the divine or an authentic relation to the divine and is thus appraised as not redemptive. Consequently, Kidlat struggles to break free from the fragrantly masked culture of passivity wrought by folk Catholicism and the vacuous utopian promise of the American Dream.

The answers to Kidlat's insightful query come in succeeding scenes in the latter portion of the film. An uninterrupted long take showing a wooden horse figure, a recollection object[29] carved out of the rifle of Kidlat's war-hero father and mounted on Kidlat's *jeepney* (a colorful passenger vehicle

Figure 9.2 " . . . we see a surrealist rendering of the face of the American on a stained glass window. The backlit window gives the image an ethereal, divinized radiance. Kidlat's face, more softly lit, is seen in the foreground, frame left."

commonly used in the Philippines as a means of mass transport) as it passes through a Paris artery, signifies the end of Kidlat's dreams of progress. Paris here is completely unrecognizable, a city that has imploded in its own hypercapitalistic rubble in a way that resembles Lars von Trier's depiction of postwar Germany as a dark watery grave in *Europa* (Denmark, 1992). What is established here is that the promised utopia of progress turns out to be a dystopic dead end. The dynamic movement of the horse figure against the backdrop of a static Paris in ruins signals a transformation in Kidlat's character. His resolve to be liberated from the "perfumed nightmare" has become a praxical imperative.

In the final reckoning of the mock farewell party prior to his departure for the United States, Kidlat refuses to allow passivity and subservience to be the order of the day as he unmasks the nightmare behind his dreams of western-style progress. Rendered in magic realism, he literally blows away at the masked Western guests. In an analogous sequence, Kidlat invokes the same superhuman powers when he boards one of the giant chimneys in Paris and causes it to fly to the heavens by the power of his breath. Reprising the myth surrounding his father's superpowers that enabled him to literally blow away accosting American sentries in the aftermath of the Treaty of Paris, Kidlat has himself become an embodiment of Kaya's prophetic and liberating proverb: "When the typhoon blows off its cocoon, the butterfly embraces the sun. . . . Where is your true strength, Kidlat? Where is your real strength? The sleeping typhoon must learn to blow again."

That the character of Kidlat would embody the utopian vision of the liberative typhoon is hinted at early on in the film. In the opening sequence, in which he is shown symbolically pulling a toy jeepney through the bridge in Balian, Kidlat asserts self-reflexively—"I am Kidlat Tahimik. I choose my vehicle and I can cross this bridge." The reference to self agency is clear but what also provides a clue to the subsequent turn of events is the very name "Kidlat Tahimik." Translated as "silent lightning," the ironic word-play carries utopic connotations—Kidlat Tahimik is a gathering tempest, a revolution waiting to happen. *Perfumed Nightmare* metaphorizes the typhoon as a utopian signifier for social change in a way reminiscent of Vsevold Pudovkin's similar but more literal use of the "storm" as a metaphor for anticolonial revolution in the climactic denouement of *Storm Over Asia* (Russia, 1928).

Utopia, in this sense, is grounded in the dissatisfaction over the status quo perpetuated by the current world order. The alienating situation, in the case of *Perfumed Nightmare*, the postcolonial trauma and its manifold expressions, yields liberative potential, the power to reimagine the possibility of a new emancipative order. The concept is akin to theologian Edward Schillebeeckx's notion of "negative experiences of contrast,"[30] the dialectical tension between the human quest for justice in a world that is running short of it. Schillebeeckx argues that it is the very experience of injustice that yields cognitive power when it brings about indignation and protest, the refusal to acquiesce to situations of meaningless suffering and disordered relations. The experience of a positive moment found within the crucible of critical negativity provides the oil for the rekindling of human hope and for the possibility of praxis.

Additionally, I am convinced that *Perfumed Nightmare* does not discount the role of divine agency as a catalyzing force toward the fulfillment of the utopian vision and the desired social change. The last frame of the film's closing credits shows a postage stamp, a child's artwork depicting Kidlat sitting by his magical spaceship in some cosmic environment. This cinematic clue validates that Kidlat had reached some celestial destination. Taken in conjunction with the several allusions to liberative cosmic powers in the film, for example, the liberating typhoon, the supernatural breath that enables Kidlat to "fly" to the heavens, I equate this quasireligious hint with what the filmmaker Tahimik refers to as the precolonial value of *Bathala Na*.[31] Translated as "May God's will be done," *Bathala Na* holds utopian significance because it is posited on the belief that when one offers his or her best efforts to a worthwhile endeavor, the divine cosmic forces cooperate. As such, *Bathala Na* represents the marriage of human and divine agency. *Perfumed Nightmare*'s open-ended ambiguity is not nearly as graphically mystical as that of Stanley Kubrick's anti-positivist science fiction opus *2001: A Space Odyssey* (1968) but it is no less cosmic; the allusion to a divine power "greater than ourselves" undeniably factors into the utopian vision of the film.

Thus it becomes clear in the postcolonial universe of *Perfumed Nightmare* that authentic religion is a verb as much as it is a noun—it is the empowering ground principle that enables the Filipino to break free from the enslaving cocoon of colonially infused "religion" into a new, emancipative sociocultural vision. It is the rediscovery of the divine presence in the eye of the liberative storm. Reverberating in the voice of the wise Filipino guru Kaya, God's interlocution quickens the Philippine postcolonial quest—"Where is your true strength, Kidlat? Where is your real strength? The sleeping typhoon must learn to blow again."

Notes

1. Clodualdo del Mundo, "Philippines," in *The Films of ASEAN,* Jose F. Lacaba, ed. (Manila: ASEAN Committee on Culture and Information, 2000), 89.

2. Renato Constantino, *Neocolonial Identity and Counter-Consciousness: Essays on Cultural Decolonization,* Istvan Meszaros, ed. (London: Merlin Press, 1978), 65.
3. Jose F. Lacaba, introduction to *The Films of ASEAN,* Jose F. Lacaba, ed. (Manila: ASEAN Committee on Culture and Information, 2000), xiii.
4. Roy Armes, *Third World Film Making and the West* (Berkeley: University of California Press, 1987), 151–152.
5. Stephen Crofts, "Concepts of National Cinema," in *The Oxford Guide to Film Studies,* John Hill and Pamela Gibbons, eds. (New York: Oxford University Press, 1998), 390.
6. Fernando Solanas and Octavio Getino quoted in Michael Chanan, "The Changing Geography of Third Cinema," *Screen* 4.36 (winter 1997).
7. Frantz Fanon, *The Wretched of the Earth,* Constance Farrington, trans. (New York: Grove Press, 1963).
8. Fernando Solanas and Octavio Getino, "Towards a Third Cinema," in *Third World Cinema,* Simon Field and Peter Sainsbury, eds. (London: Afterimage Publishing, 1971), 29.
9. Teshome Gabriel, "Towards a Critical Theory of Third World Films" in *Questions of Third Cinema,* Jim Pines and Paul Willemen, eds. (London: British Film Institute, 1994), 30–51.
10. Ibid., 40. Gabriel also explains that "the ultimate goal of Third Cinema is to present their audiences with a rational interpretation of a historically defined reality so that a line of causation can be established" (Teshome Gabriel, *Third Cinema in the Third World: The Aesthetics of Liberation* [Ann Arbor: UMI Research Press, 1979], 97).
11. Gabriel, "Towards a Critical Theory," 41.
12. Benito M. Vergara, Jr., *Displaying Filipinos: Photography and Colonialism in Early 20th Century Philippines* (Quezon City: University of the Philippines Press, 1995), 25.
13. Rizal's passion and crucifixion on the cross of colonial oppression finds cinematic expression in the acclaimed Filipino film *Bayaning 3rd World* (Third world hero), which satiricizes the guileful politics of Spanish colonial Catholicism in the revered martyr's lifetime.
14. Benigno P. Beltran, *The Christology of the Inarticulate: An Inquiry into the Filipino Understanding of Jesus the Christ* (Manila: Divine Word Publications, 1987), 5. Additionally, Anscar Chupungco rightly points out that "popular" does not refer to the "popularity" of a given religious practice. In the context of its use, the appellation is meant to distinguish folk religious practices from official, church-sanctioned liturgy. Anscar Chupungco, *Liturgical Inculturation: Sacramentals, Religiosity, and the Catechesis* (Collegeville: Liturgical Press, 1992), 101.
15. Beltran, *The Christology of the Inarticulate,* 5.
16. Ibid., 115.
17. Similarly, studies have indicated that Filipinos had become so conditioned to the image of Christ as Caucasian that the representation of Christ as a Filipino failed to generate acceptance in the Philippines. Ibid., 128.

18. Gabriel, *Third Cinema in the Third World*, 18.
19. D. R. SarDesai, *Southeast Asia: Past and Present* (Boulder: Westview Press, 1994), 144.
20. Robert N. Bellah, "Civil Religion in America," in *Religion in America*, William G. McLoughlin and Robert N. Bellah, eds. (Boston: Houghton Mifflin Company, 1968), 3–23.
21. Ibid., 10.
22. Ibid., 14.
23. Charles W. Kegley Jr. and Eugene R. Wittkopff, *American Foreign Policy*, 5th. ed. (New York: St. Martin's Press, 1996), 35–36.
24. Gabriel Kolko, *Main Currents in Modern American History* (New York: Pantheon Books, 1976), 286–287.
25. Constantino, *Neocolonial Identity and Counter-Consciousness*, 134–135.
26. Ted Lerner suggests that the fascination with beauty pageants among a number of Filipinos is a colonial influence. "Some say it has something to do with the Philippines' Spanish heritage. The country had been colonized by the Spanish for nearly 400 years and in most Latin and South American countries today, beauty pageants are also a national obsession. Some Filipinos say that the idea, like so many in their country, came from America and that Filipinos just gave their full attention to it." Observing the 1994 Miss Universe Pageant, the second time the event was held in Manila, Lerner notes that this obsession was capitalized on by the media, who covered the event "like it was the moon landing" ("The Eye of the Beholder: 1994 Miss Universe Pageant in the Philippines," *Transpacific* 9 [October 1994]: 58).
27. In *Perfumed Nightmare*, Kidlat is tasked to transport the statue of San Marcos to church via his jeepney. The Marcos-U.S. link is established in the scene, in the ambient sound of a radio broadcast of Marcos delivering a speech as Kidlat narrates, "My most important passenger is San Marcos. . . . it is said that when the Americans were bombing the Japanese in the war, San Marcos protected us from the mad American bombs (Marcos fought in the allied forces in World War 2). . . . I know that when there will be an atomic war, San Marcos will protect me from the H-bomb."
28. William G. McLoughlin and Robert Bellah, introduction to *Religion in America*, McLoughlin and Bellah, eds. (Boston: Houghton Mifflin Company, 1968), xvi.
29. Laura U. Marks defines the recollection object as "an irreducibly material object that encodes collective memory," correlative to the Deluezian conception of the "radioactive fossil," which is an "indexical trace of an object that once existed." Laura U. Marks, *The Skin of the Film: Intercultural Cinema, Embodiment, and the Senses* (Durham: Duke University Press, 2000), 77.
30. Edward Schillebeeckx, *Jesus: An Experiment in Christology*, Hubert Hoskins, trans. (New York: Crossroad Publishing, 1995), 479.
31. *Bathala Na* is the rerooting of the more common expression *Bahala Na* ("let come what may"), which is, Tahimik argues, a colonial "bastardization" of the original value, here taken in a negative, defeatist sense as a shirking of responsibility, a fatalistic resignation to the status quo, which is left in the

hands of the divine. *Bahala na* is the resultant attitude shaped by centuries of colonial conditioning that contributed to the legitimization of the unequal master-slave equation that characterized the relationship between the colonizer and the colonized. Tahimik, "Midlife Choices: Filmmaking vs. Fillmaking," in *Primed for Life: Writings on Midlife by 18 Men*, Kalaw-Tirol, ed. (Pasig City: Anvil Publishing, 1997), 41.

Chapter Ten

Pathologies of Violence:

Religion and Postcolonial Identity in New Zealand Cinema

Janet Wilson

Introduction: Puritanism and Postcolonial New Zealand

In the essentially nonconformist, secular society of New Zealand in which the "civilizing" culture of Britain has traditionally been only a thin veneer, religion has obtained an uneven purchase, no doubt contributing to the settlers' sense of "cultural emptiness."[1] Statistics show that church attendance has always been lower than in Australia; and since the "watershed year" of 1967 and increased secularization, observance in mainstream religions has declined, although minority charismatic movements and Pacific Island congregations have been dynamic.[2] Social problems associated with the pioneering and settler past in which Christianity played an ambivalent role—being either embraced or ignored—have emerged in the form of aberrant psychologies and pathologies of violence. This is evidenced, for example, in a string of bizarre murders through the twentieth century, in the literary tradition's preoccupation with the outsider—in which the "Man Alone" motif is the quintessential myth—and marginalization in general, and in the uneasy perception of being excentric, a nation at the edge of the world, all suggest some distortion of social norms.[3]

The development of New Zealand's cinema can be correlated to this somewhat decentered, negative syndrome, for local films have persistently challenged the construction of the average suburban lifestyle: From the larrikin, outsider stereotypes of the road-show movie *Good-bye Pork Pie*

(1980) and the small-town conmen of *Came a Hot Friday* (1984), it was but a short step to movies of the 1990s about disturbed or deviant individuals and dysfunctional families.[4]

The scenes of family violence in movies directed by Jane Campion, Lee Tamahori, and Peter Jackson—the triumvirate that has internationalized New Zealand cinema—stamp the films as antipodean melodramas. Through disoriented characters who have lost their moral bearings, who misinterpret or defy social values, succumbing to irrational emotions or resorting to primitive violence, they explore the blurring of boundaries between self and Other, between the so-called normal and abnormal.

This chapter examines four New Zealand films for their images of dislocated subjectivities, which, in relation to issues of gender and the family unit in a postcolonial society, might be read as representative of New Zealand's changing national identity. The vengeful mood of *The Piano* (1993) and *Heavenly Creatures* (1994) suggests a distortion of the moral code of Puritanism, which in *Heavenly Creatures* appears in the spiritual, religious dimension of the daughters' alternative fantasy worlds and their romantic longing for life through death. *Broken English* (1997) and *Once Were Warriors* (1994), by contrast, go beyond violence and the family-in-crisis motif to provide alternative sources of spiritual meaning and images of domestic and social cohesiveness.[5]

New Zealand's celebrated "cinema of unease," using the country's most marketable assets—its spectacular landscape and quirky Kiwi humor—includes the individual peculiarities and self-destructiveness associated with Puritanism on the one hand and the fragmentation of Maori culture under colonialism on the other.[6] The "dark and anguished side of New Zealand cinema,"[7] as of its novels, now almost a critical commonplace, suggests "something as yet unnamed" associated with "the cultural dominance of evasiveness and guilt about the nation's history."[8] As this history can be interpreted according to the dominating category of gender—for colonization included women as well as Maori—in ways comparable to the dominance of race in the United States and South Africa and of class in the United Kingdom, issues to do with gender, often controlling representations of racial difference, are central to the postcolonial rehabilitation of national identity.[9] Bleak-black dramas emerge in narratives of women who transgress (the daughters in *Heavenly Creatures,* Ada in *The Piano*) and men who abuse (Jake in *Once Were Warriors* and the father in *Broken English*). Their dark side can be seen as an unresolved residue from colonialism, an unexamined element in the New Zealand psyche, and to that extent a continued identifying signifier of the nation's culture to overseas audiences. Coupled with its ongoing attack on Puritan ethics, Kiwi cinema's representation of this "darkness" as oscillating between the banal and comic provides a basis for developing new structures of identity.

As Australian film also implicitly condemns "the well off mature, heterosexual unit" because it "signifies the endemic non-violability of a certain way of life," the dysfunctional family might be seen as a feature of antipodean cinema, identifying its brand of humor.[10] Jane Campion had already made it central to her art-house signature in the portrait of the psychotic daughter in *Sweetie* (1989). Comic situations based on the gruesomeness of family ties in *Muriel's Wedding* (1994) and on gay relationships impacting on the nuclear family in *The Adventures of Priscilla the Queen of the Desert* (1994) have widened the emotional repertoire and social range of Australian cinema. While contemporary horror movies and psychological thrillers that draw on perverse sexual behavior and tales of violence might suggest a fashion for dysfunctional families, nevertheless the topsy turvy family unit provides one format by which the down-under cinema can compete with Hollywood.[11] Jane Smith, identifying a generic sameness in New Zealand film—"domestic drama with a certain edginess about history"—has noted that the distilling of large social issues into a concentration on character conflict bears resemblances to Hollywood cinema.[12] Her argument that sensationalizing domestic conflict deflects attention from larger issues, such as the socially divisive neocolonialism of globalization, and of the nation's relationship to the rest of the world, is echoed in recent criticism of the film industry's refusal in the 1990s to fund social documentary-type films that might draw attention to social inequalities.[13] Yet the major films confirm the pattern that had already appeared in the literature, caused by the unweaving of the strands that constructed colonial society; local formats representing individuals at odds with their society that locate as sources of social ills either the "spiritually self maiming" Puritan ethos or, alternatively, ethnicity trapped in its own minority status.

All these films are inflected by a postcolonial critique of New Zealand society that lifts up the carpet to expose the shortcomings of its founding myths: the "pastoral paradise and the just city," linked to the breathtaking, unspoilt landscape, the myths of egalitarianism, lack of class distinction, and the racial harmony.[14] They can be interpreted further in terms of current debates about home and belonging, race relations, and migrancy. Since the late 1970s, when the myth of racial equality was exploded following the revisions of the Treaty of Waitangi (the country's founding document by which sovereignty was ceded to the British Crown in 1840) and the convening in the 1980s of the Waitangi Tribunal to deal with Maori land claims, criticism has broadened to include other grievances: Some radical Maori now call for independent sovereignty.[15] The 1980s and early 1990s were also a period of radical economic change as New Zealand was propelled from its largely agrarian economy into the free market, deregulated world of late global capitalism. Although the cinema's focus on upheaval within the family unit undoubtedly reflects the high degree of domestic violence that occurs in some sections of New Zealand society, it can also can be linked to this postcolonial repositioning of the nation as the attempt to make reparations for the appropriations of its colonial past ushered in the ideology of biculturalism, and as the free market economy known as Rogernomics simultaneously widened the gap between rich and poor.[16] The narratives of exceptional events involving unusual individuals can be interpreted as metonymic of colonialism's dislocations—settler fragmentation, Maori disenfranchisement—for the film industry presents a world of radical dissonance, of skewed social norms. And if this focus on personal drama unwittingly endorses neocolonial practices and attitudes of the present, as Jane Smith claims, then this only reflects the limits of postcolonial critique. Revisiting the past by invoking the Treaty to restore land that was wrongfully taken or the indigenous culture that was neglected often means reinscribing many features of colonialism under a different guise.[17]

New Zealand's geographical remoteness and prolonged economic and cultural dependence on the United Kingdom until the 1960s mean that religion other than as a form of worship has not achieved great prominence in the life of the nation. As a country best known for its sporting achievements, it has produced few religious leaders or philosophical thinkers; religion has not featured prominently in its cinema either, which remains resolutely secular in its social critique. Instead its rural, pioneering traditions led to a pragmatic do-it-yourself approach in devising provisional solutions to practical problems; this is epitomized in "vernacular metaphors" such as the number 8 fencing wire used in the joke finale of Roger Donaldson's Smash Palace (1981).[18] The new society was identified with a "transported" Puritanism, a doctrine that originated in seventeenth-century English society and became most powerful in Victorian England. Puritanism, as it moved with British settlers to New Zealand, has taken on the status of another national myth and an explanation of settler morality. Pakeha (white New Zealander) society has developed an ambivalence toward this "transported" Puritanism, which became identified with British hegemony—a form of the cultural cringe—and, as Pakeha society became increasingly secularized, toward piety in general.

New Zealand Puritanism is a code of social respectability linked to mainstream Christianity: Anglicanism, Methodism, Plymouth Brethren, and Scottish Presbyterianism (Catholicism was treated as a minor, separate faith, often socially stigmatized). But its repressed emotion, powerful work ethic, and moral rectitude made Puritanism "self-maiming," "a flawed source of spirituality."[19] Measuring excellence according to British middle-class behavior, as has been pointed out, increased the individual's potential for guilt and fragmentation and inhibited emotional development.[20]

Puritanism was most deeply entrenched in relation to sexual deviance. The novelist Jane Mander denounced the ethos as "this awful disease," and the New Zealand novel originated in opposition to Puritanism, and in reaction to mainstream society's valuing of heterosexuality and the nuclear family.[21] The short stories of Frank Sargeson, a covert homosexual writer from a rigid Puritan background, pioneered the vernacular tradition; Maurice Gee extensively treats Puritanism in the "Plumb trilogy," and his creation of Plumb, a Presbyterian minister who cannot tolerate his son's homosexuality, illustrates the religion's worst features. Its damaging effects are most recently charted in the novels of Noel Virtue, a homosexual writer reacting to his Plymouth Brethren upbringing.[22]

The Piano (1993) and Heavenly Creatures (1994)

Both films show affinities with the New Zealand literary tradition in their critique of bourgeois society and their affirmation of the marginal; both explicitly foreground female subjectivity. *Heavenly Creatures* concerns the true-life murder by schoolgirl Pauline Parker (played by Melanie Lynskey) and her friend Juliet Hulme (played by Kate Winslet) of Pauline's mother, Honora Rieper (as Honora and Herbert Rieper, Pauline's father, never married, Pauline was convicted under her mother's maiden name of Parker), with a brick wrapped in a stocking. Director Peter Jackson relocates respectable middle-class Christchurch society's shock and revulsion at this gruesome deed and complicates the position of the viewer by introducing a sympathetic portrayal of the girls' *folie a deux*.[23] *The Piano* redefines the romantic commonplaces of Victorian repression and liberation, represented by Ada McGrath (Holly Hunter) in the erotically charged, adulterous love triangle with her husband, Alasdair Stewart (Sam Neill), and the Maori-Pakeha settler, George Baines (Harvey Keitel), by showing her sexuality as transgressive and excessive. Both use a varied stylistic repertoire, self-consciously redefining and commenting on different genres. Jackson uses tourist bureau newsreel footage to introduce 1950s Christchurch as the most British of the New Zealand cities. Exact locations—the Hulme family home in Ilam and the classrooms of Christchurch Girls' High School—create a contrast to the hyperbolic, computer-generated images of the girl's fantasy Fourth World, or heaven, and the parallel world of Borovnia.[24] The delinquent daughters are aligned with the exhilarating powers of the imagination, middle-class conformist Christchurch society with stuffy British conservatism. Campion also contrasts diegetic settings and landscapes with a distancing antirealism to suggest the sensibility of the Victorian female encountering a crude settler society, and inflects her romance with Gothic elements.[25] Ada's newly awakened desires, for example, work in tension with images of her incarceration in the house by Stewart: The two scenes in which she strokes her naked husband on the bed are shot in a saturated golden light. The signatures of both directors validate the life of the senses and the imagination as empowering expressive modes.

The Piano begins in a critique of colonialism, in particular Scottish Presbyterianism, although its real focus is on female desire, from a twentieth-century "feminist" perspective.[26] Opening in 1850s Glasgow, but moving to colonial New Zealand, the buttoned-up characters of Ada McGrath and Alasdair Stewart are defined at first through a negative Victorian lens. Ada's muteness, occurring at the age of six when she first started playing the piano, is due to a "dark secret," as her "mind's voice" tell us. It makes her comparable to the dispossessed colonial subject whose history, having been silenced, remains invisible. But unlike the Maori, who as Linda Dyson points out, are cast in the colonial stereotype of noble savage,[27] and therefore have no access to such self-representation, Ada's self-imposed silence is a strategy rather than a disability,[28] a "declaration of her marginalization from phallogocentric discourse."[29] Campion also stresses her vulnerability within the tangled structures of patriarchal power. Raised without a mother she lacks the opportunity that the mother-daughter relationship provides to develop that sense of mirroring on which identity based.[30] Bearing a child, Flora, out of wedlock, she represents a problem for her father, who arranges her marriage—as a mail-order bride—to the ambitious Scot Alasdair Stewart in return for a handsome financial settlement. Ada's piano provides her with an alternative mode of expression that is an erotic-creative outlet for her passionate nature; her close relationship with Flora, who can speak for her by communicating in a private sign language, provides another form of discourse.

Stewart, in contrast to Ada, represents the Scottish settler's displaced consciousness, for his behavior can be aligned with the violent subjugation caused by the colonial moment of rupture from the old world; in exemplifying the problems of adapting to the new world he is also represented as a victim of his culture. Symbolizing the straitjacketed Victorian patriarch, literally too big for his tight-fitting and awkward-looking clothes, and attempting to control his environment and to acquire land, he is ridiculed by the camera.[31] Stewart's "Protestant utilitarianism," allowing little appreciation of aesthetic values, leads to the second masculine contract involving Ada, his trading her piano with Baines in return for an 80-acre block of land. His increasing emotional alienation is suggested by his voyeuristic peering at Baines and Ada's lovemaking through a hole in the floor of Baines's hut. By such deliberate misalignments, which set him up as an object of the viewer's critical gaze, his masculinity is further diminished.

Campion hints at a Polynesian alternative to Victorian sexual mores in Ada's lover, George Baines, who has "gone native" and functions as an interpreter, moving between Maori and British cultures. Baines's more relaxed attitudes, his sensuality, and his lifestyle align him suggestively with the Maori; the green and blue tones of his dwelling, surrounded by native trees and ferns, and his facial markings resembling tattoos all evoke a precolonial existence and semiwarrior status. The flowering of Ada's sexuality, represented in the exchange of sexual favors for piano keys as her intimacy with Baines develops, is therefore represented as in tune with the natural, indigenous world.

In much of the heated controversy surrounding *The Piano*, Campion has been accused of neocolonialism in using the Maori as backdrop, representing them through a colonial gaze as happy-go-lucky, ineffectual, sexually crude, even effeminate; yet, this was a choice deliberately made in deference to the film's controlling critical framework, which explores Presbyterian repression relocated in a colonial climate.[32] As Ada's desire drives the plot and as the articulation of desire through her relationship with Baines ultimately establishes her within dominant phallogocentric discourse, the narrative necessarily follows the logic of unravelling the adulterous love affair and by implication the cultural critique in which it is nested. Ada's silence suggests that just as Puritanism contains the seeds of its own destruction, so it breeds alternative ways of adapting to new conditions. With an aesthetic sensibility that contrasts to the Protestant virtue of controlling the emotions, she rides roughshod over social convention in favor of a greater passion and intensity of feeling than Protestant culture usually permits.[33] The willfulness of her childhood decision to become mute, "a dark talent" according to her father, proves to be self-contradictory when after her decision to follow her piano overboard, she involuntarily detaches herself and rises to the surface. To her surprise her desire to live overturns her focus on silence and death.

The Piano's melodramatic moments, foregrounding a punitive approach to sexuality, betrayal, and marital failure, serve both structural and aesthetic purposes. In terms of the film's critique of colonialism, of which the romantic entanglements can be seen as metonymic, they register the disruption and relocation of that ideology. The moment of violent subjugation associated with Stewart—the settler's abrupt brutal severance from family and home that is the effect of migration—is replayed in two crucial scenes: The mock decapitation of the shadow figures in the Victorian melodrama of "Bluebeard's Castle," acted out by the Scottish settlers, foreshadows, with its overlay of social chaos, Stewart's severing of Ada's finger when he hears of her betrayal. These contrasting but parallel scenes of violence are counterbalanced by the imagery of Ada's resurrection from the sea, and the imaging of the sea itself as a place from which new meaning can emerge [fig. 10.1]. Stewart's decision to hand over Ada to Baines acknowledges the logic of his own violence; it decrees a break with the past and to that extent a rejection of its inhibiting protocols and assumptions. In this new world artifacts such as the piano are associated with bourgeois British society and ultimately dispensed with. The new world thus becomes a land of new possibilities, as Linda Hardy has argued, enabling "natural occupancy," that is, "the making of a settlement without a colony."[34]

Heavenly Creatures, in contrast to the idealized, fictional world of *The Piano,* is a psychological reconstruction of the Parker-Hulme matricide that occurred in Christchurch on June 11, 1954: This lurid murder became a cause celebre in New Zealand, and as the mental state of the two girls was exhaustively investigated at the time of their trial, medical records and transcripts of the trial itself have provided material for several books and accounts.[35] The charge that they were lesbians was dismissed from the trial, although this speculation has fuelled a recent account: Intense adolescent psychosexual relations may be homoerotically charged but are usually sexually unfulfilled.[36] Peter Jackson and his scriptwriter, Fran Walsh, reconstruct the drama from the point of view of Pauline Parker, using her diaries and taking the title from her poem, "The Ones I Worship" in which she imagines herself as another daughter of the Hulmes: "'Tis indeed a miracle, one must feel, / That two such heavenly creatures are real, ... /

Figure 10.1   "These contrasting but parallel scenes of violence are counterbalanced by the imagery of Ada's resurrection from the sea, and the imaging of the sea itself as a place from which new meaning can emerge."

And these wonderful people are you and I."[37] In stressing the intensity of the friendship, Jackson and Walsh image it in terms of powerful libidinal desires.

Jackson had already made his name as a satirist of New Zealand bourgeois society, attacking middle-class norms such as the masculine ideal of mateship in his comedy splatter movies, *Bad Taste* (1987) and *Braindead* (1992), and manipulating Kiwi iconography in order to subvert its most sacred emblems: the Queen, Empire, and Puritan propriety. As in his splatstick movies, Jackson encourages the audience to laugh at what is considered normal, privileging transgression by suggesting that normality itself is uncivilized.[38] In *Heavenly Creatures* the critical viewpoint is controlled by invented "alternative" dimensions: Juliet's exotic Fourth World, or "heaven," which contains "non-Christian" saints such as Mario Lanza and James Mason, and the parallel kingdom of Borovnia, made of plasticine models of castles, dungeons, princes, and kings. To their teacher's outrage Juliet mocks the British royal family in an essay read out in class about the imaginary royal family of Borovnia. Through the plasticine Borovnians the adolescents hit back at society's moral guardians. The minister who visits Juliet in the hospital and the psychiatrist whom Pauline visits with her mother and who introduces the taboo word "homosexual" in order to explain the girls pathological attachment are eviscerated by the murderous prince of Borovnia, Diello. The camera cuts to a poster on the psychiatrist's wall of a kiwi icon—illustrating how to be a healthy kiwi—representing the "official" understanding of sexual difference as "abnormal." As Barbara Creed points out, Jackson's style of antipodal inversion—the descendants of the colonizers hypocritically practice barbaric practices under the guise of being normal—offers perverse pleasure in the way his characters rise up and destroy the very values of the Motherland that made them what they are.[39]

But Jackson goes beyond critique by entering into the febrile imaginations that the girls' friendship unleashes, signaling to them their unique genius, of which their illnesses are symptomatic: Pauline has suffered from osteomeylitis, Juliet from tuberculosis. As Rueschmann points out, Jackson breaks the mold of melodramatic realism by foregrounding their fecund creativity and delirious excitement as they "bond" to the sound of Mario Lanza in an enraptured "chase" scene, which culminates in a seminaked repose in each other's arms on the grass of Hadley Park. The scene is created using computer graphics technology and special effects with a heavily scored sound track.[40] Hyperreal effects appear when the Hulmes announce their imminent departure to England for a conference, so launching the entry into fantasy proper: Juliet discovers the key to the Fourth World, with its technicolor unicorns and gigantic painted butterflies, marking the event as the day of the death of Christ. Always about to veer out of control because of their fragile states—a recurrence of Juliet's tuberculosis, Pauline's growing desperation at being parted from her and dislike of her own family—the relationship is increasingly constrained by parental concern and disapproval and further confused for Pauline by a haphazard sexual liaison with one of her parent's boarders. Distraught at the Hulmes's decision to separate them and send Juliet to South Africa "for the good of your health," they conceive the mad ambition to go to Hollywood to sell their stories. These mood swings are reflected in the wild behavior of Borovnian society, itself representing Pauline's feverish state of mind as fantasy changes into nightmare. Jackson subtly interweaves elements of the horror movie; the Ilam mansion eerily silhouetted in moonlight and circled by its picket fence recalls similar scenes in *Halloween*. The mock birth of the monstrous prodigy, Diello, son of Deborah (Juliet) and Charles (Pauline), recalls other grotesques who exist on the border of normal and abnormal sexual desire and suggests the difficulty of assuming a proper gender role; embodying their frustrated desires Diello engineers a decapitation that anticipates the murder itself, as this fantasy world takes over the unmanageable real one.[41] Orson Welles, originally rejected from the pantheon of saints, returns to haunt them as the odious Harry Lime in the sewers and gutters of Vienna.

In representing Pauline's obsessive desire to belong to Juliet's family, formulated when the Hulmes decide to return to England, Jackson deploys a third style: Black-and-white film with a sepia tint projects the hopelessness of such an expectation, creating a never-never, soundless world of shipboard departure, site of the hoped-for reunion with the Hulmes. Occurring in the film's opening, almost superimposed on the vivid, bloodspattered faces of the two girls running toward a kiosk in the park after the murder, it shows them running toward the Hulme parents; repeated as the film's concluding sequence, it anticipates the dire consequences, spelt out by the final terse inscription, society's verdict on the decision to "moider moder," that the condition of their release from prison in November 1959 was that they never see each other again.[42] By reversing the chronology of events, starting with the melodramatic announcement of Honora Rieper's death at the film's beginning and the enactment of the murder at the end, and juxtaposing both against the black-and-white scenes, Jackson provides a critical frame by which the gap between their fantasies and reality may be measured. As Pauline's trauma deepens, her perceptions becomes more deluded: The caring but careworn Mrs. Rieper, who tries actively to help her stubborn and resistant daughter, is cast as the abject, bad mother, while the aristocratic, glamorous, but essentially self-preoccupied Hilda Hulme appears as a model of elegance, an image of desire. The cries from both Juliet and Pauline of "Mummy Mummy" in the sepia sequence show the "psychic splitting and ambivalence toward the maternal figure."[43]

In reality the seeds of dysfunction lie within the Hulme family, for Hilda's adultery with Mr. Perry, one of her clients, is tolerated by her husband, who opts for a ménage a trios while being simultaneously elevated to the top rank of Christchurch society as Rector of Canterbury College. To Pauline as well, "Dr. Hulme is the noblest person I have ever known of." The loss of family values in fact begins with earlier events. Juliet's anxiety about being abandoned by her parents is based on their previous committal of her to sanatoria in the Caribbean and elsewhere overseas. Finally, the film dramatizes the intersecting tensions among the girls, their families, and their conformist society through an insidious representation of class differences: Pauline is seduced by the glamour that the Hulmes, newly arrived from Britain, represent (when she first visits their house in Ilam, Juliet appears as a princess) and that Dr. Hulme's preeminence in Canterbury College, suggested by the 16-room stone mansion family residence, embodies. Ironically, Mrs. Hulme, prominent in welfare work, is a marriage counselor, while the more solid relationship of the working-class Riepers, who make ends meet by taking in boarders, is not sanctioned by marriage. The personal drama reinscribes and critiques another stereotype associated with Puritanism: the "colonial cringe" before superior British culture. In that most snobbishly Anglophone of cities, Christchurch, founded as a model of English society at a time when New Zealand's image was of a "better Britain," such distinctions were all too rigorously enforced.[44]

Once Were Warriors (1994) and *Broken English* (1997)

Once Were Warriors, more than any other film in the 1990s, exposed the underbelly of New Zealand society. At the same time, structural juxtapositions to the domestic scenes of brutal violence offer reinterpretations of national myths, creating a broader cultural context within which to read such myths. *Broken English* is sometimes seen as a pale imitation of the earlier film in its accent on domestic violence within a minority culture.[45] But its focus on the Maori as *turangawaewae* (people of the land), in contrast to the uprooted, dispossessed migrant communities from the Pacific Islands, Hong Kong, China, and Croatia who have sought asylum in New Zealand, explores a different set of tensions: the historical and political realities of war-torn former Yugoslavia are pitched against the local romance. Both films offer images of healing: *Broken English* privileges positive cross-cultural relations over the images of dislocated settlement, as in the fate of the Asian woman who owns the restaurant in which

Nina (Aleksandra Vujcic), the Croatian migrant, works: Nina agrees to an "arranged" marriage with Clare's (Jing Zhao) partner so they can gain New Zealand residency. *Once Were Warriors* points selectively to "authentic" sources of Maori culture in order to recover personal autonomy and domestic harmony and to define a sense of community. Both narratives suggest that the position of the ethnic minority is strengthened without actually being integrated into mainstream society.

Both *Once Were Warriors*, the biggest box office success in New Zealand cinema history (until Peter Jackson's two films of *The Lord of the Rings)*, and its sequel or coda, *What Becomes of the Broken Hearted?* (1999), use the urban wastelands of South East Auckland as the setting for the dislocated Heke family. Although the film broke new ground in representing Maori life in terms of social problems and in foregrounding domestic violence (which earlier films like Barry Barclay's *Ngati* (1987) did not), its raw realism and negative stereotyping of Maori men in particular made it controversial among both Maori and Pakeha.[46] The problems that the Maori suffered under colonization are writ large: Jake "the Muss" Heke's economic dependence on the state, his excessive dependence on alcohol, and, most powerfully, his dependence on his fists, for his assault on Beth demonstrates the loss of equality between men and women that precontact Maori society had practiced.[47] The search for identity of his son, Nig (Julian Arahanga), through joining the Toa Aotearoa gang, echoes his father's plight. Yet their dilemmas also reflect contemporary realities of poor, dysfunctional Maori families.[48] In contrast to Pakeha emotional repression, Puritan guilt, and fragmented consciousness, the Maori pathology is one of loss of autonomy through amnesia, by blocking out the unpleasant reality of the present, by forgetting what they had been. Jake—played in each film by Temuera Morrison—exemplifies in *Once Were Warriors* the decline and degeneration of the ideal of warriorhood: the loss of tribal cohesiveness and *mana* (spiritual power), in images of the failed father, of muscular masculinity, and of the urbanized enslaved Maori. Like that other antihero, Stewart in *The Piano,* his physical and emotional destructiveness makes him an outsider to the society within which he is ostensibly "central": He reigns supreme with his fists in the stamping ground of the Royal pub, just as Stewart rules in his Scottish settlement, where he builds up a miniature, mud-saturated empire. The fate of Jake the outcast is explored in *What Becomes of the Broken Hearted?,* although this film lacks the extended critique of colonialism that the earlier film offers.[49] Like *The Piano, Once Were Warriors* can be interpreted through the postcolonial interrogation of agency, identity, and authenticity.[50]

The film *Once Were Warriors* is a rewrite and reinterpretation of the book by Alan Duff for the multiplex audience, "its subversive message packaged as mainstream product."[51] Although the novel's focus switches from Jake to his wife Beth (Rena Owen), who, in the terms of one critic, discovers "the resolve to scrape the shit of her circumstances off her shoes" and reunite the dysfunctional family unit, it remains a drama of "gender conflict."[52] The film opens onto images of urban poverty and ethnic marginalization: Beth's nearly empty shopping trolley, the squalid state houses on Pine Block, the abandoned derelict car that Toots (Shannon Williams), the friend of the Heke's eldest daughter, Grace (Mamaengaroa Kerr-Bell), lives in, and Jake's arrival at home on the dole, which is only $17 less than he earned on wages. But it is 13-year-old Grace who is the victim. We see her reading a story about a *taniwha* (monster) to her younger siblings under the very tree on which she will later hang herself; the story anticipates the monstrosity of her rape, still to come. It is the problematic parental relationship that accelerates the decline into tragedy. Jake badly beats up Beth at a late-night party and other family disasters pile up: Boogie (Taungaroa Emilie) is confined to a remand home after he is picked up from the streets; the family misses an opportunity to visit him there on an outing because of Jake's disappearance into the Royal, for which he is reprimanded by Beth; and then there is the final tragedy of Grace's rape and her suicide.

Strategically interspersed with the family story are other visual images that self-reflexively comment on the film's violent content and stylistic practice; as Anthony Adah points out, these function as a structural counterpoint to the spiral of disasters, ensuring that violence is not merely gratuitous or reductive of social stereotypes of the Maori.[53] The opening "billboard hoax"—the shot of New Zealand's magnificent scenery, in fact an advertisement for ENZPOWER, which the camera then cranes back and down from to reveal the motorway below and the squalid slums on its edges—is commonly read as signaling the deep split between the "pastoral paradise" myth and the social reality [fig. 10.2].[54] Adah argues that the poster represents a "rape of the land" due to the colonial desire for a national history of "breathtaking" New Zealand, and that it illustrates the collision between "the desired unitary history and the resisting history of everyday lives"; he also aligns it with "cultural rape," Pakeha exploitation of the Maori.[55] The theme of the dysfunctional family is also repositioned in the idealizing distant shot of Beth's ancestral village, which the Hekes see bathed in glowing light. Any nostalgia for a precontact past, however, is dispelled by the revelation that Maori society was caste ridden and that Jake is descended from a line of slaves whereas Beth is *ariki* (high class).[56] By advancing this critique, the film avoids stereotyping the Maori as guardians of *mana* and of cultural riches, for it hints that recuperation of authentic Maori society, and the cultural revival associated with Maoritanga in New Zealand society today, is not a solution. Nevertheless it distinguishes among the different choices available for assuming Maori identity:

Boogie's "correct" use of the *taiaha,* a traditional weapon of war, under the training of the social welfare officer, contrasts with the ersatz tattoos that Nig and other gang members wear as signifiers of ethnicity; Beth's decides to hold Grace's *tangi* (funeral) in her village but then returns to the housing estate. Turning to indigenous ceremony, belief and ritualistic practice are represented as forms of living between cultures—as suggested by the fact that Beth's face after she decides to return home dissolves into rather than is replaced by the moko of a carved figure in her village. Maori spirituality does not provide an alternative sacred site, for the film delineates solutions that work in the present: Beth's resolve to make a life for herself and children without Jake signals the move toward closure. The communal family meal, which includes Toots, in the site for Grace's posthumous communication, through her diary, of her rapist's name, and her transcendent meaning, signified by her name, is recognized.[57]

Broken English, dealing with issues of migration and domestic violence filtered through the narrative of young love, offers itself as a complement to *Once Were Warriors*: Where Jake shows the tragic consequences of neglecting paternal duty and ignoring the past, in the happy outcome of *Broken English,* Eddie (Julian Arahanga, Nig in *Once Were Warriors*) proves that Maori men do make good fathers and that harmonious coexistence between the races is possible. Eddie is linked to the land through the image of the tree that symbolizes his *whakapapa* (genealogy). He digs up and replants the tree, finally, in the forecourt of Nina's family

Figure 10.2 "The opening 'billboard hoax'—the shot of New Zealand's magnificent scenery, in fact an advertisement for ENZPOWER, which the camera then cranes back and down from to reveal the motorway below and the squalid slums on its edges—is commonly read as signaling the deep split between the 'pastoral paradise' myth and the social reality."

home, where the showdown with her father occurs. It comes to represent the essence of family, symbolic of the love affair's growth into marriage and the birth of their child. His outfacing Nina's father, Ivan Vujcic (Rade Serbedzija), and brother, Darko (Marton Csokas), using Maori terms of contempt and *haka*-like gestures, reveals a modern-day warrior disorienting the enemy. Conflict in the family and the society is stirred by Nina's father, whose volatility concerning his daughters' sexuality and whose assertions of masculine superiority within the domestic circle can be transposed to a reading of the migrant's disorientation. The parallels between the domestic and political crises are obvious: There is evidence of war in Vukovar, which the family has just fled—wrecked cars, bombed buildings; Nina's voiceover in the film's opening describing how she felt; and a home video of the distress suffered by friends and family left in Vukovar, which the Vujcic family watches.

The film reinterprets ethnic stereotypes ironically: Unlike in *Once Were Warriors*, the Maori are defined through their relation to the land as guardians and repositories of indigenous epistemology, but Eddie is still searching for his destiny: His *mana*, evident in his *haka* (war dance), is linked to the *whakapapa* tree. His older brother, a tour guide (Temuera Morrison, Jake in *Once Were Warriors*), has a knowledge of the sea and can interpret the behavior of dolphins. There is a hierarchy of "belonging": Nina is outwardly nationalistic, acquiring a sense of status by having a New Zealand mother; she and Eddie, who has the greatest claim to belonging, become the prototypes of normality in forming a nuclear family. The Croatians are the new arrivals whose Eastern European culture sets up tensions with their Polynesian neighbors, most obviously in the different musical repertoires showcased in colorful, competing backyard parties but also in the Polynesian tradition of roasting a pig on a spit, in contrast to the Maori custom of steaming pig in a *hangi* (earthen oven). The Asians in the film have economic status (Nina is paid handsomely for agreeing to "marry" Clare's Chinese boyfriend), but compared to the Croatians they seem to lack the cohesion of a community.

Cross-cultural conflict stems from intergenerational tensions, most specifically Ivan's refusal to accept that mixed love affairs and marriages within his family are inevitable. Conversely, the problems of the star-crossed lovers in relation to the film's exposure of a rigid patriarchy in Croatian society point up the unease and complexity of racial and ethnic relations. Further links are made to the historic situation, for Nina's imprisonment in Auckland parallels the imprisoned lives of those in war-torn Croatia. *Broken English* locates itself outside mainstream Pakeha society but, unlike *Once Were Warriors*, is not so much a postcolonial critique as a portrait of contemporary multicultural, multilingual Auckland, which is in the process of becoming a new home to immigrants and refugees, tolerating ethnic diversity, and, as may be inferred from the film's title, "permitting communication where it was previously unknown."[58]

Conclusion: New Beginnings

Christopher Sharrett argues that violence can be seen an artifact with ideological assumptions rather than as a given function of human nature, a perspective that offers a way of defining the meaning of the darkly dysfunctional family within the larger identity structures of New Zealand society.[59] Adah also sees conceptualizing violence as a way of articulating the desires and anxieties prevalent in identity formation, because it probes the complex contradictions that shape human agency, the limits of rationality, and the existential issues that tie us to other humans and to the broader social world.[60] Although in the cinema of the 1990s the personal does not overtly become political, its subversive ideology illustrates forms of self-empowerment and social agency that are being produced from a variety of cultural sites, and the break from British and American values which it defines confirms the major decolonizing shifts in New Zealand society over the last 30 years.

Images of dysfunctional families in these films destabilize the fixed moral standpoints of religious, political, and social values engrained in the colonial constructions of race, ethnicity, and gender and help break down the binary "them" and "us" opposition that dominates the Provincial period (1930–1960). However, in each film the function of violence differs. *The Piano* and *Heavenly Creatures* both resist and redefine the repressive social and ethical codes of Puritanism, whereas domestic violence in *Once Were Warriors*, and, to a lesser extent, in *Broken English,* drawing on symbolic resources of narrative that are only recently available to Maori and other ethnic minorities, renegotiates identity issues; it is linked to the political struggles of minority cultures, to nativism or tribalism, and to the assertion of cultural specificity. But, with the exception of *Heavenly Creatures,* they all suggest that violence, with its proximity to death, initiates a healing process and a new beginning; this is imaged in motifs of birth or rebirth that involve a new or "restored" use of language. In *The Piano,* Ada opts to live after falling overboard; rising from the sea, she recovers her voice and so by implication can take on her new life with Baines.[61] In *Once Were Warriors,* Grace, after her death, acquires a sacred dimension, symbolized in the sacrificial, religious meaning of her name, confirming the message of hope in Beth's reform and aim to reunite her family. *Broken English* ends with the literal birth of Nina and Eddie's daughter and metaphorically suggests the discovery of new linguistic forms from the shards of English, Maori, and Croatian. In *Heavenly Creatures* the birth of the monster, Diello, polarizes the worlds of Borovnia and 1950s Christchurch and cements the daughters' reversal of the Christian ideas of heaven, the saints, and religion. Like Jackson's earlier cult movies, this threat to the dominant ideology is removed in the film's conclusion.[62] In each case the retrieval of women's invisible stories—Grace's diary, Pauline's diary, Ada's silenced voice, and Nina's voiceover account of her experience of the Croatian war—helps represent this future, by way of dislocating and repositioning the unstable male Pakeha norm through which New Zealand culture and society traditionally has been represented.

And in promoting an essentially secular vision of the nation they can all be aligned with significant postcolonial novels of the 1980s: Keri Hulme's *the bone people* (1983), in which the mute child Simon's belief in a new beginning helps shape the bonds of *aroha* (love) and the alternative concept of family with which the novel ends; Patricia Grace's *Potiki* (1986), which weaves the hidden history of the Maori *whanau* (extended family) into a new pattern of past, present, and future, anticipating through the vision of the maimed child Potiki future retaliations against the Pakeha; and Janet Frame's *The Carpathians*, with its autistic child Decima, whose name signals her nine-tenths "non-being" but, by extension, the decimation of Maori culture during colonization. This film concludes with the visionary belief that artists, with their access to memory and desire, should be guardians of the nation's future.

Notes

1. Barbara Creed, "*Bad Taste* and Antipodal Inversion: Peter Jackson's Colonial Suburbs," *Postcolonial Studies* 3.1 (2000): 67; Linda Dyson, "The Return of the Repressed? Whiteness, Femininity and Colonialism in *The Piano*," *Screen* 36.3 (autumn 1995): 269.
2. Michael Hill and Jenny Barnett, "Religion and Deviance," in Paul F. Green, ed., *Studies in New Zealand Social Problems*, 2d. ed. (Palmerston North: Dunmore Press, 1994), 231; Allan K. Davidson, *Christianity in Aotearoa: A History of Church and Society in New Zealand* (Wellington: New Zealand Education for the Ministry, 1997), 170–71, 177–78.
3. The key text is John Mulgan, *Man Alone*, 1939; for its importance in the literary tradition see Lawrence Jones, *Barbed Wire and Mirrors: Essays on New Zealand Prose*, 2d. ed. (Dunedin: Otago University Press, 1990), 295–312.
4. Ian Conrich, "In God's Own Country: Open Spaces and the New Zealand Road Movie," in *New Zealand—A Pastoral Paradise?*, Ian Conrich and David Woods, eds., Studies in New Zealand Culture 6 (Nottingham: Kakapo Books, 2000), 31–38.

5. Luisa Ribeiro, review of *Heavenly Creatures, Film Quarterly* 49.1 (fall 1995): 33. Quoted by Eva Rueschmann, *Sisters on Screen: Siblings in Contemporary Cinema* (Philadelphia: Temple University Press, 2000), 104.

6. The term is Sam Neill's in his film *Cinema of Unease: A Personal Journey* (1995); see Helen Martin and Sam Edwards, eds., *New Zealand Film: 1912–1996* (Auckland: Oxford University Press, 1997), 184.

7. David Callahan, "The Functional Family in New Zealand Film," in *New Zealand—A Pastoral Paradise?,* Ian Conrich and David Woods, eds., Studies in New Zealand Culture 6 (Nottingham: Kakapo Books, 2000), 97.

8. Nick Perry, *Hyperreality and Global Culture* (London and New York: Routledge, 1998), 8.

9. Bev James and Kay Saville-Smith, *Gender, Culture and Power: Challenging New Zealand's Gendered Culture* (New York: Oxford University Press, 1994), 16; quoted by Jane Smith, "Knocked around in New Zealand," in *Mythologies of Violence in Postmodern Media,* Christopher Sharrett, ed. (Detroit: Wayne State University Press, 1999), 382; see also Jacqui True, "'Fit Subjects for the British Empire?' Class-ifying Racial and Gendered Subjects in 'Godzone' (New Zealand)," in *Women out of Place: The Gender of Agency and the Race of Nationality,* Brackette F. Wiliams, ed. (London: Routledge, 1996), 115.

10. Meaghan Morris, quoted by Callahan, "The Functional Family in New Zealand Film," 104.

11. Deborah Chambers, *Representing the Family* (London: Sage, 2001), 92, 99.

12. Smith, "Knocked around," 391.

13. See Leonie Pihama, "Repositioning Maori Representation: Contextualising *Once Were Warriors,*" in *Film in Aotearoa New Zealand,* 2d. ed., Jonathan Dennis and Jan Beiringa, eds. (Wellington: Victoria University Press, 1996), 191–92; Barbara Cairns, "Looking the Other Way: New Zealand Feature Film Production in the 1990s," paper delivered at "New Zealand, Identities, and Globalisation," the New Zealand Studies Association conference held at New Zealand House, London, July 2, 2002. See the report in *British Review of New Zealand Studies* 13 (2001/2): 124–31.

14. Bob Consedine, "Inequality and the Egalitarian Myth," in *Culture and Identity in New Zealand,* David Novitz and Bill Willmott, eds. (Wellington: IGP Books, 1989), 174; Lawrence Jones, "Versions of the Dream: Literature and the Search for Identity," in *Culture and Identity in New Zealand,* Novitz and Willmott, eds. (Wellington: IGP Books, 1989), 184, 189.

15. See Gregory Waller, "Embodying the Urban Maori Warrior," in *Places through the Body,* Heidi J. Nast and Steve Pile, eds. (London and New York: Routledge, 1998), 338–39.

16. See James and Saville-Smith, *Gender, Culture, and Power,* 63–69; Greg Newbold, "Violence," in *Studies in New Zealand Social Problems,* 2d. ed., Paul F. Green, ed. (Palmerston North: Dunmore Press, 1994), 207; Celia Biral, "Problems within the New Zealand Family," in *Studies in New Zealand Social Problems,* 2d. ed., Paul F. Green, ed. (Palmerston North: Dunmore Press, 1994), 253–276. The under-reporting of violence, especially of domestic violence is well attested.

17. Smith, "Knocked around," 382.

18. Perry, *Hyperreality and Global Culture*, 13.
19. Trevor James, "Beyond Puritanism: Post-Colonialism's 'Awful Disease' in the Novels of Maurice Gee," in *"And the Birds began to sing": Religion and Literature in Post-Colonial Cultures,* Jamie S. Scott, ed. (Amsterdam-Atlanta, GA: Rodopi, 1996), 104.
20. An example is the condemnation of the New Zealand accent in the early twentieth century and the introduction of elocution lessons to impose a uniform one; see Bill Willmott, "Introduction: Culture and National Identity," in *Culture and Identity in New Zealand,* Novitz and Willmott, eds. (Wellington: IGP Books, 1989), 4.
21. Jane Mander, *The Story of a New Zealand River* (Christchurch: Whitcombe and Tombs, 1960 [1920]), 27, cited by James in "Beyond Puritanism: Post-Colonialism's 'Awful Disease,'" 103.
22. Patrick Evans, "The Provincial Dilemma: After the God Boy," *Landfall* 117 (March 1976): 34. Evans points out that the most important characteristics of the New Zealand novel are "parents who are Puritans and children who are alienated."
23. On the film's dual narrative mode, which elicits viewer sympathy while simultaneously encouraging a critical distance, see Rueschmann, *Sisters on Screen,* 104; Barry Keith Grant, *A Cultural Assault: The New Zealand Films of Peter Jackson,* Studies in New Zealand Culture 5 (Nottingham: Kakapo Books, 1999), 16–17.
24. Martin and Edwards, *New Zealand Film: 1912–1996,* 177.
25. Estella Tincknell, "New Zealand Gothic?: Jane Campion's *The Piano,*" in *New Zealand—A Pastoral Paradise?,* Ian Conrich and David Woods, eds., Studies in New Zealand Culture 6 (Nottingham: Kakapo Books, 2000), 109.
26. The debate over whether *The Piano* is "feminist" is as heated as that over its treatment of the Maori as colonial Other; see for example, Estella Tincknell, "New Zealand Gothic?: Jane Campion's *The Piano,*" 117–118 who argues that it operates only in relation to the project of feminism.
27. Dyson, "The Return of the Repressed?," 267–76.
28. Naomi Segal, "The Fatal Attraction of *The Piano,*" in *Scarlet Letters: Fictions of Adultery from Antiquity to the 1990s,* Nicholas White and Naomi Segal, eds. (Basingstoke and New York: Macmillan and St. Martin's Press, 1997), 205–210. Segal argues that Ada cannot reverse this strategy (205).
29. David Baker, "Mud-Wrestling with the Angels: *The Piano* as Literature," *Southern Review* 30.2 (1997): 191–92.
30. Tincknell, "New Zealand Gothic?," 110–111.
31. Stella Bruzzi, *Undressing Cinema: Clothing and Identity in the Movies* (London and New York: Routledge, 1997), 58.
32. Leonie Pihama, "Ebony and Ivory: Constructions of Maori in *The Piano,*" in *Jane Campion's The Piano,* Harriet Margolis, ed. (Cambridge: Cambridge University Press, 2000), 130, quoting from Kim Langley's interview with Campion, "Dark Talent," *Vogue* (Australia) (April 1993): 140, that Campion "was determined not to compromise herself artistically in order to be politically right on."
33. Baker, "Mud-Wrestling with the Angels," 180–81.

34. Linda Hardy, "Natural Occupancy," *Meridian* (special issue: *Asian and Pacific Inscriptions: Identities, Ethnicities, Nationalities*) 14.2 (1995): 214.

35. See, for example, Tom Gurr and H. H. Cox, "Death in a Cathedral City," in *Couples Who Kill*, selected by Richard Glyn Jones (London: Virgin Publishing Ltd., 1993), 211–228.

36. See Julie Glamuzina and Alison Lurie, *Parker and Hulme: A Lesbian View*, 2d. ed., introduced by B. Ruby Rich (New York: Firebrand Books, 1995), 110–133, for accounts and studies.

37. Quoted by Rueschmann, *Sisters on Screen*, 108.

38. Barry Keith Grant, "Second Thoughts on Double Features: Revisiting the Cult Film," in *Unruly Pleasures: The Cult Film and its Critics*, Xavier Mendik and Graeme Harper, eds. (Guildford: Fab Press, 2000), 27.

39. Creed, "*Bad Taste* and Antipodal Inversion," 63.

40. Rueschmann, *Sisters on Screen*, 103, points out that this scene counterpoints the scene of running through the park after the murder of Honora Parker.

41. Barbara Creed, *The Monstrous Feminine* (London: Routledge, 1994), 11.

42. See Glamuzina and Lurie, *Parker and Hulme*, 100–109, on the sentence.

43. Rueschmann, *Sisters on Screen*, 109. She points out that Pauline's craving can be linked to the Freudian "Royal Family," when a child believes that he or she really belongs to a more socially elevated family.

44. On New Zealand as "New Britian" in the 1880s, see James Belich, *Paradise Reforged: A History of the New Zealanders from the 1880s to the Year 2000* (London: Penguin Press, 2002); on the myth of the superior origin of New Zealanders as "best British" see Jacqui True, "Fit Citizens for British Empire?," 108–09.

45. Laurence Simmons, "Language and Magical Realism in *Broken English*," *Illusions* 26 (winter 1997): 10–16.

46. Davinia Thornley, "White, Brown or 'Coffee'? Revisioning Race in Tamahori's *Once Were Warriors*," *Film Criticism* 25.3 (spring 2001): 22–36; Leonie Pihama, "Repositioning Maori Representation," 191–92.

47. Powhiri Rika-Heke, "Margin or Centre? Indigenous Writing in Aotearoa," *The Poet's Voice* 2.1 (June 1995): 35–50.

48. Newbold, "Violence," 207.

49. Anthony Adah distinguishes between Lee Tamahori's postcolonial project in *Once Were Warriors* and the recolonizing of the Maori screen that Ian Mune undertakes in directing *What Becomes of the Broken Hearted?*" (Anthony Adah, "Post- and Re-Colonizing Aotearoa Screen: Violence and Identity in *Once Were Warriors* and *What Becomes of the Broken Hearted?*," *Film Criticism* 25.3 [spring 2001]: 52). I am indebted to Adah's reading of the film.

50. Thornley, "White, Brown or 'Coffee'?" 22–26; Smith, "Knocked around," 386; Waller, "Embodying the Urban Maori Warrior," 338–39.

51. Thornley, "White, Brown or 'Coffee'?", 26; the novel *Once Were Warriors* by Alan Duff was published by Tandem Press in Auckland in 1990.

52. Peter Calder, "Would-Be Warriors: New Zealand Film Since *The Piano*," in *Film in Aotearoa New Zealand*, 2d. ed., Jonathan Dennis and Jan Beiringa, eds. (Wellington: Victoria University Press, 1996), 185.

53. Adah, "Post- and Re-colonizing Aotearoa Screen," 46–53.

54. Smith, "Knocked around," 386; Waller, "Embodying the Urban Maori Warrior," 337–38; Thomas Spooner, "*Once Were Warriors* (1994), and its Challenge to New Zealand Myth," in *New Zealand—A Pastoral Paradise?*, Ian Conrich and David Woods, eds., Studies in New Zealand Culture 6 (Nottingham: Kakapo Books, 2000), 91–2.

55. Adah, "Post- and Re-colonizing Aotearoa Screen, 49–50.

56. On the *mana* and rights of high-ranking women in traditional Maori society, see James and Saville-Smith, *Gender, Culture, and Power,* 25–26.

57. Waller, "Embodying the Urban Maori Warrior," 341.

58. Simmons, "Language and Magical Realism in *Broken English,*" 12.

59. Christopher Sharrett, "Introduction," in *Mythologies of Violence in Postcolonial Media*, Christopher Sharrett, ed. (Detroit: Wayne State University Press, 1999).

60. Adah, "Post- and Re-colonizing Aotearoa Screen, 46–48.

61. Tincknell, "New Zealand Gothic?," 116–117, claims that Ada undergoes an "existential transformation" and that the conclusion offers "a new *narrative* not a recovery of authenticity'; Segal, "The Fatal Attraction of *The Piano,*" 206, describes Ada's "graphic birth out of the amniotic bubble."

62. Grant, "Second Thoughts on Double Features," 15–27.

Chapter Eleven

Santería and the Quest for a Postcolonial Identity in Post-Revolutionary Cuban Cinema

Edna M. Rodríguez-Mangual

"African Spirit Worship Has Powerful Hold on Cubans: Catholics Embrace Santería,"[1] reads one of the many headlines during the visit of Pope John Paul II to the island in January 1998. During that time around 300,000 people gathered in Havana's Plaza of the Revolution to greet the pope. It was a "history-making," five-day visit, an article in *The Christian Century* pointed out, as Fidel Castro himself welcomed the Roman Catholic leader.[2] During his talks, the pope spoke out for greater religious freedom within Cuba, meanwhile condemning the long-lasting U.S. economic embargo against Cuba. Everyone had big hopes for what this visit could mean for the island, since social, political, and religious issues were brought forth. Nonetheless, when a group of Santería *babalawos* requested a special meeting with John Paul II they were denied by the Cuban Catholic leaders, the same leaders that stood alongside the pope asking for greater religious freedom. So, even with greater freedoms to practice religion, there yet remains a hierarchy of those religions both within the political government and within the religious structures.

This strange, political-religious paradox of the rhetorical acceptance of Santería—and, relatedly, of Afro-Cuban people and culture—is constantly met by a veiling of the visibility of black culture and religion within the national imaginary. This paradox can be traced throughout a history of Cuban film production, and in this chapter I will explore some of the visual aesthetics that Cuban national cinema has been developing in a post-revolutionary age, and how revisions to the historical processes of the nation converge with religious representations in Cuba's quest for a postcolonial identification. I argue that the portrayal of hybridity—mixed culture, mixed religion, "blackness" in general—in contemporary Cuban film becomes a strategy to define a distinctive postcolonial identity among Cubans. Many recent films produced within the island include representations of the popular syncretized religious beliefs as an essential part of Cuban everyday life and culture. No matter what the plotline of the film, Santería religious practices are mixed within the main themes. In romances, dramas, or films with a strong social critique, Santería myths and rituals have become a constant refrain even while they are treated indirectly or in passing. After some brief background into religious practices in Cuba, I will show some of the parallels among film production, national identity construction, and Santería religious representations.

Religion in Cuba

Cuba's Marxist, materialist, and atheist society once dismissed religion as an opiate for the masses, at least officially—hidden religious practices among the population have always been very common. All that has changed since the collapse of the Soviet-led trading block in the early 1990s. Today, religious affiliations are an open subject, due to the fact that the government has introduced liberalizing reforms such as the acceptance by the Fourth Congress of the Cuban Communist Party to admit "believers" as party members in 1990. And Santería, in particular, has become a highly popular and in-demand commodity by foreigners and scholars visiting the island. With its already hybrid makeup of Iberian Catholicism and West African religious traditions, Santería becomes an intriguing point of departure from which to think through a contemporary postcolonial identity.

The Catholic religion was brought to Cuba by the Spanish colonizers and was practiced by nearly half of the population prior to the 1959 revolution. Today two-thirds of the population is baptized Roman Catholic,[3] but the number who actually practice the religion is much lower. Furthermore, many of these also practice the syncretized version, Santería, with its many denominations (Rule of Osha, Rule of Palo Monte, the Abakuá Secret Society, and so on), which developed early on in the colonial process when African slaves were forcibly converted to Catholicism. A growing number of Cubans are also found attending Protestant services on Sunday mornings, with Pentecostalism particularly on the rise.[4]

So now, five years after the landmark visit by the pope, relations between the government and the Catholic Church are in very good standing, at least according to Catholic Cardinal Jaime Ortega in Havana, who affirms that 250 houses have been opened as places of worship and now function as parishes.[5] But changes are not organic since the Church is still considered a private entity; for example, the school system is still religion free. So, a number of contradictions remain with regard to religious tolerance and visibility. More freedom has been given to the Catholic Church, yet there is a strong separation from public social and political structures. And Santería, which everyone knows about and is widely practiced, is still pushed to the sidelines by the Catholic authorities. There thus remains an uneasy relation between the government, the official orthodoxy of the Catholic Church, and the widespread practices of Santería. In these tensions, a national identity is continually being reformed.

However, one event in particular may be an indicator for recent changes, as it points out the always-glimpsed yet never fully visible presence of Santería. In order to commemorate the five-year anniversary of the pope's visit, and in homage to the patron saint of Cuba, an art exhibit was organized that presented the work of 40 artists under the title "Virgen de la Caridad del Cobre: Ruega por nosotros" (Our Lady of Charity: Pray for us). This was the first exhibition of its type in the island and begins to suggest how religious themes and imageries are occupying more and more public spaces than ever before, not excluding cinematic representations.

La Virgen de la Caridad del Cobre is an important icon in the national imaginary of the island. According to different versions of her apparition, it was during the first years of the seventeenth century (the exact date changes in each version) that the image of the Virgin appeared to Juan Moreno and to the brothers Joyos in the Caribbean sea after being saved from a storm. Significantly, her dress was dry in spite of being in the middle of the sea. The many versions of the story are interesting in themselves since sometimes Juan Moreno is said to be a black slave, and sometimes a *mestizo,* and the two brothers, while usually two indigenous men, are other times represented as white. Another version asserts that there was a white, a black, and an indigenous man, each of them representing the ethnic groups of the people of Cuba. There is a popular belief accompanying this last version that claims that when the Virgin spoke to them she said that in her heart blacks, whites, indigenous, and *mestizos* were all equal. That is why they all needed to love each other, and the miracle goes as far as to explain that this is why in Cuba there have never been any racial problems. In 1916 La Virgen de la Caridad officially became the patron saint of the island, and her festival day was set for September 8.

Nowadays it is hard to think about her image floating in the sky above the stormy sea and the three men on the boat without also imagining represented images of the sensual Oshún, the Yoruban deity with whom La Virgen de la Caridad is syncretized, or better, "synopticized."[6] Oshún is the *orisha* of love, femininity, and rivers; she embodies coquetry, grace, and female sexuality. The synthesis between Oshún and the Virgin has been so thorough that the celebration on September 8 is now devoted to both deities, which have become two and the same in the popular Cuban imaginary. But there is still a difference, since the African celebration day for Oshún is officially September 11, and while there are many masses and visits to churches on September 8—especially to the Cathedral of the Cobre near Santiago—the Santerían *Toque de tambores* (playing of the drums) and the masses for Oshún take place on September 11. Despite the difference in dates, Santería rituals and Catholic services for the Virgin and Oshún have been overlapped rather than opposed, and the same santeros who visit the Catholic churches dressed in their white clothes—displaying in their necklaces all the colors of the different *orishas*—also participate in the *Toque de tambores*. This is but one example of many denoting the ritual interrelations between Catholicism and Santería that play prominent roles in the national-mythic structures of Cuban identity. Such spectacles have not gone unnoticed by filmmakers.

Early Cuban Cinema through the Revolution

A brief consideration of the history of Cuban cinematic production will show that, as in society itself, the filmic representations of religious practices on the island have usually followed a political and social agenda. When the film industry started in the first half of the twentieth century, the difficulties of establishing a national cinema under the colonial rule of the United States made its development almost impossible. Just as the U.S. colonized Cuba politically, so did Hollywood colonize Cuban film production. According to John King, there was little commercial cinema made in Cuba, and the most common image of the island in Hollywood and Mexican movies was that of an exotic paradise where all fantasies were possible, a "fantasy island," if you will.[7] One melodrama by director Ramón Peón is one of the exceptions to this, and worth reviewing since it marks the transition from the silent-film era to the prerevolutionary sound era.

In 1930 Peón directed one of the last silent feature films, *La Virgen de la Caridad,* which shows the political and social agenda of the period.[8] Yeyo (Miguel Santos), a young man who lost his father during the War of Independence in the 1890s, falls in love with the local chieftain's daughter Triana (Diana Marde). Triana's father, Don Pedro (Francisco Muñoz), opposes the romance because he wants his daughter to marry someone with greater monetary capital. Meanwhile, Fernández (Guillermo de la Torre) returns from Spain after a period of absence. He falls for Triana and falsifies the ownership documents of La Bijirita, the land that rightfully belongs to Yeyo and that once upon a time belonged to his own father. Don Pedro likes this foreigner with money and power and approves the marriage of Triana and Fernández. Only a miracle can save Yeyo and Triana's love affair now, and La Virgen de la Caridad intervenes in the name of justice.

After an establishing shot of the newspaper *El Mundo,* one of the more reliable sources of the time (in which it is indicated that La Birijita's case is being clarified in court), the camera frame shows Yeyo's grandmother (Matilde Maun) holding a picture of La Virgen de la Caridad. She cleans the glass and Yeyo hangs the frame on the wall. The image is a significant prop in the film, for later on, when Yeyo has lost all hope of keeping the land and the woman he loves, he prays to this image of the Virgin as his last resource. Meanwhile, in the penultimate scene, someone is trying to hang a painting by the Spanish artist Murillo on the other side of the wall. When the hammer hits the wall, the image of the Virgin falls and breaks. In an ironic manner it seems as if La Virgen de la Caridad is responding to his prayers, impotent to help. But behind the broken picture frame Yeyo finds the title papers where he is listed as the legal owner of the property: This piece of evidence gives him back his land and makes possible the marriage with Triana.

Despite Peón's questioned level of achievements as a filmmaker, this film is interestingly made, with shots from a variety of angles and differing length, just as it is highly ideological in nature.[9] García Canclini reminds us that film was one of the most important media to contribute to the organization of narratives of identity in national societies during the first half of the twentieth century.[10] In *Virgen de la Caridad del Cobre,* the allegorical romance between Yeyo and Triana is a forbidden one and becomes impossible due to the presence of the foreign usurper. However, in this foundational melodrama the real *guajiro,* heir of the founding fathers who fought for the independence of the island, is the one who, at the end, receives what rightly belongs to him.

By 1930, a number of Cubans in the pseudorepublic had grown some resentment and opposition toward the control of the island by the U.S. government, and particularly its support of the highly corrupt dictatorship of Machado. His government pleased foreign interests, and from around 1929, 50 percent of U.S. sugar imports came from Cuba. However, soon after, the great depression deeply affected the foreign capital coming into the island. As the economic situation changed drastically, the opposition just grew stronger. In this light, *La Virgen* made an argument for an economy based on local ownership with a localized, noncorrupt authority. Simultaneously, the religious aspects—La Virgen de la Caridad as the savior and the one who makes justice possible—appeal to the popular cultural beliefs. At this point in time, this Virgin cannot be identified, at least openly, with Oshún, since Afro-Cuban religious practices still belonged to the underground.

Although there were many films made before the Revolution (over 100), in reality it was not until the 1960s that a national cinema fully developed in the island, just as Santería came to be a more open subject and was able to be practiced in limited public displays. Cinema became an especially vital medium with which to narrate the new social and political organization after the Revolution of 1959. On the one hand the Revolution funded this development by, among other things, creating the ICAIC (Instituto Cubano de Arte e Industria Cinematográfica) and the Cinemóvil (a mobile cinema unit that brought filmed documentaries into the rural areas of the island in order to document and classify the population), and by bringing world-renown directors like Chris Marker to teach the new filmmakers how to make films. The Revolution also proclaimed a nonracist agenda and pretended to integrate blacks and their culture into the mainstream social agenda.

On the other hand, the Revolution came at the same time that the so-called "new" Latin American Cinema grew up in different parts of South and Central America. This movement was due, in part, to the success of the Cuban Revolution and its rejection of North American imperialism, but also grew because of what filmic production might mean for the future of all Latin American identities. In manifesto after manifesto in these new movements, the filmmakers were clear about theorizing their own practices distinct from the colonial, monopolistic ones of Hollywood. As King points out, "the various manifestos all point to a distinctive break with the past and with dominant hegemonic discourses."[11] King also considers that the remarkable work by Tomas Gutiérrez Alea between 1968 and 1970 is a good example of the maturity of this new cinema. (Even so, Gutiérrez Alea had studied film at the Centre Sperimentale in Rome back in the fifties, and the manifestoes that proclaimed the value of local production were yet influenced by established European film aesthetics.)

Despite revolutionary changes and the pursuit of new cinematic forms, during the second half of the century there was still a lack of filmic representations of Santería and Afro-Cuban culture in Cuba. Perhaps this is because soon after the Revolution religious practices were prohibited. Or perhaps many of the changes of revolutionary Cuban society—equality of race and gender—were merely rhetorical and the otherness of Afro-Cubans actually had little part to play in the revolutionary imaginary of the nation. Without fully resolving this ambiguity, I turn now to look at the post-revolutionary status of Santería visibility in film, noting its usefulness in the construction of national identity, after colonialism and after the Revolution.

Seeing Santería after the Revolution

Santería did not disappear from the antireligious, revolutionary social order, for there were still several films and documentaries with themes of religion and syncretism made during the sixties. Among them were the short documentaries *Abakuá* and *Cultura Aborigen* (1963) by Bernabé Hernández, and *Acerca de un personaje que unos llaman San Lázaro y otros llaman Babalú* (About a character some people call Saint Lazarus and others call Babalú, 1968) by Octavio Cortázar.[12] In this latter documentary, the question of who is this Saint Lazarus is never answered with certainty, but one thing comes across, and it is that whichever Lazarus this may be from the Christian tradition (and there are several), he has an alter ego in the African deity Babalú Allé.

Important reconstructive narrations of the history of Afro-Cubans were filmed during the 1970s. In his book on Gutiérrez Alea, Paul A. Schroeder argues that there were two main reasons for the ICAIC to focus on history during this period. The first one was that the First National Congress on Culture and Education in 1971 had the aim of ensuring social awareness among the population, since, despite the success of the literacy campaign during the sixties, there was still a low educational level of the population at large: "Alea's historical films are therefore part of a larger project to understand the material basis of contemporary society."[13] The second reason that Schroeder provides for the historical emphasis is because of the atmosphere of oppression that remained after the *quinquenio gris*. This was a five year period (1971–76) in which many circumstances—including censure and the repression of artists, summed up by the famous words of Fidel: "With the Revolution everything, against the Revolution nothing"— stopped the search for new forms of expression that had flourished during the sixties. "Under these circumstances, it is not too surprising that filmmakers would choose historical subjects over contemporary ones."[14] Schroeder also underlines how "[t]he reconstruction of history implies its correction."[15]

In the seventies, three important films emerged that were central to bringing Santería and Afro-Cuban tropes and images into the cinematic (and thus also national, since they were government funded) imaginary. These films allowed a space for Afro-Cuban subjectivity that is constitutive of Cuban identity itself. They are: *Una pelea cubana contra los demonios* (A Cuban struggle against the demons; dir. Gutiérrez Alea, 1971), *Los días del agua* (days of water; dir. Manuel Octavio Gómez, 1971), and, later, *La última cena* (The last supper; also by Gutiérrez Alea, 1976). Coincidentally, and significantly, each of these films is a reenactment of a historical event in Cuban history.

Chanan correctly points out that *Una pelea cubana contra los demonios* presents a visual attack on stable and established filmic techniques of cinematography and editing.[16] The unstable movements of the hand-held camera shots make it hard to identify visually with any character in the film, or either ideological side—church versus landowner, Catholic practices versus paganism. The film is based on the 1959 book of the same name by Fernando Ortiz and recounts a documented story that in the film takes place in 1659—Schroeder notes that the original date (1672) was changed in the film to coincide with 300 hundred years of the Revolution. The story goes that a local priest (Jose Rodríguez) wanted to move the inhabitants of his coastal town to an interior part of the island, claiming that the move would keep pirates and heretics away from the community. In Ortiz's book, the priest's motivations are purely materialistic since he wants to move the town to a place where the priest himself owns the land, while in the film his motivations are more fully religious. Nonetheless, in the film the skeptical landowners who would benefit from the current location oppose the move and the ideology of the church. It becomes a battle between the theology of the Inquisition and the witchcraft of the illiterate, between the social and economic forces of the time, both in the seventeenth century and in the twentieth.

The priest, Father Manuel, exorcises both spirits and the people of the town through conventional Christian rites, but when these do not seem to work African rituals are performed by slaves, as in the case of the purification of Laura, the mayor's wife. Laura, who is raped by pirates who attack the town, becomes hysterical, and the priest's interpretation of her behavior is that she is possessed by the devil and needs him to exorcise her. However, the priest himself also rapes her later, and, traumatized, she looks for relief in a slave who not only purifies her but also performs an abortion and a ceremonial bath in a river. The lines between corruption and morality are blurred, and a sense of confusion permeates the entire film, aided by distorted images and dissonant music. There is no salvation at the end: Father Manuel gets away with moving the town, and the collective hysteria prevails. Father Manuel burns the remains of the town and then kills himself. Christianity does not serve as a positive agent of social change, especially in the distorted way it is being manipulated here, and its African counterpart, as a marginalized practice, does not have much power to change anything. The film becomes a comment on what happens to religious consciousness when it becomes entangled with materialistic motives. This is of course reminiscent of the centuries-long colonization process in Latin America—the sword and the Bible, the conquest and the evangelization all at once—and recurs as a theme in the other two key films of the seventies mentioned above.

Los días del agua is another "hallucinatory allegory" of the clash between economic and political forces versus popular religious practices.[17] Antoñica Izquierdo (Idalia Anreus) becomes a popular saintly healer after allegedly having cured her own son without the help of traditional medicine since the local doctors do not offer relief to the poor community to which she belongs. From the beginning, the opening images offer a ritualized perspective through a close up of burning candles and syncretized altar images. After the title sequence, the viewer sees Antoñica getting rid of the medications on the altar. She tells her husband that they will not need them anymore, nobody will, because from now on she will heal the people for free: The Virgin has commanded her to heal the sick.

The story takes place in Barrios de los Cayos de San Felipe, a province of Pinar del Río, in 1936. An establishing shot shows the houses of the town, the poverty, and the natural beauty of the site all at the same time. As in *Una pelea cubana contra los demonios*, the subjective point of view of the camera is hard to identify with. The narration is sometimes framed by the point of view of a journalist, Lino (Raúl Pomares), who becomes the narrator of the film at times and who little by little grows convinced of the enormous power of Antoñica—not of any supernatural power but of her extraordinary power to lead people politically just because they believe in her. But as he interviews people, the point of view shifts. The viewer is alternately connected to those who believe in her power to heal, and to those who think her power comes from hell. There are those who also feel threatened by her since she is capable of destabilizing the established power of the church, and of doctors, pharmacists, and politicians who do little to actually help sickness in the society. Antoñica's power not only heals but also prevents sickness and purifies the soul. She also offers hope, and this is the biggest threat of all to the establishment.

The sanctuary where Antoñica heals by administering holy water becomes a fair as well. People start coming from all over, and Tony, a businessman, quickly takes advantage of the situation to make money, again mixing the economic and the religious. He is the narrator of the Virgin's apparition to Antoñica, and his voiceover becomes a sound bridge as the viewer is presented with surreal images of Antoñica's encounter with the Virgin Mary and with representations of evil and good. These images of the Virgin are unusually paganlike and not the typical ecstatic Christian images found in churches.

At several points in the film, crosscuts create a visual confusion for the viewer, just as they function formally to synthesize Christian and Santería practices. At one point the viewer sees images of the priest preaching at a church mixed with shots of *babalawos* and *babalochas* doing *despojos* (a sort of purification rite), and divining cowerie shells while syncretized altars of Santería appear in the background. After this collage of images, the film presents a Santería procession, while the drums and their Yoruba chants interface with a Christian procession. The processions meet together when they each turn a corner and run into each other. Syncretism takes place visually as they intercept each other's paths [fig. 11.1]. Their former separateness becomes integrated.

But Antoñica and her followers are in the middle ground of these two more organized religious practices, and the boundaries between what is divine and what is diabolic come clashing together. The collective hysteria shown in the film undermines the sacred aspects of Antoñica's rituals, and the prayer that goes along with the water rites is certainly profane: "Perro maldito al infierno" (Damn dog to hell). The phrase could also be interpreted metaphorically, since in the end the "damn dog" is equated with governmental power against Antoñica and her people.

When a person who Antoñica has supposedly cured is found dead, she is accused of murder. Alberto Labrado, a candidate for the provincial governor and a friend of Lino, takes the case, sets her free, and uses her to gain popularity for his candidacy. Once in power, he sends the army to attack and move the people out of Los Cayos. On the one hand they do not serve his purposes anymore, and, on the other, they actually threaten his new interests. Tony starts packing his business and counsels everyone else to do so. But Antoñica's followers are convinced that her power can defeat the

Figure 11.1   " . . . the film presents a Santería procession, while the drums and their Yoruba chants interface with a Christian procession. The processions meet together when they each turn a corner and run into each other. Syncretism takes place visually as they intercept each other's paths. Their former separateness becomes integrated."

army. At that point Tony confesses that he staged the miracles of healing in order to make money. Confronted with this, Antoñica professes that she is more powerful than God and the Virgin, and that her power resides in her mind and not in the holy water. She resolves that she will fight the army with her mind; she does not need anyone. Her followers, on the other hand, respond with violence. In the end, Antoñica becomes a heretic due to the power that has corrupted her as well. Fanaticism and repression become entangled one more time. The film also offers no resolution, no single moral standpoint from which to judge.

As with his *Una pelea Cubana*, Gutiérrez Alea's *La última cena* (The last supper) also portrays a corrupt Christianity, made so by the lust for economic and material gain. This is by far the most simplistic film of the three historical films of the 1970s discussed so far. Its form of narration follows a classical mode; however, it has many layers of parables inside parables that end in a moral message against slavery and against religious manipulation, which the other two films lack. This one condemns and provides answers, presenting ideas in a very clear manner. The straightforward approach paid off, says Schroeder, since "*The Last Supper* became Cuba's first international box office success, and critics are in general agreement on what the film means."[18]

The film is full of religious images that comment on the tension between the Catholic doctrine professed by the ones in power and the reality of lived economic practices. During the title sequence the camera pans and tilts over baroque paintings of Christ ascending to heaven with angels carrying his cross, images of Saint Francis, and images of the Madonna and Child. The low-tone music emulates Gregorian chants, helping to set the mood for something sacred. Before the action starts the viewer is advised: "The event shown in this film took place in a Havana sugar-mill during Holy Week at the end of the eighteenth century." The incident is recorded in Manuel Moreno Fraginal's famous book *The Sugarmill*, which is another reinterpretation of Cuban history from a Marxist point of view written after the Revolution.[19]

After the peaceful title sequence, a full-screen title announces "Miércoles Santo" (Wednesday of Holy Week), which is immediately followed by images of violence in the sugar-mill. Sebastián, a determined and stubborn slave, has escaped again, which is why the overseer, Don Manuel, arrives late to his encounter with señor Conde, Count of the House of Bayona, and the owner of the land, played by Nelson Villagra. But Sebastián is caught soon after, and as punishment Don Manuel cuts off Sebastián's ear and feeds it to a dog.

While the film overall is cynical toward the perversions of Catholicism, there are actually two sympathetic main characters: a straightforward priest who is trying to teach Christianity to the slaves and care for their well being, and Monsieur Gaspar Duclé, who represents the technological, rational aspects of the sugar industry. He does not side with anybody, does not show loyalties, and follows his instincts on what works and what doesn't. Don Gaspar shows the count the new system he has developed in order to produce more cane sugar, but advises him that in order to increase the production they will need more hands to work, more slaves. This is dangerous because, as he explains, they can overcome the white people in number. The film takes place during the 1790s, just a few years after the uprisings of black Haitians on the neighboring island.

After all the references to the stages of the evolution of the sugar industry and its consequences, the stage is set for the rest of the film. The second part is announced: "Jueves Santo" (Maundy Thursday). Ironically, the first shot after the chapter title is a close up of the count feeding a bird in a cage. The cage takes half of the screen, and the count says, "Now that I have fed you, you must sing to your master." This is a premonition of the scene to come: a recreation of the Last Supper of Christ with slaves standing in for the disciples. The mise-en-scène emulates Leonardo's *Last Supper* [fig. 11.2], with the count sitting in the middle of the table, surrounded by his slaves. His purpose is to show them how good he can be, and to teach them manipulated and distorted concepts of Christianity: that they must respect and serve their master as God requires.

The count washes the feet of the slaves first and then invites them to sit at his table. On the one hand, he shows compassion, setting Pascual free and

Figure 11.2 "The mise-en-scène emulates Leonardo's *Last Supper*, with the count sitting in the middle of the table, surrounded by his slaves. His purpose is to show them how good he can be, and to teach them manipulated and distorted concepts of Christianity: that they must respect and serve their master as God requires."

telling Antonio that he can return to the village where he belongs. On the other hand, he makes a mockery out of the reenacted last supper. Every time the count begins to talk and tell one of his parables, religious music starts playing, but the morals that come out of his preaching are deformations of Christianity. The film becomes pure dark comedy as the master preaches equality to a group of slaves, telling them that true happiness consists of suffering the overseer's cruelty with patience in the name of God.

Yet, the film achieves a certain revision of history by giving a voice to the slaves and by representing their subjectivity. These slaves have their own personalities and thoughts. For example, Antonio and Bangoché respect their master and believe in his good deeds, while Negro Conguito always expresses himself in *mucandas,* combining dance and song in his story-telling, and also offers his own interpretations of suffering and hunger among blacks. Sebastián is the critical character that at first seems to play the part of Judas, who does not recognize his master. The two even break bread together and at one point the count asks Sebastián to recognize him, but he instead spits on the count's face. By not recognizing his master, he is able to escape his destiny as a slave and forge a path toward liberation. This leads Schroeder to discuss Sebastián's character as the real Christlike character, thus reversing roles with the count, who, on this view, becomes the Judas figure.[20] After all, the next day the count is the one who betrays his own words.

One of the more important aspects of this reenactment is the visual representation of syncretism. As Schroeder puts it, "[it] dramatizes the transculturation between Europe and Africa as it has played itself out in Cuba."[21] For example, when the count tells the story of Saint Francis, the slaves recognize him instead as Orula. And Sebastián also offers his own version of creation when he tells the parable about how when Olofi (creator of the world in the Santería tradition) made the world, Truth and Lie were also created. These two became confused because Lie cut off Truth's head and put it on his own body. This explains why the truth sometimes gets confused with lies, and is directly relevant to the figure of the count.

The day after the "last supper," on Good Friday, the count leaves the mill early in the morning so he does not need to fulfill his promises about the slaves not having to work on the holiday. Don Manuel wakes the slaves for work, but they do not want to work because it is Good Friday and the count has told them they will not have to work. Don Manuel does not respect anything that the count has promised, and the slaves start to rebel. The priest tries to get help from the count, and here is where all the count's religious hypocrisy becomes obvious. In the end, he tracks down and kills all the slaves, including the very ones who had been seated at the table the night before. He cuts off their heads and displays them publicly next to a cross on a hill—a place visually similar to Golgotha—in order to teach a lesson to the other slaves.

Sebastián is the only one who escapes. Schroeder suggests that perhaps he is worthy of salvation because he is the most developed person of the group.[22] However, during a previous scene in which Don Manuel visits Don Gaspar to complain about the count's laughable enactment of the foot washing of the slaves before the supper, he also talks about Sebastián as one who has special powers, noting how he does not die even after all the punishments heaped upon him. The slave has escaped three times, and he will be healed again and rise up against us, Don Manuel prefigures. Don Manuel's words imply a sense of special, divine power in Sebastián, maintaining a similarity to Christ's supernatural powers. Sebastián has a divine connection that ultimately enables him to save himself. During the supper, he blows special powders into the count's face while he is sleeping and professes his escape. Furthermore, as he escapes at the end of the film, Sebastián's running is intercut with empowering images of a bird in flight, horses running, a flowing river, and big stones falling down a mountainside. These are images of freedom and strength, yet they also remind the viewer of an anecdote in Alejo Carpentier's novel, *El reino de este mundo*, in which Mackandal, a black slave, escapes his destiny of slavery because he also had faith, and his followers furthermore have faith in his transformation into a more religious being. Without Sebastián's transformation, the film simply falls into a historical materialistic narration—which it certainly is, in part—that only pursues the utilitarian purpose of condemning slavery and a bourgeois history. While the film is clearly critical of religion (particularly a corrupted Christianity) it nonetheless opens a space for an Afro-Cuban religiosity, which simultaneously becomes a space of resistance. Religion is seen in oppressive terms but also in liberatory terms.

The 1990s saw the production of a number of highly popular feature films in Cuba that also gained international acclaim. While not the main subject, Santería has become an increasingly visible entity that has surfaced within many recent films. For example, in hugely successful *Strawberry and Chocolate* (1993; dir. Gutiérrez Alea), Diego (Jorge Perrugoría) and Nancy (Marta Ibarra) both have altars to Santa Barbara/Changó, and pray and give offerings to them. There is a scene where Nancy consults with her Babalawo (Santero-godfather) about the future of her relationship with David (Vladimir Cruz), and the Babalawo reads the cowerie shells. Even so, these religious representations in the film are part of the mise-en-scène and little else.

In Gutiérrez Alea's last film, *Guantanamera*, the syncretic elements of Santería are overcome and the film portrays Afro-Cuban religious myths without having to compare them to Catholicism. The film portrays the parable of Oloffin and the Afro-Cuban myth about how Ikú was able to overcome immortality on earth. Santería simply exists by itself and does not rely on the legitimation of any other system.[23] And, in a more playful way, Juan Carlos Tabío's *Plaff* (1988) also presents elements of Santería when Concha (Daisy Granados) seeks advice from her santera-godmother in order to find an explanation as to why people are throwing eggs at her. In all these films, the representation of Santería is part of everyday life on the island. The main characters are not Afro-Cubans, and Santería is just a part of the overall narration of the culture.

This is also the case with the more recent *Miel para Oshún* (Honey for Oshún; dir. Humberto Solás, 2001), which can be read as the contemporary counterpart of Peon's 1930 *La Virgen de la Caridad*. Solás's film shows the political and social agenda of the later part of the Revolution, and uses the popular religious icon to make a miracle happen that will restore the sense of identity for the main character. However, in this film La Virgen de la Caridad has become Oshún. Roberto (Jorge Perugorría) is a Cuban exile who returns to the island after a 30-year absence. He has come back to find his roots, as well as an explanation as to why his mother abandoned him many years ago. He encounters his cousin Pilar (Isabel Santos), who will show him little by little the reality and truth that has been overshadowed in his life: His mother did not abandon him. Contrary to what he believed, it was actually his father who took him away from Cuba illegally, against the will of his mother—an Elián González story in reverse. He also gradually learns that by being away so long he has lost a sense of identity that can only be regained by reconnecting his new self with the land and its people. This reconnection includes his transformation from being highly skeptical of Oshún and Santería to ultimately having to accept that it is Oshún who makes a final encounter with his mother possible.

Nonetheless, there are few representations of Santería practices in the film. The only real encounter is when Pilar goes to visit her godmother and asks for help in finding Roberto's mother, whose whereabouts have been unknown for a long time. Oshún speaks through the godmother, letting them know that he will find his mother where the river meets the ocean, where Oshún meets with Yemaja. The film is another narrated journey seeking a lost mother, and through this search a lost identity is refound. While it is an *orisha* who makes the encounter possible by revealing the mother's location, the viewer never actually encounters Oshún or the honey; they remain invisible.

The ICAIC has always been deficient in black and Afro-Cuban directors,[24] however, Gloria Rolando, an Afro-Cuban independent filmmaker, is doing experimental work on themes of blackness and Santería outside the walls of the ICAIC. Her work marks a transition in the contemporary cinematic visualization of Santería. For example, *Los marqueses de Atarés* is about a carnival *comparsa* (a community of musicians and dancers) uniting expressions of the *rumberos, santeros,* and Abakuá in the Atarés neighborhood of Havana. In 2001, she also finished a film called *Raíces de mi corazón* (Roots of my heart) concerning the 1912 massacre of the "Independents of Color," a group of black men who fought for the independence of Cuba against Spain.

Rolando's work is an interesting mixture of documentary, containing certain anthropological approaches, and dramatizations. *Oggún: The Eternal Presence* (1991) is worth reviewing since it is a film that visually represents several *patakíes* (stories of *orishas*) in hagiographic ways. Shot on video,[25] the title sequence opens onto images of altars in temples and homes; the usual candles, offerings of cigars, honey and other foods, flowers, and the caldrons where the *orishas* resides, fill the screen. In the background, sacred drum music is playing. After the titles, we see a quote by Jacques Stephen Alexis (Jamaican) that reads in English: "Africa does not leave the Negro in peace, no matter from which country he is, the place where he comes or goes." A sense of pan-Caribbeanism pervades these words since they are not in Spanish or said by a Cuban, thus breaking already with the intranationalism that prevails in the other films discussed here. But also, these words call for a postcolonial identity in a manner akin to Stuart Hall's theorizations, whereby Africa is the imaginary source of origin where all the blacks would like to return, even if this return is not possible in reality.[26]

The film is framed by the narration of Lázaro Ross, an Afro-Cuban man who tells the stories of Oggún. At times he sings the stories because he is being trained as an Akpwon Yoruba, a singer to the gods, and is himself an initiate of this *orisha*. A little way into the film, there is a switch from a documentary style to a dramatic style where we see Oggún (José L. Kindelan) burning metals and constructing his tools, while Oshún (Teresa Alfonso), the sensual god of love, is seen dancing. Oshún seduces Oggún with her enchantments, dancing naked and putting honey all over her body. The images then switch back to the documentary style when we see a group of people in contemporary Cuba dancing and singing together. In this switch, the soft focus of the dramatized *orisha* story turns into a hard focus: the bright, defining light of the documentary narration. The film continues to alternate between the narrator, the *patakíes,* which dramatize more *orisha* stories (the second is the marriage between Oya and Oshún, and the consequent betrayal of Oya when she is seduced by Changó), and the singing and dancing of the contemporary group of people, who are celebrating the *orishas.* The effect is an interwoven narration of history and mythology bearing on present life in Cuba. Despite the dramatization of the *patakíes,* the *orishas* are never given voice. The narrator speaks for them.

It is important to note that there is no syncretism presented here: These representations are from the Yoruba tradition, the Yoruba language is spoken at times, and there is a sense of connection with Africa—its legends of kings and lands, and its history—without the countervailing presence of Catholicism, and nothing pointing to the historical setting of blacks in Cuba. Santería is represented in its own universe, and there is a sense of universalism that breaks with any barriers of locality and specificity.

Questions are thus provoked here: Who is the intended audience of such a representation? Who did Rolando have in mind when filming *Oggún*? Her work seems to be pointing toward a real postcolonial black subjectivity that has not been made visible in such a way before. Yet, at the same time, it is clearly a production designed in many ways to "educate" (or entertain) a public who is foreign to the concepts of Santería religiosity, and it presents an exoticised, clean-cut version of Afro-Cuban religion for outsiders. The exoticizing of Cuba in part derives from its very real Afro-Cuban presence, a presence that is only more mysterious since it has been kept hidden. Yet, in revealing more of Afro-Cuban culture and religion, filmmakers run up against the ideological problems of representation.

This brief survey of the presence of religion, specifically Afro-Cuban religion, within Cuban cinema leads me to a couple conclusions. First, representations of Catholicism as much as Santería are pivotal because they help define a sense of cultural identity that has been neglected at times for political and ideological reasons. Filmmakers thus contribute to a project of recovery, of representing what has fallen out in the continually revised history of Cuba. "Catholicism," Schroeder suggests, "has been the single most important institution throughout Cuban history," meanwhile, Santería "seems to have secured its place as the *de facto* religion of Cuba . . . [because] it is free of the unproductive disputes over doctrine and ortho-doxy that plague Catholicism and Marxism."[27] Tensions thus remain between the more dominant and orthodox Catholicism and the more popular practices of Santería.

Finally, we must ask why there have been so many films depicting Santería practices as something vital but at the same time marginal to the Cuban collective imaginary. I suggest that filmic images of Santería, and Afro-Cubans in general, however fleeting, are inserted as a critical attempt to forge a new, postcolonial identity that the Revolution claimed in the name of the unity of the nation—all people, all races, all classes—but perhaps has never completely fulfilled. To openly portray Afro-Cuban cultural practices and talk about racial problems would be to admit there is still prejudice and racial inequality. The place for Afro-Cubans and their (religious) practices is still being contested. However, the hybrid nature of political identity mixes with the hybrid religious identities, pushing for-ward to an ever-new sense of Cubanness. The ideology of *mestizaje* and *mulatismo* that continues to prevail in the national cultural agenda of the Cuban imaginary may explain this intersection between Santería and Catholicism, as well as explain the abiding interest in syncretism itself. The fact is that what is still relatively more prominent in Cuban social structures is an ambiguity of sorts, and this very ambiguity is reflected and represented in national film productions.

Notes

1. Michael Warren, "African Spirit Worship Has Powerful Hold on Cubans: Catholics Embrace Santería," from ABC News online, available at http://more.abcnews.go.com/sections/world/pope_cuba/cuba_journal_12498.htm.
2. *The Christian Century* (no author specified) (February 4, 1998), available at http://www.findarticles.com/cf_dls/m1058/n4_v115/20350171/p1/article.jhtml.
3. Alice L. Hageman, "Introduction," in *Religion in Cuba Today,* Alice L. Hageman and Philip E. Wheaton, eds. (New York: Association Press, 1971), 31. Although this information is taken from a book published in 1971, the numbers have not changed much; according to Anita Snow, chief of the Associated Press in Havana, currently 40 percent of Cubans are today baptized Catholics. See "Spirits High for Pope's Cuba Visit," available at http://www.s-t.com/daily/01–98/01–20-98/b06wn060.htm.
4. Hageman, "Introduction," 31. See also Fred D. Bloch and Constantino Torres and their electronically published book *Doing Business with Cuba,* 1997, available at http://www.edutourstocuba.com/cuba/cuba_lang.html.
5. In *Granma International Digital,* "Recuerdan visita del Papa a la isla," January 13, 2003, available at http://www.granma.cu/espanol/ene03/lun13/ortega.html.
6. I use the term "synopticized" here to highlight the often visual hybridizing of these different traditions. In Santería, as in many so-called "syncretic" religions, there is often a visual similarity established before any recourse to parallel "beliefs." See, for example, my short photo essay, cowritten with S. Brent Plate, "From Salamalecun Malecunsala to Amen: Seeing Syncretism in Cuba," in *Religious Studies News,* March 2002.
7. John King, *Magical Reels: A History of Cinema in Latin America* (London: Verso, 1990), 145.
8. *La Virgen de la Caridad,* dir. Ramón Peón. (Cuba, 1930).
9. Michael Chanan, *The Cuban Image: Cinema and Cultural Politics in Cuba* (London: BIF Publishing, 1985), 60.
10. Néstor García Canclini, "Will There be Latin American Cinema in the Year 2000?" in *Framing Latin American Cinema,* Ann Marie Stock, ed. (Minneapolis: University of Minnesota Press, 1997), 246.
11. John King, *Magical Reels,* 66.
12. Michael Chanan, *The Cuban Image,* 262.
13. Paul A. Schroeder, *Tomás Gutiérrez Alea: The Dialectics of a Filmmaker* (New York: Routledge, 2002), 68.
14. Ibid., 70.
15. Ibid., 89.

16. Chanan, *The Cuban Image,* 213.
17. Ibid., 261.
18. Schroeder, *Tomás Gutiérrez Alea,* 67.
19. Ibid., 78.
20. Ibid., 86.
21. Ibid., 83.
22. Ibid., 88.
23. For more on *Guantanamera* and the retelling of Santerían myths, see Edna M. Rodríguez-Mangual, "Driving a Dead Body through the Nation: Death and Allegory in the Film *Guantanamera,*" *Chasqui* 31 (May 2002): 50–61.
24. Sergio Giral, one of the few black directors in the island, produced a trilogy of films about slavery in the seventies as well. They are all based on literary sources, and the slaves in these productions are also seen in a new way, as characters who have a subjectivity and historical agency. Another key exception is Sara Gómez, who died young after only having helped direct *De cierta manera* (1977).
25. During the 1980s and 1990s, as video technologies became more accessible, many young filmmakers started to make videos, thereby changing the aesthetic ideas promoted by the ICAIC. However, these productions continue to lack channels of distribution, and therefore it is difficult to add them to the cultural imaginary I am trying to trace here.
26. See, among other places, Stuart Hall, "Cultural Identity and Diaspora," *Identity and Difference,* Kathryn Woodward, ed. (London: Sage Publications, 1997), 51–59.
27. Schroeder, *Tomás Gutiérrez Alea,* 134.

Chapter Twelve

"The Eyes of All People Are Upon Us":

American Civil Religion and the Birth of Hollywood

Kris Jozajtis

Introduction

Although serious writing on religion and the cinema can be traced back at least as far as the late 1960s, with a considerable expansion having taken place over the last decade or so, this literature has, if truth be told, made little impact on the mainstream of either film and media studies or religious studies. Overwhelmingly theological in its orientation and based almost entirely on the analysis of films as "texts," scholarship on religion and film and religion has grown into a lively subfield of its own, without ever really gaining the credibility of its parent disciplines.[1] This is especially apparent in work on American culture, the world's most important market for film production and reception.

With its distinctive evangelical tang, the United States is by any conventional measure the most "religious" nation in the developed world. Yet students of film have only rarely sought to consider how the nation's distinctive economy has shaped the movies.[2] Similarly, the much-needed examination of the ways in which a media-saturated cultural environment has come to shape religious beliefs and practices in America is still in its infancy.[3] Concentrating on the contemporary scene, however, even this emerging scholarship has tended to overlook the social and historical importance of the movies. And, in those rare instances where the broader social context within which both film and religion are consumed is invoked, though not necessarily examined, the particular historical forces that have shaped both American society and American cinema are usually taken for granted.[4] This, I would argue, needs to change if the discussion of religion and film is to gain a wider constituency.

In what follows, I want to suggest that scholars interested in religion and film have much to gain from a more rigorous examination of the particular national context that has shaped the American cinema. Based around a necessarily brief reexamination of D. W. Griffith's epochal *The Birth of a Nation* (1915), one of the most influential *and* notorious movies ever made, this chapter highlights how the beginnings of Hollywood were informed by broader, long-term developments in the cultural and religious economy of the United States. Faith-based positions may well have an advantage when it comes to prompting an initial engagement with the religious ideas, images, references, and stories articulated routinely within Hollywood since Griffith's picture was unleashed upon the world. But there is, I believe, a wider social and political resonance to Hollywood's treatment of religion that does not depend on any preexisting religious orientation for it to be deemed relevant. Recognition of this, though, demands a shift in focus from the issue of religion to the issue of national identity and the processes whereby nationhood is established and maintained. For it is the nation that furnishes the economic, political, and social context within which religion and cinema interact.

"The New Israel": Religion and U.S. National Identity

Acknowledging the immense economic, political, and social power still bound up with notions of nationhood from a media studies perspective, Philip Schlesinger argues that questions regarding national identity should not be taken for granted within contemporary discussions of culture and communication. Rather, they ought to be seen as something foundational to them, and explored accordingly. Like Benedict Anderson's celebrated conception of the "imagined community," Schlesinger understands the nation "as a particular kind of collective identity . . . constituted at a given strategic level of society." Serving to construct an "us" and exclude others, it is functionally dependent upon the effective communication of stories, symbols, and traditions through which we imagine ourselves, both spatially and temporally, as participants in the broader drama of national life. Especially important in this respect is the "continual" and "selective" mediation of the temporal relationship between the nation as collected in the present and the past. Obviously, the media have a crucial role to play in this process, and accounts of how a collective feeling of national belonging is developed and maintained often emphasize the importance of shared myths and narratives in furnishing the sense of continuity or "tradition," without which a nation simply cannot exist. But, as Schlesinger stresses, "national cultures are not simple repositories of shared symbols to which the entire population stands in identical relation. Rather, they are to be approached as sites of contestation in which competition over definition takes place." As integral as the media and other cultural activities such as education and sport are to the elaboration of a national identity, therefore, they are nonetheless subject to the shifting power relations of the national process.[5]

A similar approach can also be taken to the study of religion. Instead of taking religion to be *sui generis*, as something which in its essentials transcends the kind of temporal and geographical specifics associated with the modern nation-state, one might insist that the institutions, practices, stories, and other cultural forms associated with the category of religion are not to be abstracted from historical circumstance.[6] Hence, the emergence of the nation-state as the most important and powerful form of social organization associated with modernity can also be seen as a key aspect of the same broad historical process that has not only brought about religious change but also stimulated the specialized study of religion. In religious terms, moreover, the defining moment of this process came in 1791, when the First Amendment was included in the American Bill of Rights.

As Tocqueville recognized early on, the formal separation of church and state enacted in the First Amendment ensured, somewhat paradoxically perhaps, that in contrast with much of Europe, religion in the United States would remain a vital social resource.[7] Far from marking the end for religion and religious institutions, disestablishment furnished the conditions for the development of a vibrant, diverse, and intensely competitive religious economy that has thus far confounded the widespread assumption that secularization (as the death of religion) would be one of the defining characteristics of modernity. Instead, and building on a mythology of religious freedom and virtue associated with New England Puritanism, setting aside and protecting religion in the American context made it a defining aspect of the national process: "One Nation under God"; a "Chosen People"; a "New Israel."

The religious and biblical imagery that pervades American political rhetoric prompted Robert Bellah to develop the Tocquevillean perspective and argue that the symbols and rituals of U.S. nationhood actually represented "an elaborate and well-institutionalized civil religion," beyond denominational factionalism, which served to provide "an understanding of the American experience in the light of ultimate and universal reality." At the heart of Bellah's famous article was an idealistic insistence on the primacy of the individual citizen's conscience over the possible injunctions of the state. Thus he cited John F. Kennedy's assertion that "the rights of man come not from the generosity of the state but from the hand of God," and highlighted the way in which these rights are "more basic than any political structure and provide a point of revolutionary leverage from which any state structure may be radically altered."[8] As the flood of responses to Bellah's notion of an American civil religion confirms, such formulations indicate the problems inherent in the defining and theorizing of "religion."[9] Nevertheless, Bellah was surely correct when he pointed out that

> most of what is good and most of what is bad in [American] history is rooted in our public theology. Every movement to make America more fully realize its professed values has grown out of some form of public theology, from the abolitionists to the social gospel and the early socialist party to the civil rights movement under Martin Luther King and the farm worker's movement under Caesar Chavez. But so has every expansionist war and every form of oppression of racial minorities and immigrant groups.[10]

In these terms, therefore, religion can be seen as a key "second language" within the "argument" that comprises the national "tradition."[11] Thus, as elitist and prescriptive as Bellah's original conception was—his thesis avoided the role of popular culture entirely—it remains important and useful because it reminds us of the utter centrality of religion, the category of the religious, and the attendant questions of existential meaning that accompany debates surrounding American national identity. What, then, of American cinema?

The Progressive Era: Protestantism and Early American Cinema

Despite the visibility of religious ideas, narratives, and symbols in the work of such quintessentially "American" filmmakers as Cecil B. DeMille, Frank Capra, and John Ford, to mention but a select few, and the decisive role played by the Catholic Church as the industry came to adopt the Production Code during the 1930s, there is little writing that considers the emergence of motion pictures as both a reflection of and an influence upon the complex religious economy of the United States. This is odd. Reflecting upon the initial success of movies in a United States experiencing the transformations wrought by large-scale immigration, industrialization, urbanization, and the dissolution of Protestant hegemony leads Garth Jowett, for example, to argue that far from being "a lucky innovation, arriving merely at a propitious time," cinema actually "answered a deep social and cultural need of the American people."[12] In the early decades of the twentieth century, motion pictures were not simply a new and compelling form of entertainment. They also provided ideas, information, stories, and new forms of social activity to an uncertain, multicultural, and rapidly changing America. In a sense, therefore, the American cinema might even be seen as an appropriately modern mechanism of "orientation," in the religious sense of that term proposed by Charles Long: "that is, how one comes to terms with the ultimate significance of one's place in the world."[13] Be that as it may, the point to be stressed here is that Hollywood did not develop independently of the religious dimension to American life but, rather, in dialogue and negotiation with it.

The emergence of cinema as both a medium and a social and cultural phenomenon during the early part of the twentieth century coincided roughly with a time of massive change in American Protestantism. Up to the late nineteenth century, "Protestantism presented an almost unbroken front in its defense of the social status quo."[14] Prerevolutionary efforts to establish America as a "Christian" nation may have failed; nevertheless, the constitutional separation of church and state enshrined in the First Amendment had ensured that the United States would indeed develop as a Protestant nation. From around 1880 onward, however, social changes began to undermine the hegemonic influence Protestant denominations had hitherto enjoyed: the Civil War, immigration, industrialization, urbanization, and rural depopulation; public schools were spreading Enlightenment ideas, while evolution and new critical approaches questioning scriptural authority became established within the increasingly secular universities; unionization was taking place and the social problems of a free market economy were becoming ever more apparent.[15]

The public response of the Protestant churches to change was a growth in social criticism, which found its wider expression via the reform movements of the so-called Progressive Era. Clearly, it would be misleading to explain the complexities of the Progressive Era as little more than the result of a crisis within American Protestantism. The large-scale and multifaceted nature of the historical forces that were transforming the United States at the time defy such simplifications. Nevertheless, in terms of its cultural expression and elevated moral tone, progressivism was very much a product of, and legitimated with reference to, the American Protestant tradition. Given the widely acknowledged prominence of churchmen such as Josiah Strong, Walter Rauschenbusch, and William Jennings Bryan within the various reform movements, not to mention Woodrow Wilson, the "Protestant Pope," as well as the rhetoric of "Christian principles," "confessions of faith," "crusades," and "social purity" routinely employed by the progressives, there is a sense in which American public life of the time took on the characteristics of a nationwide religious revival.[16]

In fact, the Evangelical flavor of the reform period disguises the fact that at no time was there an especially unified or coherent "progressive" program. It may be the case that as U.S. society grew more complex, as well as more powerful and prosperous, progressivism represented what Robert Wiebe has described as a "search for order."[17] Yet, in terms of social origins, tendencies, and the causes they adhered to, progressives were relatively diverse. The moral stridency of progressive rhetoric could only partially disguise the era's ambiguities, contradictions, and paradoxes. Instead, progressive invocations of the "old-time religion" support arguments that the problem reformers sought to solve was the problem of *progress*: "specifically, how American society was to continue to enjoy the fruits of material progress without the accompanying assault upon human dignity and the erosion of the conventional values and moral assumptions on which the social order appeared to rest."[18] What progressives appeared to want was nothing less than a reconstitution of the crumbling Protestant empire in a radically new set of circumstances. *The Birth of a Nation* was to articulate this desire in startling form.

Whilst the pictures of D. W. Griffith, the most famous filmmaker of the period then and now, are, quite obviously, a product of their time, the evangelical tang to the Progressive Era is often ignored in the discussion of them.[19] Lary May, however, emphasizes the importance of the director's Southern Methodist background in describing how the so-called "father of film" gave aesthetic form to the assumptions, tensions, and dilemmas of the Progressive Era in its quest to affirm a traditional moral order in the face of rapid change. Stressing the "explicitly Protestant tone" of Griffith's films, he notes, "reporters referred to [Griffith] as the 'messianic savior of the movie art, a prophet who made shadow sermons more powerful than the pulpit.'" Indeed, Griffith saw himself as being "above politics" and portraying feelings "bred in the bone." Yet although such attitudes might have sat comfortably with the innate conservatism of the reformers, Griffith also believed that the cinema was "a moral and educational force" and "the universal language" predicted in the Bible. And the director's particular and essentially religious understanding of "realism," that the camera was a neutral but necessarily active instrument of truth and its revelation, led him away from the conventions inherited from the traditions of the stage toward the development of a style that succeeded in dramatizing the lives of real people in real settings. On this basis, May argues that as important and influential as Griffith's working methods were, his interest in the technical aspects of the medium was really a function of the director's moral vision and his quest to "show God's will surfacing in the chaos of material life."[20]

Positing the cinema as an agent of moral transformation also represented a positive response to progressive worries about the moral worth of the cinema. The early silent period was to some extent characterized by a complex negotiation between, on the one hand, a motion picture industry keen to maintain its profitability and, on the other, a loose coalition of civic-minded reformers and clergy seeking to regulate or at least control the social impact of the new medium.[21] Indeed, for all the moral concerns articulated in his pictures, Griffith's movies were often antagonistic toward "meddling" reformers. For Griffith, it was the still underdeveloped medium of film, rather than the campaigns and movements of progressives, that offered the greatest possibilities for the moral regeneration of America as the churches began a slow retreat from the mainstream of national life. In this respect, Griffith's own concerns reflected a deeper change within American religion wherein religion was increasingly seen as something private. By the time he had begun to make films, Griffith's own religious orientation had shifted away from his original Methodism, and he would eventually become a freemason, holding "no strong sectarian beliefs."[22] Thus, while the religious allegories in several films, including *The Birth of a Nation* and *Intolerance* (1916), support Richard Schickel's assertion that Griffith "harbored somewhat loftier, somewhat more romantic, somewhat vaguer religious sentiments," this aspect of the director's work cannot be aligned with the reform movements of the Progressive Era in as straightforward a way as May appears to claim.[23]

For Scott Simmon, Griffith's pictures reflect a view of reformers as meddlers who "exacerbate the conditions they profess to ameliorate." Like May, Simmon argues that Griffith's movies were informed by a belief in the medium's capacity for moral reform, and he admits "that Griffith's world remained a religious one." Nevertheless, the director's relationship with the reformers was characterized by antagonism, Simmon contends, "because he [wa]s battling them over common ground. Both [we]re claiming the territory of moral instruction . . . newly open for contention because of the evident retreat of organized religion." Drawing on accounts of American culture that stress the "feminization" of the Protestant tradition and a privatistic "shift from a Protestant to a therapeutic orientation within the dominant culture," Simmon proposes Griffith's work as "representative of another, more complex cultural transformation in America: the breakup of Puritan unity (in which spirituality had been expressed through work) for more purely practical manifestations of moral reform." Thus, he reiterates the profound significance attached by the director to the development of both the form and status of motion pictures:

> Griffith's real ambitions for the movies as art were inextricably tied into [the] claim . . . that art is a truer guide to moral reform than is any organized society

of reformers. Put a little more strongly, art . . . now fills the reformist role that was once reserved for organized religion, a role that organized reformers can only counterfeit and pervert.

The suggestion here is that Griffith understood the medium of film not just in terms of art but as something that might perhaps succeed religion in the provision of moral guidance and "ceremonies of community."[24]

On occasion, Griffith's religiosity led him into excess. The inability to "resist flying in angels on wires or Christ himself to beatify grand finales," most famously in *The Birth of a Nation,* leads Simmon to suggest that the director's "most literal religious imagery plays quite inauthentically," and thus query "how much of Griffith's darker world of God and fate was genuine devotion, how much conventional piety, and how much another scheme to legitimate movie art."[25] Yet, one might also argue that such problems reveal the confusions of the filmmaker because they reflect the contradictions of his time. Griffith's career as a director began and developed at a time when the traditional hegemony and moral authority associated with American Protestantism had been called into question by the cultural upheavals wrought by non-Protestant immigration, large-scale industrial development, and rapid urbanization, as well as the fundamental ideological challenge of positivist science. In the cinema, itself a product of scientific development, this positivist worldview was reflected in the assumed and largely unconsidered "realism" of the screen image. Still, for all its problems, Protestant Christianity remained the basic symbolic currency of American public life. The early motion picture industry was indeed controlled, almost entirely, by white, Anglo-Saxon, Protestant men.[26] Griffith, it would appear, responded to his cultural environment by attempting to reconcile the apparent veracity of the movies with the traditional, Bible-based conception of the absolute, widely accepted across America as the ultimate source of national legitimacy. Perhaps the inauthenticity Simmon detects in Griffith's pictures arising from overt and literal deployment of Christian imagery indicates the inherently problematic nature of such a project: squaring belief in a pragmatic and economically effective empiricism with faith in an invisible yet still personified moral order.

The Birth of a Nation: Griffith and the Lost Cause

If any one film can bear the weight of the wider argument being made here regarding the importance of the national culture in determining the nature of relations between religion and film, *The Birth of a Nation* is that film.[27] Not only did it, and the huge box office success it enjoyed over several decades, mark a watershed in terms of the development of the American film industry, but it can also be seen as "almost a myth of origin" for the serious study of cinema itself.[28] Yet, where it was once described as "the incontestable keystone movie in the history of American cinema,"[29] Griffith's picture, which depicts the Ku Klux Klan as patriotic heroes who restored the "natural" order in the wake of black emancipation, tends now to be remembered as little more than an expression of unreconstructed Southern white supremacism [fig. 12.1]. Indeed, apart from a provocative piece by Russell Merritt, recent treatments of *The Birth of a Nation* have done little more than restate the obvious.[30] Contemporary scholars appear baffled as to why such a racist piece might once have been so important and popular. Addressing the film in terms of the religious and cultural context that informed its production, and positing the film as a response to a crisis in American Protestantism, the following discussion reasserts the importance of *Birth*. It contends that the racism of the picture was not an end in itself but a function of the director's largely successful attempt to enact a transformation of how Americans might continue to a understand themselves as a "chosen people." In that sense, *The Birth of a Nation* marked an important turning point within the history of the American civil religion.

By 1914, spurred by the success of longer Italian-made feature films, often with religious themes, like Guazzoni's *St. Francis* (1911) and *Quo Vadis* (1912), Antamoro's *Christus* (1914), and Pastrone's *Cabiria* (1914),[31] Griffith's aspirations for the medium led him to embark upon his most ambitious production yet, an adaptation of *The Clansman,* Thomas M. Dixon's best-selling, but unapologetically racist, "historical romance of the Ku Klux Klan" set in the reconstruction period. Right from the portentous decision to begin filming on July 4, Griffith understood the project as more than just another "sausage," as he dubbed his earlier short films for the production company Biograph.[32] Mindful, perhaps, of the approaching fiftieth anniversary of Appomattox, Griffith not only supplemented the original source with material from Dixon's novel *The Leopard's Spots* (1902) as well as the stage play of *The Clansman* (1906), but also chose to preface his film with a lengthy section devoted largely to the Civil War itself. It is in the director's particular regional, white, Southern standpoint on the history he sought to depict, his passionate identification with the fate of the white South during and after the Civil War, that we find the key religious meanings articulated by the film.[33] For Griffith, "setting the record straight" on the Civil War and Reconstruction represented an opportunity to revitalize the traditions of Protestant America via the modern technology of film.

As the first Southerner elected to the presidency since the Civil War, the victory of Woodrow Wilson in 1912 symbolized the apparent reconciliation that had taken place between the North and South since 1865. For some sections of American society though, the reintegration of the South into the life of the nation merely reflected the unwanted resurgence of ideals and values that the Civil War had supposedly put an end to. Just as progressive reforms were essentially for whites only, Wilson came to preside over a nation in which many blacks were effectively disenfranchised, and Jim Crow was the norm.[34] In terms of race relations, therefore, *The Birth of a Nation* merely reflected and reinforced certain trends in American life. That said, we should recognize attempts to play down or separate out the film's depiction of blacks from its other qualities as misguided.[35] Racism is fundamental to the film in terms both of form and content. As "obvious" as the racism of *Birth* is, however,[36] there may yet be value in reconsidering D. W. Griffith's denials of racist intent, both in the

Figure 12.1   "Griffith's picture, which depicts the Ku Klux Klan as patriotic heroes who restored the 'natural' order in the wake of black emancipation, tends now to be remembered as little more than an expression of unreconstructed Southern white supremacism."

film itself (via intertitle at the beginning of part two) and in the public debate that followed the picture's release.[37] Whilst they clearly fail(ed) to mitigate the picture's negative portrayal of African Americans, taking the denials seriously leads one to recognize the racism of the film as a consequence of the way Griffith sought to mobilize a cultural authority deriving from the South's sense of itself as the conscience of an America in the throes of modernization.

The longstanding furor engendered by the racism of *The Birth of a Nation,* and the necessary condemnation of that racism which has emanated from various quarters, has in recent times led away from any recognition and/or consideration of the movie as a sincere expression of the trauma experienced within the American South as a result of defeat in the Civil War.[38] Indulging a tendency to stereotype the white South in a way that merely reverses what was played out in Griffith's picture, the current critical orthodoxy would ask us to believe that the once extensive popular appeal of the film rested entirely upon its now embarrassing white supremacist standpoint. The complexities and contradictions of the movie are all subordinated to its racism, while its long-term importance and influence are played down. Yet, the sad fact remains that racist "othering" is by no means as aberrant as we might wish it to be. Moreover, while boundaries dividing "us" from "them" are crucial in the construction and maintenance of social groups, they do not in themselves explain the attractive force that serves to bind a society "from within."[39] Thus, although Fred Silva admits that Griffith shared "with many Southern writers and apologists a failure to confront the race issue honestly," he argues that "without excusing the obviously racist sentiments of *The Birth of a Nation,* the viewer must recognize that Griffith presented the values of a conquered people who viewed the rubble of what they had conceived as a civilized, moral way of life."[40] This cultural orientation, commonly known as the "Lost Cause," is derided by some commentators as one of many clichés via which the Civil War is remembered in America "not as history but as legend."[41] That may be true up to a point. But, dismissing the Lost Cause in such a way ignores the deeper significance attached to the Lost Cause as the South came to terms with defeat. What I want to indicate here is the trope of victimhood Griffith's picture is organized around, and the way in which the film transforms oppressor into underdog.

For Charles Reagan Wilson, the cultural translation of white southerners' shared need to make sense of defeat evolved into something he dubs "the religion of the Lost Cause" or, echoing Robert Bellah, "Southern civil religion." By no means the first to engage with the mythic aspects of the Lost Cause, Wilson lays particular emphasis on the position and role of the clergy within what H. L Mencken came to describe as "the Bible Belt."[42] Thus, instead of dismissing the Lost Cause as mere "myth" or "legend,"

Wilson argues that "judged by historical and anthropological criteria, the civil religion that emerged in the postbellum South was an authentic expression of religion."[43] Whilst subsequent work challenges such attempts to cast the Lost Cause in religious terms,[44] the theoretical understanding of religion Wilson applies to the extensive empirical evidence he marshals in support of his thesis is rooted in fairly conventional notions of religion as a response to chaos, disorder, and sociocultural crisis; as manifest in symbols, myths, and rituals; as dividing existence into two realms, the sacred and the profane, via which members come to perceive their society as having a sacred or holy quality. As Wilson notes, "for postbellum southerners such traditional religious issues as the nature of suffering, evil, and the seeming irrationality of life had a disturbing relevance."[45]

In adapting Bellah's notion of an American civil religion above and beyond the denominations to the specific historical context of the postbellum South, Wilson lays great emphasis upon the active and popular creation of, as well as participation in, ceremonies articulating the Lost Cause during the half century or so after Appomattox. In his analysis, there is an almost Catholic richness to the material culture of the Southern civil religion and the significance attached to a whole pantheon of Southern saints via pilgrimages, relics, rituals, and a range of institutions (including the Ku Klux Klan) extending beyond the Protestant churches that remained the bedrock of the distinct cultural environment of the South.[46] For a filmmaker like Griffith, moreover, the materiality described by Wilson provided a tangible basis for the translation of the word-based, Protestant traditions undergirding the social and moral order into the visual forms of the silent motion picture. Crucial in this respect was the way in which a distinctively Southern appropriation of the jeremiad, a rhetorical form more usually associated with the Puritan tradition, helped proponents of the Lost Cause celebrate Southern culture by defining it in relation to the North.

In Sacvan Bercovitch's classic account, "the American jeremiad" is "a mode of public exhortation . . . a ritual designed to join social criticism to spiritual renewal, public to private identity, the shifting 'signs of the times' to certain traditional metaphors, themes, and symbols." And he argues that it "has played a major role in fashioning the myth of America." Originating in Europe, where it "pertained exclusively to mundane, social matters, to the city of man rather than the city of God," its purpose was transformed by the Puritans of New England in order "to direct an imperiled people of God toward the fulfillment of their destiny, to guide them individually toward salvation, and collectively toward the American city of God." According to Bercovitch, the cultural and social utility of the American jeremiad within the nation's civil religion derived from its capacity to enable a reconciliation of the changes demanded by the developmental processes of Americanization and modernization with the religious values represented in the Puritan tradition, a critical commentary on the present made legitimate in the terms of a mythohistorical past. Delivered on special ritual occasions, it fulfilled a hegemonic function in the classic Gramscian sense.[47]

In the postbellum South, the jeremiad was deployed in the service of the Lost Cause by clergymen concerned at the threat to a distinct white Southern identity carried in the economic, political, and social changes coming from the victorious North. Typically, it was delivered on those occasions that mourned or celebrated the Confederacy, rituals recalling the blood sacrifice of the Civil War. Hence, the dedication of monuments, the burial of veterans, Confederate Memorial Day, etc., "all brought forth the Lost Cause sermon, prophesying Southern doom if virtue was not preserved." As already indicated though, such prophetic affirmations of Southern identity were expressed in terms defined in relation to the North. Indeed, its regional twist gave it a profoundly antimodern tone. Even before the war, the white South had developed "a new image of itself as a chivalric society, embodying many of the agrarian and spiritual values that seemed to be disappearing in the industrializing North." This "cultural nationalism" presaged the political nationalism of the Confederacy. The Civil War, however, cast serious doubt over the whole idea of a separate Southern identity. Asserting the importance of this identity, the Lost Cause jeremiad urged constant vigilance to preserve it. Noting that "a major theme of the Lost Cause jeremiad was the wickedness of the Yankees," Wilson describes how ministers

> cautioned Southerners to learn from the evil North. The danger of the South's future degradation was readily embodied in the North's image, with some ministers even teaching that the South must serve as a model to the corrupt North. By maintaining Confederate virtue in the postbellum world, the South would be an example to the North in future days of reform. This was a Southern mission worth achieving.

Moreover, although reconciliation between North and South came as the Civil War moved ever further into the past, the white South did not abandon the religion of the Lost Cause or the prophetic functions that attended it.[48]

The turn of the century marked a revival of the American civil religion in the South. Important in this respect was Southern support for the Spanish-American War. Yet, despite such Northern-led encroachment onto the terrain of the Lost Cause, it did not signal the latter's disappearance. Instead, white Southern preachers suggested that "because of its historical experience . . . the South was quintessentially American. As the rest of the nation had changed because of industrialism, urbanization, immigration, and other forces of modern America, the South had remained most like the nation of the Founding Fathers."⁴⁹ Only as a result of the white South's willingness to fight and sacrifice for liberty and constitutional rights in the Civil War when the North was "going after other gods" did traditional American values and institutions survive.⁵⁰ For white southerner's, interpreting the Lost Cause in this way enabled them to renew their participation in the life of the nation whilst retaining pride in their own regional identity. Addressing the nation as a whole, it is this revived and religiously based cultural authority that Griffith, with the aid of Thomas Dixon, sought to mobilize in *The Birth of a Nation*.⁵¹

Blood Sacrifice: The ReBirth of the American Civil Religion

That *The Birth of a Nation* promoted traditional white Southern attitudes to race is indisputable. The film not only portrays freed blacks as unfit for full citizenship but posits (black male/white female) miscegenation as a threat to the integrity of the American nation. As one or two commentators have pointed out, however, *Birth* should not be seen as a response to a race crisis. The incidence of racial violence had gone into something of a decline since its peak in the 1890s, reflecting perhaps the degree to which African Americans "had been rendered both politically impotent and socially invisible."⁵² In context, therefore, it makes more sense to see how white progressives might have used blacks as powerful visual symbols of the chaos apparently threatening America. Sympathy for the southern perspective on race not only grew with each successive wave of non-Protestant, non-Anglo-Saxon immigrants or black migrants to the cities but fitted neatly with the then-prevalent social scientific ideology of Social Darwinism.⁵³ Reexamining the way in which Griffith set out his white supremacist thesis therefore reveals the extent to which it was intended to act as a means rather than an end in itself.

Immediately after the opening titles, and Griffith's own "plea for the art of the motion picture," the very first image of the film shows a Puritan minister blessing the trade in Africans, which, the film asserts, "planted the first seed of disunion." Probably citing a now-absent title from this prologue, an early and sympathetic reviewer of the film comments "but when slave trading was no longer profitable to the North the 'traders of the seventeenth century became the abolitionists of the nineteenth century.'" Hence there follows a short scene depicting "a typical Northern congregation" with a preacher demanding freedom for the slaves. In some prints, the preacher inspires a white matriarch to offer her arms to a black child, but she pushes him away as soon as he reaches her, presumably in response to his body odor.[54] It is a somewhat surprising and unsettling opening to the film. The Puritan North, the traditional touchstone of American nationalist sentiment is being portrayed as misguided and full of meddlers and hypocrites. Such antagonism toward the North might have been understandable given the South's living memories of defeat and humiliation in the Civil War. As the film goes on to make clear, however, there was more to Griffith's opening gambit than mere rancor.

Having thrown the integrity of the Yankees into doubt, the rest of the first half of the film sets about affirming the moral authority of the white South. Equivalences are established between the South and Lincoln, the closest thing to a Christ figure within Bellah's civil religion, as they are both sacrificed to the cause of emancipation. Not only is the hero, Ben Cameron (Henry B. Walthall), linked to Lincoln by the contrivance of a presidential pardon after he is falsely accused of being a spy, but his willingness to sacrifice all for what is an already Lost Cause in battle marks him out as a fitting successor to Lincoln as a savior once the latter is assassinated. After his sister, Flora, sacrifices herself to preserve her honor after being chased by the freed black soldier Gus, it is Ben Cameron's unimpeachable moral status, among other things, that Griffith uses in seeking to transform the ride of the Klan from a bigot's fantasy of revenge to a quest for justice on a national scale.

By the end of the film, with harmonious union between the whites of North and South having been restored by the Ku Klux Klan, Ben Cameron and Elsie Stoneman, daughter of the misguided Northern politician Austin Stoneman (modelled on Thaddeus Stevens) are rewarded with the sight of Christ ushering in the kingdom of God followed by a vision of "a city upon a hill." [Fig. 12.2] This is a clear reference to one of the most famous sermons of the American Puritan tradition, John Winthrop's *A Modell of Christian Charity* (1630), a reminder to those who would soon found Boston of their responsibilities to God: "The eyes of all people are upon us."[55] Furthermore, as camp, dated, or even ridiculous as this final sequence might appear to us now, it remains an important indicator of the sensibilities and intentions that shaped the film. For it is the film's own commentary on what its makers hoped to have achieved during the intervening three hours.

The overriding goal of *Birth* is a revitalization of American nationalist feeling by first recalling the national blood sacrifice of the Civil War and, subsequently, mythologizing the "redemption" of the South. It almost goes without saying that, for all Griffith's denials of racist intent, this aim is predicated upon an understanding of the sacred core of U.S. national identity as fundamentally white and constructed in opposition to blacks. The genius of the film, however, lies in its invocation of the Lost Cause, most obviously through Ben Cameron's evident willingness to sacrifice himself on the battlefield. Moral authority thus established, Griffith went on to portray the white South as an oppressed people thirsting for justice and liberty. Seeking thereby to justify the violent white supremacism of the Ku Klux Klan, *The Birth of a Nation* reworked the Puritan and revolutionary traditions of the United States in romantic visual terms well suited to the emerging consumer society. Whether this development can be thought of as something authentically "religious" depends, of course, on how one understands the term "religion." What is worth suggesting here, nonetheless, is that the development and growth of the supposedly "secular" medium of cinema in America offered up an important public space for the renegotiation and transformation of American national identity, its civil religion if you will. The creation of a cultural arena that was free, to some extent, from Protestant suppositions as to the primacy of the word would provide certain non-Protestant groups, white Catholics and Jews in particular, with a point of entry into the American cultural mainstream. In the work of such

Figure 12.2   " . . . with harmonious union between the whites of North and South having been restored by the Ku Klux Klan, Ben Cameron, and Elsie Stoneman . . . are rewarded with the sight of Christ ushering in the kingdom of God followed by a vision of 'a city upon a hill.'"

luminaries as Ford, Capra, Louis B. Mayer, and the Warner brothers, this fresh blood would, in turn, regenerate and revitalize the cultural roots of U.S. nationhood and American religion via the screen.

By furnishing an actual, albeit crude, and not metaphoric vision of the kingdom to come, not only for Ben and Elsie, but also for the audience, Griffith was staking a claim on behalf of the film industry for those aspects of the national imagination that had hitherto been largely the preserve of historians, political orators, and the Protestant churches. Griffith's audacious attempt to shift the symbolic and, thus, religious foundations of U.S. nationalism from Massachusetts Bay to somewhere south of the Mason-Dixon line was a sign that in practical terms the narratives via which Americans continued to understand their significance as a "chosen people" or "New Israel" would derive less and less from the pulpit and the Bible and ever more from the "stories in pictures" produced in the studios of Hollywood. Indeed, we might understand the popular appeal of *The Birth of a Nation* as resting not on the supposed attraction of its white supremacist viewpoint (as compelling as that might be to some) but, rather, on its reaffirmation of *faith* as the basis of national life. In the face of the cold hard historical forces of modernization, rationalization, and the rise of the corporate order, *Birth* offered a vision of America in which moral autonomy survives and the victims of change could still regain control of their lives and communities through direct action. Walthall's Ben Cameron should have been killed as he charged the Union guns, but instead, against all odds, he rose again to establish a template for the righteous male rebels who continue to bestride American cinema to this day: think the Ringo Kid (John Wayne) in *Stagecoach* (1939, dir. John Ford), Harry Callahan (Clint Eastwood) in *Dirty Harry* (1971, dir. Don Siegel), and John McLane (Bruce Willis) in *Die Hard* (1988, dir. John McTiernan) and its various sequels. Lost causes abound in Hollywood, and the compelling fiction mobilized by Griffith in *The Birth of a Nation* furnished American cinema with a narrative formula that has, over the years, encouraged its audience to believe that, for all the transformations wrought by modernity and the emergence of the United States as the preeminent world power, the "self-evident" principles upon which the nation was founded survive intact, at the heart of American culture, and that their country remains "like a city upon a hill."

Although the social, political, and cultural implications of *The Birth of a Nation* are many, full discussion of them will have to wait. What the preceding discussion of the film is intended to highlight, however, are the potential riches available to scholars prepared to acknowledge the sociological and historical importance of the nation in their work, not only on religion and film, but also on the complex interaction between the media and religion in culture. For example, the expansion of the commercial mass media in the United States during the twentieth century was not accompanied by the same waning of belief and decline in the influence and power of religious institutions that took place in Europe. Hence, we might go beyond an interest in, or fascination with, the religious ideas, images, and references readily found in American cinema to enquire how far the movies, along with other media, actually served to bolster faith and religious practice as the norm in American culture. Addressing such issues, and the potentially awkward questions that follow, would allow the discussion of religion and film to gain a wider currency beyond the theological ghetto. To do this, though, requires that some of us tear our eyes from the glory of the screen and pay attention instead to the big picture *outside* the movie house.

Notes

1. For an astute historical overview of the field and discussion of how dependent most writing on religion and film has been on a shared framework of religious commitments and beliefs, see Steve Nolan, "The Books of the Films: Trends in Religious Film Analysis," *Literature and Theology* 12.1 (1988): 1–12.
2. There are of course exceptions to this general neglect of American religion in film studies. Probably the most developed work in this area describes the role of the Catholic Church in the struggles over movie censorship. See for example, Gregory D. Black, *Hollywood Censored: Morality, Catholics, and the Movies* (Cambridge: Cambridge University Press, 1994); Frank Walsh, *Sin and Censorship: The Catholic Church and the Motion Picture Industry* (New Haven and London: Yale University Press, 1996); and Francis G. Couvares, "Hollywood, Main Street, and the Church: Trying to Censor the Movies before the Production Code," in *Movie Censorship and American Culture*, Francis G. Couvares, ed. (Washington and London: Smithsonian Institution Press, 1996). However, only Couvares seeks to locate the basis for Catholic involvement in the censorship debate within the broader religious economy of the United States. Similarly, Babington and Evans's study of the biblical epic makes the point that it is impossible to understand the significance of that most derided of genres without engaging with its origins in "the unique context of American religion" (Bruce Babington and Peter William Evans, *Biblical Epics: Sacred Narrative in the Hollywood Cinema* [Manchester: Manchester University Press. 1993], 12). Whilst often tending toward a somewhat one-dimensional view of religion, i.e. as institutional, hegemonic, and reactionary, there is also some useful work examining the religious influence upon early and silent cinema. See for example, Richard Maltby, "*The King of Kings* and the Czar of all the Rushes: The Propriety of the Christ Story," *Screen* 31.2 (1990): 188–213; Roland Cosandey, André Gaudreault, and Tom Gunning, eds., *Une Invention du Diable? Cinema des Premiers Temps et Religion* (An invention of the devil? religion and early cinema) (Sainte-Foy: Les Presses De L'Université

Laval/ Lausanne: Éditions Payot Lausanne, 1992); William Uricchio and Roberta E. Pearson, *Reframing Culture: The Case of the Vitagraph Quality Films* (Princeton: Princeton University Press, 1993).

3. The work of Stewart Hoover and associates is particularly important here. Introducing an important collection of essays, Hoover and Knut Lundby argue for a "more complex understanding" of "media, religion, and culture . . . as an interrelated web within society" (Stewart M. Hoover and Knut Lundby, eds., *Rethinking Media, Religion, and Culture* [Thousand Oaks: Sage, 1997], 3). For further developments see Stewart M. Hoover *Religion in the News: Faith and Journalism in American Public Discourse* (Thousand Oaks: Sage, 1998); David Morgan, *Visual Piety: A History and Theory of Popular Religious Images* (Berkeley: University of California Press, 1998); David Morgan, *Protestants and Pictures: Religion, Visual Culture, and the Age of American Mass Production* (New York: Oxford University Press, 1999); Jolyon Mitchell, *Visually Speaking: Radio and the Renaissance of Preaching* (Edinburgh: T & T Clark, 1999); Bruce David Forbes and Jeffrey H. Mahan, eds., *Religion and Popular Culture in America* (Berkeley: University of California Press, 2000); Stewart M. Hoover and Lynn Schofield Clark, eds., *Practicing Religion in the Age of the Media: Explorations in Media, Religion, and Culture* (New York: Columbia University Press, 2002).

4. See, for example, Joel W. Martin and Conrad E. Ostwalt, eds., *Screening the Sacred: Religion, Myth, and Ideology in Popular American Film* (Boulder: Westview Press, 1995); Margaret R. Miles, *Seeing and Believing: Religion and Values in the Movies* (Boston: Beacon Press, 1996); Albert Bergesen and Andrew M. Greeley, *God in the Movies: A Sociological Investigation* (New Brunswick, NJ: Transaction Publishers, 2000).

5. Philip Schlesinger, *Media, State and Nation: Political Violence and Collective Identities* (London: Sage, 1991), 173–74; and Benedict Anderson, *Imagined Communities: Reflections on the Origins and Spread of Nationalism*, rev. and extended ed. (London: Verso, 1991). See also Ernest Gellner, *Nations and Nationalism* (Oxford: Blackwell, 1983); Eric Hobsbawm and Terence Ranger, eds., *The Invention of Tradition* (Cambridge: Cambridge University Press, 1983); Eric J. Hobsbawm, *Nations and Nationalism Since 1780: Programme, Myth, Reality* (Cambridge: Cambridge University Press, 1990); Homi K. Babha, ed., *Nation and Narration* (London: Routledge, 1990); and Anthony D. Smith, *National Identity* (London: Penguin, 1991). For an especially useful recent overview of the sociological background to the study of nations and national identity orientated specifically toward the study of "national cinemas," see Philip Schlesinger, "The Sociological Scope of 'National Cinema,'" in *Cinema and Nation: Interdisciplinary Approaches to Nationalism and National Identity*, Mette Hjort and Scott MacKenzie, eds. (London: Routledge, 2000), 19–31.

6. For a critical account of how the notion of sui generis religion has been routinely reproduced by scholars seeking to validate the field of religious studies within the academy, see Russell T. McCutcheon, *Manufacturing Religion: The Discourse on Sui Generis Religion and the Politics of Nostalgia* (New York and Oxford: Oxford University Press, 1997).

7. Alexis de Tocqueville, *Democracy in America*, J. P. Mayer and Max Lerner, eds., trans. George Lawrence (New York: Harper and Row, 1966 [1835]).

8. Robert N. Bellah, "Civil Religion in America," *Daedalus* 96 (1967): 1–21.

9. See, for example, Russell E. Richey, and Donald G. Jones, eds., *American Civil Religion* (New York: Harper & Row, 1974); Robert N. Bellah, *The Broken Covenant: American Civil Religion in a Time of Trial* (New York: Seaburg Press, 1975); John Wilson, *Public Religion in American Culture* (Philadelphia: Temple University Press, 1979); George A. Kelly, *Politics and Religious Consciousness in America*, New Brunswick, NJ: Transaction Inc., 1984); Wilbur Zelinsky, *Nation into State: The Shifting Symbolic Foundations of American Nationalism*, (Chapel Hill: University of North Carolina Press, 1988); and Phillip E. Hammond, Amanda Porterfield, James G. Moseley, and Jonathan D. Sarna, "Forum: American Civil Religion Revisited," *Religion and American Culture* 4.1 (1994): 1–23.

10. Robert N. Bellah, "Religion and the Legitimation of the American Republic," in Robert N. Bellah and Philip E. Hammond, *Varieties of Civil Religion* (San Francisco: Harper & Row, 1980), 15.

11. Robert N. Bellah, Richard Madsen, William M. Sullivan, Ann Swidler, and Steven M. Tipton, *Habits of the Heart: Individualism and Commitment in American Life* (Berkeley: University of California Press, 1985).

12. Garth Jowett, *Film: The Democratic Art* (Boston and Toronto: Little, Brown and Company, 1976), 35.

13. Charles H. Long, *Significations* (Philadelphia: Fortress Press, 1986).

14. Henry F. May, *Protestant Churches and Industrial America* (New York: Harper & Row, 1949), 91

15. Phillip E. Hammond, "In Search of a Protestant Twentieth Century: American Religion and Power Since 1900," *Review of Religious Research* 24.3 (1983): 281–294.

16. Martin. E. Marty, *Pilgrims in Their Own Land: 500 Years of Religion in America* (New York: Penguin, 1985), 337–71.

17. Robert Wiebe, *The Search for Order, 1877–1920* (New York: Hill and Wang, 1967).

18. Richard M. Abrams, "The Failure of Progressivism," in *The Shaping of Twentieth Century America: Interpretive Essays*, 2d. ed., Richard M. Abrams and Lawrence W. Levine, eds. (Boston: Little, Brown and Company, 1971), 209.

19. For example, Stanley Corkin's analysis of *The Birth of a Nation* does ground the director's aesthetic sensibility in "the reigning impulses of Progressivism" but ignores the significance of the religious background to the reform movements. Stanley Corkin, *Realism and the Birth of the Modern United States: Cinema, Literature, and Culture* (Athens, GA. and London: University of Georgia Press, 1996), 4.

20. Lary May, *Screening Out the Past* (Chicago: Chicago University Press, 1983), 68, 61, 74.

21. See for example, May, *Screening*, 43–59; William Uricchio and Roberta E. Pearson, "Constructing the Audience: Competing Discourses of Morality and Rationalization During the Nickelodeon Period," *Iris* 17 (1994): 43–54; William Uricchio and Roberta E. Pearson, "'The Formative and Impression-

able Stage': Discursive Constructions of the Nickelodeon's Child Audience,"
in *American Movie Audiences: From the Turn of the Century to the Early
Sound Era,* Melvyn Stokes and Richard Maltby, eds. (London: British Film
Institute, 1999), 64–75; and Lee Grieveson, "Why the Audience Mattered in
Chicago in 1907," in *American Movie Audiences: from the Turn of the
Century to the Early Sound Era,* Melvyn Stokes and Richard Maltby, eds.
(London: British Film Institute, 1999), 79–91.

22. Richard Schickel, *D. W. Griffith: An American Life* (New York: Simon and
    Schuster, 1984), 33.
23. Ibid.
24. Scott Simmon, *The Films of D. W. Griffith* (New York: Cambridge University
    Press, 1993), 147–53. See also Ann Douglas, *The Feminization of American
    Culture* (Garden City, NJ: Doubleday, 1988); T. J. Jackson Lears, *No Place
    of Grace: Antimodernism and the Transformation of American Culture,
    1880–1920* (New York: Pantheon Books, 1981).
25. Simmon, *Griffith,* 152.
26. May, *Screening,* 251–52.
27. Obvious points of entry into the extensive literature on *The Birth of a Nation*
    are Fred Silva, ed., *Focus on* Birth of a Nation (Englewood Cliffs, NJ: Prentice-
    Hall, 1971), and, for a collection that includes more recent critical perspectives
    on the picture, Robert Lang, ed., *"The Birth of a Nation": D. W. Griffith,
    Director* (New Brunswick, NJ: Rutgers University Press, 1994).
28. Clyde Taylor, "The Re-Birth of the Aesthetic in Cinema," in *The Birth of
    Whiteness: Race and the Emergence of U.S. Cinema,* Daniel Bernardi, ed.
    (New Brunswick, NJ: Rutgers University Press, 1996), 16.
29. Philip French quoted by David Robinson, sleeve notes to *The Birth of a Nation,*
    directed by D. W. Griffith (London: Connoisseur Video, 1993).
30. Russell Merritt, "D.W. Griffith's 'The Birth of a Nation': Going after Little
    Sister," in *Close Viewings: An Anthology of New Film Criticism,* Peter
    Lehman, ed. (Tallahassee: The Florida State University Press, 1990), 215–37.
    See also, for example, Richard Dyer, "Into the Light: The Whiteness of the
    South in 'The Birth of a Nation,'" in *Dixie Debates: Perspectives on Southern
    Cultures,* Richard H. King and Helen Taylor, eds. (London: Pluto Press, 1996),
    165–76; Linda Williams, "Versions of Uncle Tom: Race and Gender in
    American Melodrama," in *New Scholarship from BFI Research,* Colin MacCabe
    and Duncan Petrie, eds. (London: British Film Institute, 1997), 111–139; and
    Cedric J. Robinson, "In the Year 1915: D.W. Griffith and the Whitening of
    America," *Social Identities* 3.2 (1997): 161–192.
31. Schickel, *D. W. Griffith,* 186.
32. Griffith's cameraman Billy Bitzer quoted in Iris Barry, *D. W. Griffith: Ameri-
    can Film Master,* revised by Eileen Bowser (New York: The Museum of
    Modern Art/Doubleday, 1965), 19.
33. Although Kentucky was not a secessionist state during the Civil War, and
    eventually sided with the North, Griffith's family were slave owners prior to
    the war, his father fought for the Confederacy, and the family shared many of
    the hardships that befell the defeated South. As Griffith wrote in his autobiog-
    raphy, "one could not find the sufferings of our family and our friends—the

dreadful poverty and hardships during the war and for many years after—in the Yankee-written histories we read in school. From all this was born a burning determination to tell some day our side of the story to the world" (D. W. Griffith and James Hart, eds., *The Man Who Invented Hollywood: The Autobiography of D. W. Griffith* [Louisville: Touchstone. 1972], 26).

34. Thomas R. Cripps, "The Reaction of the Negro to the Motion Picture, 'Birth of a Nation,'" in *Focus on* Birth of a Nation, Fred Silva, ed. (Englewood Cliffs, NJ: Prentice-Hall, 1971), 111.

35. For a discussion of this tendency within serious writing on film see Taylor, "The Re-Birth of the Aesthetic in Cinema."

36. Pierre Sorlin, *The Film in History: Restaging the Past* (Oxford: Basil Blackwell, 1980), 30; Janet Staiger, *Interpreting Films: Studies in the Historical Reception of American Cinema* (Princeton, NJ: Princeton University Press, 1992), 152.

37. See for example, D. W. Griffith, "The Motion Picture and Witch Burners," reprinted in *Focus on* Birth of a Nation, Fred Silva, ed. (Englewood Cliffs, NJ: Prentice-Hall, 1971), 96–99, and D. W. Griffith, *The Rise and Fall of Free Speech in America* (Los Angeles: D. W. Griffith, 1916).

38. For objections to the racism of the picture voiced upon its initial release, see Rolfe Cobleigh, "Why I Oppose 'The Birth of a Nation,'" in *Focus on* Birth of a Nation, Fred Silva, ed. (Englewood Cliffs, NJ: Prentice-Hall, 1971), 80–83; and Francis Hackett, "Brotherly Love," in *The Birth of a Nation: D. W. Griffith, Director*, Robert Lang, ed. (New Brunswick, NJ: Rutgers University Press, 1996), 161–163. Recent accounts of the film's representation of race are not hard to find, but for one of the most insightful and wide-ranging analyses, see Michael Rogin, "'The Sword Became a Flashing Vision': D. W. Griffith's 'The Birth of a Nation,'" in *The Birth of a Nation: D. W. Griffith, Director*, Robert Lang, ed. (New Brunswick, NJ: Rutgers University Press, 1996), 250–93.

39. Karl W. Deutsch, quoted in Schlesinger, "The Sociological Scope of 'National Cinema,'" 20.

40. Silva, *Focus*, 7.

41. Lang, *"The Birth of a Nation,"* 3. The term can be traced back at least as far as Edward A. Pollard's (1867) *The Lost Cause: A New Southern History of the War of the Confederates* (New York: E.B. Treat and Co. Publishers, 1867), which cast the defeat of the South in tragic terms without any renunciation of white supremacism. Thus Lang's dismissal of the Lost Cause reflects the traditional liberal suspicion of the Confederate legacy and its influence upon American culture. Such a position, however, is by no means a consensual one, as evidenced by recent controversies over the flying of the Confederate flag from state capitols in South Carolina and Mississippi, and the writings of modern apologists for the South. Indeed, whilst the attempt to portray the South in a more complex and sympathetic way is most closely associated with conservatives such as John Shelton Reed, coeditor of the journal *Southern Cultures* (see also John Shelton Reed, *Whistling Dixie: Dispatches from the South* [San Diego: Harcourt Brace Jovanovich, 1992]; John Shelton Reed, *Surveying the South: Studies in Regional Sociology* [Columbia: University of Missouri Press, 1993]), this partial rehabilitation has also found support from less likely sources. See, for example, the marxist account in Eugene D.

Genovese, *The Southern Tradition: The Achievement and Limitations of an American Conservatism* (Cambridge, MA: Harvard University Press, 1994).

42. Charles Reagan Wilson, "The Religion of the Lost Clause: Ritual and Organization of the Southern Civil Religion, 1865–1920," *The Journal of Southern History* 46.2 (1980): 219–238; and Charles Reagan Wilson, *Baptized in Blood: The Religion of the Lost Cause* (Athens, GA: University of Georgia Press, 1980). See also, George B. Tindall, "Mythology: A New Frontier in Southern History," in *The Idea of the South*, Frank E. Vandiver, ed. (Chicago: University of Chicago Press, 1964), 1–15; and Rollin G. Osterweis, *The Myth of the Lost Cause, 1865–1900* (Hamden, CT: Archon Books, 1973).

43. Wilson, "The Religion of the Lost Clause," 232.

44. Gaines M. Foster, *Ghosts of the Confederacy: Defeat, the Lost Cause, and the New South* (New York: Oxford University Press, 1987).

45. Wilson, "The Religion of the Lost Clause," 232.

46. Wilson, *Baptized in Blood,* 18–36.

47. Sacvan Bercovitch, *The American Jeremiad* (Madison: University of Wisconsin, 1978), xiii, xi, 9.

48. Wilson, *Baptized in Blood,* 82, 3, 81.

49. Ibid., 167.

50. R. A. Goodwin, rector of St John's Episcopal Church, Richmond, Virginia, quoted ibid., 166.

51. Although Wilson, ibid., 100–118, stresses white supremacism and the Ku Klux Klan as key foci for the "Southern civil religion," highlights the cultural impact of Thomas M. Dixon's racist fiction, and briefly acknowledges the popularity of D. W. Griffith's adaptation of that book in *The Birth of a Nation,* he does not pursue the long-term implications of the film's articulation of the Lost Cause any further.

52. Melvyn Stokes, "Crises in History and Responses to Them as Illustrated in 'The Birth of a Nation' and 'Gone with the Wind,'" *La Licorne* 36 (1996): 72. See also, Cripps, "The Reaction of the Negro to the Motion Picture, 'Birth of a Nation,'" 111; Sorlin, *The Film in History,* 108

53. Schickel, *D. W. Griffith,* 79; Stokes, "Crises in History," 73–74

54. W. Stephen Bush, from *The Motion Picture World* 23 (March 13, 1915), in Lang, *"The Birth of a Nation,"* 176.

55. Winthrop's sermon is widely available in a number of collections, including, Robert N. Bellah, Richard Madsen, William M. Sullivan, Ann Swidler, and Steven M. Tipton, eds., *Individualism and Commitment in American Life: Readings on the Themes of "Habits of the Heart"* (New York: Harper Torchbooks, 1988), 22–27.

Contributors

Francisca Cho is associate professor of Buddhist studies at Georgetown University. Her book, *Embracing Illusion: Truth and Fiction in the* Dream of the Nine Clouds (Albany, NY: SUNY Press, 1996) examines the expression of Buddhist philosophy in a seventeenth-century Korean classic novel. Recent publications include "Leaping into the Boundless: A Daoist Reading of Comparative Religious Ethics," in the *Journal of Religious Ethics*, and "The Buddhist Theory of Social Action," in *Ideal in the World's Religions*. Her recent research and publications focus on Buddhist aesthetics as expressed through East Asian literature and film.

Linda C. Ehrlich is associate professor of Japanese, comparative literature, and cinema at Case Western Reserve University, and has published articles on world cinema in *Film Quarterly, Cinema Journal, Literature/ Film Quarterly, Film Criticism, Cinemaya, Journal of Film and Video, Ethnomusicology,* and *Journal of Religion and Film,* among others. She has coedited (with David Desser) *Cinematic Landscapes: Observations on the Visual Arts and Cinema of China and Japan* (University of Texas Press, 1994; 2d. ed., 2000). Her second book, *An Open Window: The Cinema of Víctor Erice,* appeared in the Scarecrow Press Filmmakers Series in 2000. She is currently finishing an anthology of essays on sculptural images in the cinema entitled *A Particular Slant of Light.*

Kris Jozajtis completed his Ph.D. on religion and film in American culture at the University of Stirling in 2001. Since that time he has taught at Stirling in the departments of religious studies and film and media studies. His work on the use of media in religious education in schools prompted worldwide interest, and he is currently writing a book based on his doctoral dissertation. He is also developing a career in radio, as a producer and presenter of his own show for Heartland FM. He lives in Stirling with his partner and four children.

Philip Lutgendorf has taught in the University of Iowa's Department of Asian Languages and Literature since 1985. He regularly offers Hindi language classes as well as courses on written and oral narrative traditions of South Asia, including Indian film. His book on the performance of the epic Ramayana, *The Life of a Text* (Berkeley: University of California Press, 1991) won the A. K. Coomaraswamy Prize of the Association for

Asian Studies. He received a Guggenheim Fellowship in 2002–03 for his book project on the popular "monkey-god" Hanuman, which he has also treated in several articles.

Birgit Meyer is a senior lecturer at the Research Centre Religion and Society (Department of Anthropology, University of Amsterdam). Her publications include *Translating the Devil: Religion and Modernity Among the Ewe in Ghana* (Edinburgh: Edinburgh University Press, 1999) and *Globalization and Identity: Dialectics of Flow and Closure* (edited with Peter Geschiere, Oxford: Blackwell, 1999). In April 2000 she was awarded a PIONIER grant from the Netherlands Foundation for Scientific Research for a comparative research program on modern mass media, religion, and the postcolonial state in West Africa, India, Brazil, and the Caribbean.

Paul Nathanson does research at the Faculty of Religious Studies, McGill University. Nathanson's interest in the frontier between religion and secularity, along with coming of age, led to his first book: *Over the Rainbow: The Wizard of Oz as a Secular Myth of America* (Albany, NY: SUNY Press, 1991). He has published numerous journal articles on popular culture and religion, including "Coming of Age in the Movies: Myth and Manhood in *Rebel without a Cause*" in *Gender in World Religions,* and "You Can't Go Home Again, or Can You? Reflections on the Symbolism of TV Families at Christmastime" in *Journal of Popular Culture.* He has collaborated with Katherine K. Young on several research projects, including *Spreading Misandry: The Teaching of Contempt for Men in Popular Culture* (Montreal: McGill-Queen's University Press, 2001). Their most recent project is on the moral, philosophical, and other implications of current demands for the legalization of gay marriage.

S. Brent Plate is assistant professor of religion and the visual arts at Texas Christian University, where he teaches the courses "Myth and Ritual on Film" and "Religion and Visual Culture." Recent publications include the edited volumes, *Religion, Art, and Visual Culture* (Palgrave, 2002) and *Imag(in)ing Otherness: Filmic Visions of Living Together,* coedited with David Jasper (Atlanta and Oxford: American Academy of Religion/Oxford University Press, 1999), as well as the journal articles "Looking at the Body of Death," in *Soundings*; and "The Re-creation of the World: Filming Faith," in *Dialog.* He is currently preparing a manuscript on Walter Benjamin's religious aesthetics, forthcoming with Routledge.

Lloyd Ridgeon lectures on Islamic studies in the Department of Theology and Religious Studies, at the University of Glasgow. His major publications include *Aziz Nasafi* (Richmond: Curzon Press, 1998) and *Persian Meta-*

physics and Mysticism (Richmond: Curzon Press, 2003). He has also published an article on Makhamlabaf entitled "Makhmalbaf's Broken Mirror," in *Durham Middle East Papers.*

Edna M. Rodríguez-Mangual is assistant professor of Spanish and Latin American studies at Texas Christian University. Her research and teaching focus on the intersection between cultural expressions (especially literature and film) and nation building. She is currently working on a book manuscript on the Cuban writer Lydia Cabrera, analyzing the representation of Afro-Cubans and Santeria as an alternative national discourse. Her most recent publication is the essay "Driving a Dead Body through the Nation: Death and Allegory in the Film *Guantanamera,*" in the journal *Chasqui.*

Antonio D. Sison is a Ph.D./Th.D. candidate from the Philippines currently doing research on the confluence of Edward Schillebeeckx's eschatology and Third Cinema at the Catholic University of Nijmegen. He taught at the Ateneo de Manila University, the premier Jesuit university in Asia, prior to his doctoral research in the Netherlands. Sison complements his academic interest in theology and cinema with screenwriting. His first screenplay, *9 Mornings,* a modern-day parable of conversion, was awarded second place in a national screenwriting contest and enjoyed a successful run when it was released as a film in the Philippines in October 2002.

Luis A. Vivanco is assistant professor of anthropology and director of the Latin American studies program at the University of Vermont. He holds a Ph.D. in cultural anthropology from Princeton University. He has done ethnographic research and published articles on the cultural politics of nature conservation and ecotourism in Costa Rica and Oaxaca, Mexico. He is a coeditor of *Talking About People: A Reader in Contemporary Cultural Anthropology* (Boston: McGraw-Hill, 2000) and is currently finishing a monograph on the environmental movement in rural Costa Rica.

Judith Weisenfeld is associate professor of religion at Vassar College. She is the author of *African-American Women and Christian Activism: New York's Black YWCA, 1905–1945* (Cambridge: Harvard University Press, 1997), co-editor (with Richard Newman) of *This Far By Faith: Readings in African American Women's Religious Biography* (New York: Routledge, 1996), and coeditor (with Christine diStefano and Priscilla Wald) of a special issue of *SIGNS* (1999). She is the recipient of grants from the American Academy of Religion and the NEH and has been a visiting fellow at the Institute for the Advanced Study of Religion at Yale. Prof. Weisenfeld is currently working on *Hollywood Be Thy Name: African-American*

Religion in American Film, 1929–1950 (forthcoming with University of California Press).

Janet Wilson is reader in English at University College Northampton. Her research interests are in linguistics, postcolonial writing, and New Zealand literature. Publications include the edited *Preaching in the Reformation* (Cambridge: D.S. Brewer, 1993) and *Intimate Stranger* (Wellington: Steel Roberts, 2000), reminiscences of the New Zealand writer and publisher Dan Davin. She is currently editor of *World Literature Written in English* and secretary of the New Zealand Studies Association in the United Kingdom.

INDEX